the ART & SCIENCE of
Speyfishing

*"...the art and science of
speycasting and speyfishing
with a true speyrod..."*

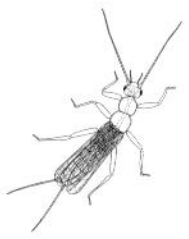

ON THE COVER...

Mike Maxwell speycasting under difficult conditions - the wind was blowing, the river level was rising and, of course, the trees were overhanging the river behind.

With close scrutiny, you might be able to see the fly leaving the water 'out of harm's way' and the blurred forward section of the line as it starts to accelerate and straighten the loop.

Inset Photograph:
Fred W. Kelly

Speyrod/Fly Photograph:
Richard J. Mayer

End Leaves Design/Photography:
Richard J. Mayer

the ART & SCIENCE of Speyfishing

Written by:
Mike Maxwell

Illustrations:
Richard Mayer

Studio Photography:
Kelly Fisher

FIRST PRINTING

PUBLISHED BY:
FLYFISHERS' ARTE & PUBLISHING

DELTA, BRITISH COLUMBIA CANADA

Published by:

FLYFISHERS' ARTE & PUBLISHING
  4713 – 46th Avenue
  Delta, British Columbia
  Canada V4K 1N2

**For additional copies or bulk orders of this book,
please contact:**

ENIGMA PRODUCTIONS
  5169 Joyce Street
  Vancouver, British Columbia
  Canada V5R 4H1

Book Design:
Richard J. Mayer

First Printing May 1995
Printed in Canada
Hemlock Printers Ltd.

ISBN 0–9699610–0–6

DEDICATION

To All Our Hardy Ancestors *who originated the fascinating and rewarding sport of fishing with long limber double-handed flyrods.*

To All My Dedicated & Accomplished Students *who have 'gone forth and spread the word' on the advantages of fishing with 'true speyrods'.*

To My Many Skilled & Experienced Angler Friends *who have endured my constant discussions on angling techniques.*

To All Who Will Come to the Sport *later and struggle through the sometimes tedious and frustrating process of learning to cast and fish with a double-handed speyrod.*

Finally ~ To Those Intelligent Anglers *who must know 'why', not just 'how to'.*

This book is for you.

Mike Maxwell
1995

ABOUT THE SPEYFISHING PATTERNS...

TELKWA STONE

Developed on the steelhead rivers of British Columbia to represent the colour, size and proportions of the *Acroneuria Abnormus* stonefly as it returns to the water to deposit its eggs. This easy-to-tie dry fly is now used on many other steelhead rivers and is a very successful Atlantic Salmon fly.

THUNDER & LIGHTNING

This beautiful wet fly is a modern hair wing version of the traditional feather wing pattern. It is used to represent small fry or minnows feeding at mid-water or rising to the surface to feed on caddis emergers and adults. My favourite wet fly.

TELKWA NYMPH

The nymphal version of the Telkwa Stone, developed to represent the *Acroneuria Abnormus* stonefly nymph feeding on the bottom, drifting downstream or migrating shoreward to hatch. The popular and realistic pattern is now used extensively on many rivers and for many species of fish.

Flies tied by MIKE MAXWELL *on Alec Jackson #5, 24 karat gold-plated spey hooks.*

ABOUT THE HOOK...

ALEC JACKSON SPEY HOOK ~ DAI-ICHI

The culmination of the hookmaker's art is embodied in the latest hook designs of veteran American angler, Alec Jackson, and the advanced metallurgy and hook-making techniques of the *Dai-Ichi Company* of Japan.

These beautiful, light wire hooks are unbelievably strong and dangerously sharp. The attention to detail of the tapered eye and the minute barb will gladden the heart of any dedicated fly tyer.

Although this thoroughbred hook is available in numerous practical colours, it is difficult to resist the temptation to fish with the 24 karat gold-plated version. The fish seem to concur.

CONTENTS

LIST OF SKETCHES ix

LIST OF PHOTOGRAPHS xi

FORWARD - TREY COMBS xv

PREFACE xvii

INTRODUCTION xxi

PART ONE ~ INTRODUCTION

CHAPTER...			
	One	Introduction to Speyfishing	3
	Two	The Development of Tubular Rods	7
	Three	The Controlled Energy Speyrod	11
	Four	The Energies of Speycasting	15
	Five	Speycasts You Will Learn	19
	Six	More About Speycasting Energies	21
	Seven	Using the Body and Arms	29

PART TWO ~ POND CASTING

CHAPTER...			
	Eight	Forward Spey	37
	Nine	Circular Forward Spey	49
	Ten	Single Spey	59
	Eleven	Double Spey	71
	Twelve	Advanced Techniques	83
	Thirteen	Speycasting in Wind	95

PART THREE ~ RIVER CASTING

CHAPTER...			
	Fourteen	Speycasting on Moving Water	101
	Fifteen	Speycasting on the Right Bank	105
	Sixteen	Speycasting on the Left Bank	117
	Seventeen	Special Casting Techniques	129

PART FOUR ~ SPEYFISHING

CHAPTER...			
	Eighteen	On Speyfishing	143
	Nineteen	About Fish Behaviour	149
	Twenty	Know Your Fish and Your River	155
	Twenty-One	Think Before You Fish	165
	Twenty-Two	Angling Techniques	171
	Twenty-Three	Hooking, Controlling and Landing Fish	179

Contents

Part Five ~ Equipment

Chapter...

Twenty-Four	Design and Construction of Speyrods	193
Twenty-Five	Selecting a Speyrod for Speyfishing	197
Twenty-Six	Reels for Speyfishing	205
Twenty-Seven	Lines and Leaders	207
Twenty-Eight	Hooks for Speyfishing	217
Twenty-Nine	On Flies and Local Rivers	221

Conclusion	225
Recommended Reading	227
List of Rod Makers	229
List of Speyline Makers	231

LIST OF SKETCHES

PART ONE ~ INTRODUCTION

SKETCH...			
	1	Overhead versus Spey	9
	2	Rope Trick	16
	3	Energies of Overhead Cast	17
	4	Energies of Forward Delivery	22 - 23
	5	Compound Curve	24
	6	Stiff Rod Delivery	25
	7	Rollcast	26
	8	Body Rock	32

PART TWO ~ POND CASTING

SKETCH...			
	9	Standard Forward Right Shoulder	40 - 41
	10	Standard Forward Left Shoulder	44 - 45
	11	Circular Forward Right Shoulder	52 - 53
	12	Circular Forward Left Shoulder	56 - 57
	13	Single Right Shoulder	62 - 63
	14	Single Left Shoulder	66 - 67
	15	Double Right Shoulder	74 - 75
	16	Double Left Shoulder	78 - 79
	17	Restrictive Backcast - Pond	88
	18	Serpentine Mend - Pond	91
	19	Reach Mend - Pond	92
	20	Water Mend - Pond	93

PART THREE ~ RIVER CASTING

SKETCH...			
	21	Double Right Bank, Right Shoulder	108 - 109
	22	Single Right Bank, Left Shoulder	114 - 115
	23	Double Left Bank, Left Shoulder	120 - 121
	24	Single Left Bank, Right Shoulder	126 - 127
	25	Serpentine Mend - River	133
	26	Reach Mend - River	134
	27	Water Mend - River	135 - 136

LIST OF SKETCHES

PART FOUR ~ SPEYFISHING

SKETCH...

28	Fish's Sight	150
29	Fish's Sight	153
30	Cross Sections - River	160
31	Longitudinal Variations	161
32	Boulders	162
33	The Game Plan	166
34	Presentations	169 - 170
35	Vectors - Effective & Useless Landing Forces	182
36	Effective Lateral Pull	185
37	Lift/Don't Bow/Walk	186
38	Tailing Fish	187
39	Break Rod	189
40	Angler Fatigue	190

PART FIVE ~ EQUIPMENT

SKETCH...

41	Rod Jointing Systems	195
42	Improved Taper	208
43	Loops	209
44	Marking Lines	210
45	Sink Tips	212
46	Recommended Knots	214
47	Speyfishing Leaders	215
48	Floating Line Leader	216
49	Sunk Line Leader	216
50	Steelhead Rivers in British Columbia	223

LIST OF PHOTOGRAPHS

Casting sequences cross-referenced with the text...

PART ONE ~ INTRODUCTION

| PHOTO... | 1 | Casting Positions - Front | 30 |
| | 2 | Casting Positions - Side | 31 |

PART TWO ~ POND CASTING

PHOTO...	3	Standard Forward Right Shoulder	38 - 39
	4	Standard Forward Left Shoulder	42 - 43
	5	Circular Forward Right Shoulder	50 - 51
	6	Circular Forward Left Shoulder	54 - 55
	7	Single Right Shoulder	60 - 61
	8	Single Left Shoulder	64 - 65
	9	Double Right Shoulder	72 - 73
	10	Double Left Shoulder	76 - 77

PART THREE ~ RIVER CASTING

PHOTO...	11	Double Right Bank, Right Shoulder	106 - 107
	12	Single Right Bank, Left Shoulder	112 - 113
	13	Double Left Bank, Left Shoulder	118 - 119
	14	Single Left Bank, Right Shoulder	124 - 125

PART FOUR ~ SPEYFISHING

| PHOTO... | 15 | Rod, Hand and Line Positions | 144 - 145 |

LIST OF PHOTOGRAPHS

Not cross-referenced with the text...

PHOTO...	Summer Steelhead	xiv
	Waterfall Pool, Varzina River	xvi
	B.C. Silver	xx
	Early Days	2
	Speyrods	6
	Taking a Break	13
	Backcast on the Pond	36
	Power Push	49
	Acceleration	71
	Final Delivery	83
	Improbable	85
	Canyon Run, Varzina River	100
	Silent Sentry	103
	Pulling the Anchor	105
	The 'Other Half'	117
	It Pays to Practise	139
	'Apprentice'	140
	Samurai Steelie	142
	Prime Fall Male	148

LIST OF PHOTOGRAPHS
Not cross-referenced with the text...

PHOTO...		
	Adult Stone	151
	A Speyfisher's Dream	159
	Tea Time Again	165
	Applying Pressure	183
	Helping Hand	184
	The Pay Off	184
	Matepedia Atlantic	188
	For the Future	188
	A Pair of Contemporaries	192
	Part of the 'Plan'	196
	Robust Brown	199
	An Angler's Artisan	202
	Old Time Reels	204
	Reel Protection	206
	Speyfishing Flies	220
	Indian Summer	221
	Old Flies	222
	Varzuga Silver	222
	Time for Contemplation	224
	God's Gift to Speyfishers	233

SUMMER STEELHEAD...

Trey Combs has spent decades on researching, teaching and writing about western North America's premier fresh water gamefish... the magnificent steelhead salmon. His recent book, 'STEELHEAD FLY FISHING', gives the most comprehensive advice on equipment, angling methods and locations ever assembled in one volume.

Anglers are indebted to Trey for popularizing the sport of speyfishing.

FORWARD

WHEN I COMPLETED 'STEELHEAD FLY FISHING', I felt that the book was sufficiently definitive to be the last I would ever write on the subject. With one notable exception, I believe that fly fishers received it in that light. The criticism I heard most often related to the use of two-handed rods in steelhead fly fishing. While I discussed their use at length and described in detail how they improved my winter fishing, I didn't illustrate how they should be cast. Readers, fascinated with the prospects of commanding home waters with these rods, considered this a serious omission.

Mike Maxwell has written the definitive book on the use of two-handed rods. I consider The ART & SCIENCE of SPEYFISHING an encyclopedia treatment of speyrods and how to cast them. In my view, this is the perfect companion volume to 'STEELHEAD Fly Fishing'.

I have fished with Mike on many occasions and I know he comes by his knowledge of speycasting honestly. He has fished in no other way for most of his adult life and for a generation he has been at the cutting edge of two-handed rod design technology.

Watching Mike demonstrate his casting skills at the streamside always frees me from the tribulations of fishing to catch fish. Whether presenting the greased line dry for summer steelhead, or running the deep swimming wet down the winter river, the speyrod in Mike's hands becomes a mesmerizing flow of energies. I know I'm witnessing a master displaying his craft.

Thanks to Mike Maxwell, fly fishers now find it possible to become more proficient at presenting their fly, and *presenting their fly under conditions that would prohibit the use of a one-handed rod*. As such, this long needed book must be considered an important addition to fly fishing literature.

Trey Combs

Photography © Joe Kambietz

WATERFALL POOL, VARZINA RIVER...

George fishing from this rock caught a 25 pound Atlantic on an upstream cast dry fly shortly after this photograph was taken... this was done moments after another angler broke a single-handed rod when he hung his backcast in the trees.

Above:

George Beatty
Varzina River,
Russia.

PREFACE

FISHING WITH A DOUBLE-HANDED FLYROD can be one of the most pleasant experiences available to contemporary flyfishers. To be able to cover all fishable water, to cast in any required direction, regardless of wind, current or obstructions behind you without wading chest deep in dangerous water, is the answer to a fly-fisher's prayers. To be able to control the shape of the line before it falls to the water, activate the fly by water mending, present the fly to the fish correctly and trigger its natural instincts to strike is the essence of flyfishing. Finally, to allow the fish to take the fly securely, to control it during its initial frantic efforts to escape, land it efficiently and humanely, and then release it virtually unharmed is the icing on the cake.

Unfortunately, learning to fish with a double-hander can be a frustrating and unrewarding experience leading to frayed nerves, tennis elbow, blasphemy and empty wallets. Adding to the confusion of the misguided beginners is the mistaken belief that using a double-handed rod will somehow make up for their inadequate single-handed casting and that the fish are always on the other side of the river. To make matters worse many anglers believe that using heavy sinking lines, lead core sink tips or magnum overweighted flies can be a substitute for their poor line and fly control techniques.

Having investigated and decided to take up the sport of fishing with a double-hander, the beginner now faces numerous other problems. Problem number one... *what style of double-handed casting and fishing will you adopt? Is it to be overhead casting and rollcasting, overhead casting with a limited form of speycasting or true speycasting?* Each of the above mentioned styles of casting and fishing require totally different types of rod, and are traditional and legitimate methods of angling. Given time, the intelligent person will eventually adopt the style and method of fishing that they enjoy the most.

In my half-century career of flyfishing, I must have fished in every incorrect, dangerous and often ridiculous fashion. This includes fishing with heavy cumbersome cane rods while wading up to my chin in rapids, medical treatment for torn muscles or removing wayward flies and serious discussions with my financial advisors, not to mention a badly bruised ego. When returning from one of my 'less than memorable' fishing trips, nagging thoughts kept running through my often bruised and confused head... *'There must be a better way'* - *'Why don't you find a better way'*.

What followed were many years of research, experiment and field testing to produce a double-handed rod and method of casting and fishing that would be successful and enjoyable. The result of my research and development was a graphite rod which allowed me to make double and single speys over either shoulder, then control the line and the fish perfectly. As the new style of rod and method of casting reminded me of using my old cane rods, I named the rod a '*true speyrod*' and the method of casting '*true speycasting*'.

My seemingly effortless casting and success in fishing with the new style of graphite rod, encouraged many anglers, from many parts of the world, to investigate speyfishing. Many of those motivated to take up what was to them a new way of casting and fishing, were already skilled in using the stiffer styles of double-hander or the traditional, but heavy, cane rod and were instrumental in developing many of the methods of casting and fishing with a true speyrod.

Having decided to adopt the sport of speycasting with a true speyrod, the beginner is then faced with the problems of learning how to cast and fish with one. This is not surprising when you remember the relatively short period of time this style of casting has been practised (*in North America*). Another problem is selecting the correct speyrod when you don't know what you are looking for. This is further complicated by the practice of some rod manufacturers calling any double-handed rod, a speyrod, regardless of what style of fishing it was intended for. Trying to speycast with a stiff rod intended for overhead casting is as hopeless as flycasting with a spinning rod.

Many prospective speyfishers are also intimidated and discouraged by listening to or watching 'recent experts' who seem to be demonstrating how clever they are, how strong they are and how difficult it all is. To illustrate this misleading state of affairs, let me recount the following frustrating experience...

When teaching speycasting and other flyfishing subjects at the International Federation of Fly Fishers annual convention in Livingstone, Montana, I was asked to attend an impromptu group of well-known anglers on the banks of the Yellowstone River. The intention of the gathering was for each of us to demonstrate our double-handed casting techniques. What followed was a performance (*by the others*), of every conceivable method of casting the line to the other side of the river without actually speycasting. Many of the methods required the use of very long stiff rods, extremely heavy shooting heads, enormous power and the occasional need to take cover from wayward lines. The significant and disappointing thing about the whole demonstration was that not one second or word was 'wasted' on line control or fly presentation. So much emphasis was given to the distance casting capabilities of the rods that it was difficult to remember that double-handed rods are for fishing with, not just casting with. What had started out as a casting demonstration had become a double-handed rod distance casting tournament which could no doubt impress an inexperienced caster, but would not fool an accomplished angler.

Let me tell you about a few of the people who attended this little 'gathering of the rods'... First there was my good friend *Jim Vincent*. Jim is built like a Sherman tank and with a double-handed rod in his hands, has just about the same fire power. He is a dedicated and expert angler, and it is difficult to understand why he was so fascinated with excessive distance casting. Then there was *Jim Green*. This Jim is a former champion tournament caster and although he is slightly built and about the same vintage as myself, was not about to be outcast by anyone - and was not. The curious thing about Jim's performance is that he had previously told me that for the past few years, he was only casting half as far and catching twice as many fish. There were further demonstrations by other double-handed distance casters, however, I will refrain from commenting on their performance or mentioning names 'out of kindness'.

On the positive side, there were some notable casting instructors present who did not demonstrate. Mel Krieger, a world recognized authority on flycasting, had the good sense not to enter into this dominant male selection process. Last and certainly not least was Joan Wulff, who was far too polite to comment, at least not to me. Joan is an accomplished angler and flyfishing instructor who is capable of casting with any type of fly rod, knows just how important line and fly control is, and how unnecessary excessive distance casting can be.

The sad thing about the gathering of distance casting 'experts' on the banks of the Yellowstone River is that many of them received their first speycasting instruction from me or had read my 'Manual of Speyfishing', published in 1988. What had gone wrong? Had rod companies led them down the wrong road? Had tournament casters muddied up the water? Could it be that true speycasting was too difficult or too time-consuming to learn? Perhaps my manual was not all that it should be and needed revising?

Since the publication of my first manual (1986), I have been continuously revising my methods of teaching or explaining both speycasting at my Vancouver speycasting courses and speyfishing at my Bulkley River school in the fall. When working with any student, it seems that the learning process was a two way street, as the instructor can also learn from the student. Many of the improvements suggested by, not always complimentary students, have been included in this revised edition.

As the art and science of speycasting and speyfishing with a true speyrod, by the controlled energy method, is now accepted and practised the world over, it is time to turn the loose leaf manual into a hard cover book.

In writing this book, I hope to motivate you to take up the wonderful sport of speyfishing and perhaps lead you through the mine field of misinformation and misconception that seem to surrounds the sport of speyfishing.

It has been said that the first piece of equipment you will need to learn any new subject on flyfishing is a shovel. Those who have worked on a ranch or farm will understand.

Here's hoping you do not find too much use for the shovel in this book.

Mike Maxwell

ps...   Don't forget to read the conclusion at the end of the book!

B.C. Silver...

Captain Pete Soverel (US Navy retired) releasing a magnificent chinook salmon 'somewhere' in northern British Columbia. Pete has been in the forefront of the resurgence of speycasting in North America and has done much to advance the art and science of speyfishing.

INTRODUCTION

ALTHOUGH YOU WILL EVENTUALLY come to the conclusion that speyfishing is a delightfully simple and logical method of angling, you could easily become confused and disappointed with the seemingly unending data that you are confronted with in this book. The problem is that the more care you take to describe a simple subject, the more difficult it appears to be and no doubt, I have fallen into this ever-present trap.

In all walks of life, there are those who approach the study of any subject of interest by reading neat little books such as 'Brain Surgery Made Easy', with the mistaken idea that if you skim the salient points of any subject, you can just 'go out and do it'. Having discovered that this approach does not work, they look around for an electronic device or machine to do it for them. Plastics and technology are a poor substitute for skill and tradition.

On the other end of the scale, there are those who become so interested in a subject that they invest their valuable time and energy in learning everything there is to know about it. Many will want to know 'how to' and 'why' a certain procedure works and then learn to 'do it' correctly, now matter how long it takes. This book will probably 'bore the waders off' the unashamed 'skimmer', however, it is hoped that it will assist the more intelligent and studious angler. Newcomers to speycasting and speyfishing, looking for a quick fix, are strongly advised to read no further.

The book is primarily concerned with teaching the art and science of true speyfishing to beginners, however, it should also be useful to casters already accomplished in the use of the overhead cast. Speycasters using the legendary heavy solid rods may also find it interesting to note how close the controlled energy speyrod, and the method of using it, compares with their traditional rods and angling techniques.

There are many experienced and accomplished anglers skilled in the art of fishing with the stiffer action double-handed fly rods who are not yet aware of the advantages, pleasure and success of using a correctly designed long powerful limber 'true speyrod'. It would be incorrect and presumptuous of me to suggest that these anglers should throw away their stiffer rods and adopt controlled energy speyrods and the methods of fishing with them.

There are also many accomplished double-handers, using the stiffer style of rod, who have become bored with their present method of casting as it no longer presents a challenge. With the greatest of respect for these lucky people, I would suggest that it is time to 'add another string to their bows' and take up the sport of casting and fishing with a 'true speyrod'.

To simplify the learning process, the material has been divided into separate parts starting with a brief history of speyfishing, through the theory of the cast, how to cast, how to fish and finally, how to select and set up your rods, reels, lines and other related equipment.

It is obvious that this book is not a novel and may be somewhat boring if taken in large doses. You will also notice that many important points are repeated in order to reinforce your memory and avoid excessive cross-referencing. Take your time and try not to proceed until you have at least a rudimentary grasp of the previous subject or lesson. Insomniacs may find that a couple of pages of theory 'taken at bedtime' is better than any sleeping potion.

It is human nature to rush out and 'have a go' the moment you start some new venture. Those of you who have attempted to erect your new 'easy-to-assemble' camping tent in a howling rainstorm will know that...

- when all else fails - *read the instructions.*
- better still - *read them before you start.*

Read on and enter the... *'wonderful world of speyfishing'*.

PART ONE ~ INTRODUCTION

CHAPTER

One   *Introduction to Speyfishing*

Two   *The Development of Tubular Rods*

Three   *The Controlled Energy Speyrod*

Four   *The Energies of Speycasting*

Five   *Speycasts You Will Learn*

Six   *More About Speycasting Energies*

Seven   *Using the Body and Arms*

EARLY DAYS...

Mike Maxwell with an early morning Kispiox steelhead, some twenty years ago.

Part One ~ Chapter One
Introduction to Speyfishing

THERE HAS TO BE A BETTER WAY - There must have been times on your favourite river when you have been unable to cast to that obvious 'fish hold' because of those wicked little breezes or that annoying bush that mysteriously grows behind you. To make matters worse, your rod may be too short or stiff to allow you to control the line and present the fly to the fish in an appetizing or appealing way. The ultimate insults are losing your hard-earned fish due to the poor shock absorbing qualities of your rod, or having the unfortunate fish die of old age before you can land it, due to the rod's lack of backbone. Many anglers will accept defeat and move to an easier casting location. Others will assume that their inadequate fly and fish control is a fact of life and make little effort to improve, or reach for their spinning or float fishing rod. By now, it is obvious that there is a better way of fly-fishing and it is, of course, casting and fishing with a speyrod.

WHAT IS SPEYFISHING? - Speyfishing is the art of combining complete coverage of the river by speycasting, complete control of the line and fly after casting, and skilful control of the fish after hooking it.

It should be realized that all stages of speyfishing are *equally important*.

- You will not reach your initial target area if your speycasting is faulty.
- You will not motivate fish with inadequate line control techniques.
- You will not land your fish with clumsy control procedures.

Speyfishing will enable you to catch fish by the most relaxed, safe and elegant method of flyfishing. It will open up your favourite river, increase your effective fishing time and provide an entirely new way of flyfishing (*for some anglers*). You will find that you will be fishing where the fish are, not just where you can backcast.

THE DISADVANTAGES OF THE SINGLE-HAND ROD - Using a single-hand rod in the traditional manner is pleasant and rewarding, and will no doubt be practised forever. However, with the greatest of respect for my friends and former single-handed casting students, fishing with a single-handed rod in the traditional overhead casting style has some disadvantages under certain circumstances. Restricted back-casting space will often force the angler into the only cast possible, not the presentation originally intended. A typical solution to this problem is a splashy fish-disturbing water rollcast. It is also obvious that the single-hand overhead caster will be severely restricted in fishing locations and must leave many interesting parts of the river unfished. Have you ever recorded how much time you wasted catching 'tree fish'.

A major disadvantage of single-handed flyrods is the difficulty of controlling the line and the fly at the extreme distance casts possible with modern graphite rods. As a general rule... *the shorter or stiffer the rod, the more difficult it is to control the line and the fly*. A second important rule... *never cast more line than you are capable of controlling*. It follows that long limber rods are better line controllers than shorter, stiffer rods. The final disadvantage of the shorter, stiffer single-hand rod is in controlling and landing fish. Many fish are lost after hooking unless the angler uses a delicate and long-winded method, bowing to the fish when it jumps and letting the fish tire itself out on long runs. This is unsporting and unhealthy for the fish. Apart from the obvious advantages of river coverage, line control and fish control, speyfishing has many other important advantages.

GETTING AWAY FROM THE CROWD - Perhaps the most significant advantage of speycasting is the ability to fish water that other anglers cannot because of obstacles such as trees or embankments behind them, deep or fast water in front of them or windy locations where the wind seems to blow from all directions at once. The ability to handle casting location obstructions will allow you to get away from the crowd and fish where you want to. As the popularity of flyfishing grows, many rivers are becoming crowded and overfished in certain popular backcasting areas. Some well-known 'pools' are so pressured that there are 'daily line-ups' to fish that particular water and constant bickering about any angler that dares to take too much time moving down the pool. The most important advantage of 'daring to go where others cannot follow' is that you will be fishing undisturbed fish.

EXCESSIVE WADING MINIMIZED - The ability to cast with very little rear clearance will allow you to stay out of dangerous deep or fast water. It will also allow you to fish that productive fish-holding water close to the bank without wading right through it and disturbing or neglecting the fish hiding there. Wading up to your chin in dangerous water to take full advantage of your recently acquired high tech waders may be very good for the 'ego', however, it is disconcerting when a speyfisher in hip waders hooks a fish close to the bank immediately behind you. Why disturb the very fish you are after with excessive wading?

FALSE CASTING ELIMINATED - Many casters enjoy falsecasting to the extent that it seems to be their only reason to be on the river. You begin to wonder if the fish will die of old age before it sees the fly. The old excuse of fishing is 'off' today, so I might as well practise my casting is a waste of time that should have been used to find out some other method of presentation or location that will interest difficult fish.

SPEYCASTING IN THE WIND - As you are probably aware, the wind starts to blow the moment you pick up your single-hand rod and will increase in velocity in proportion to the length of your double-hander. Having decided to blow, the wind will change direction and velocity constantly, and sometimes, seem to be blowing from all directions at the same time. These conditions can make fishing miserable and dangerous, however, the accomplished speycaster can continue in safety and turn the wind into an ally, not an enemy.

To illustrate speyfishing in the wind, it should be remembered that this method of fishing was developed on brawling windy rivers in the Highlands of Scotland using long heavy greenheart or cane rods and great big treble hooks.

The object of the game was to catch fish while keeping those big, ugly flies away from the more important parts of their anatomy, especially when wearing kilts.

INCREASED EFFECTIVE FISHING TIME - Effective fishing time can be defined as the length of time the fly is kept in productive water. If you record how little time your fly is out there in productive water when fishing with the overhead casting technique, you will be unpleasantly surprised.

Here are some of the reasons for speyfishing...

- No searching for backcasting areas.
- No previously disturbed fish.
- No time wasted falsecasting.
- No catching 'tree' fish.
- No dangerous wading.
- No crowded fishing locations.

To sum up, the accomplished speyfisher does not have to 'line up' to fish, does not waste time with excessive wading, does not waste time falsecasting or retying broken flies, returns the fly to the water immediately, and controls the river, line, fly and fish perfectly. One final and important advantage of using a true speyrod is that it greatly reduces angler fatigue. Those athletic people who approach speycasting as a method of exercising are welcome to borrow an old speycasting outfit of mine. This 'delicate' little cane rod is eighteen feet long and has a steel core. The rod, reel and line weigh in at four-and-a-half pounds.

THE POWER AND SENSITIVITY OF TRUE SPEYRODS - Uninformed or envious anglers are fond of saying that speyrods are unfair to fish because they have such enormous power and that you must be unable to detect the delicate touch of an interested fish. This is just sour grapes and complete nonsense. The power of a true speyrod is determined by the line weight it is designed for, not how many hands you need to cast it. A long limber true speyrod will telegraph the slightest nibbles of a very small fish. It is sometimes difficult to tell if you are being teased by a big fish or a smolt if your speyrod has been designed for this important characteristics.

WHY HAS IT TAKEN SO LONG? - There is no definitive reason why speycasting and speyfishing have taken so long to become popular in North America. Could it be that not knowing the sport existed or not realizing the advantages? Perhaps it is the difficulty of finding suitable speyfishing tackle. It could be the revulsion felt after observing a clumsy demonstration by an inexperienced caster using magnum equipment attempting to catch fish that he has driven over to the other side of the river or dredging the river bottom with a heavyweight fly. The most likely reason for not taking up the wonderful sport of speyfishing is the difficulty of finding a competent instructor.

WHERE DO WE GO FROM HERE? - It has been my objective in writing this book to try and lead you down the right road without making too many detours or ending up down a dead end street. If you take the time to study the contents, you will be able to select your equipment, and know how to perform all the necessary casts and fishing techniques. You will also be able to read the river as a speyfisher and enjoy your fishing, catching fish elegantly and intelligently with the technology of the present and the traditions of the past. Most importantly, it should enable you to spot the uninformed rod salesman or the untrained inexperienced speycasting 'instructor'.

SPEYRODS…

A 'family' of speyrods, from then and now (left – right)…

GRANT VIBRATION - *9-weight, 15'–0", solid greenheart, spliced leather thong joint, circa 1910*
HARDY PALACONA - *10-weight, 17'–0", split cane, Lockfast twist joint, circa 1905*
HARDY PALACONA - *9-weight, 14'–0", split cane, spring-loaded pin joint, circa 1965*
MAXWELL TRUE SPEYROD - *10-weight, 15'–0", graphite, internal spigot joint, circa 1995*
MAXWELL TRUE SPEYROD - *6-weight, 11'–6", graphite, internal spigot joint, circa 1995*

Part One ~ Chapter Two
The Development of Tubular Rods

THE DIFFICULTY AND COST of producing split cane rods led to the development of tubular fibreglass and later on, graphite rods. This new breed of rods is considerably lighter, easy to assemble and requires little maintenance. Those who have experienced the problem of maintaining the metal joints on large cane rods (*some resemble plumbing pipe connections*) will know that it was easy to forget and could produce a very awkward situation when finally stuck solid. It was not unusual to see an older long double-hander being carried on the roof rack of a much smaller car.

THE OVERHEAD STYLE OF CASTING DEVELOPS - It was soon realized that light tubular rods made overhead casting easy and allowed beginners to make relatively long casts. As these new stiffer rods were principally designed for overhead casting, they would not speycast adequately, however, they made excellent water rollcasts. The ability to make long rollcasts led to a style of casting based on the erroneous premise that speycasting is just 'contrived rollcasting'. Fishing with these stiffer double-handers is limited in application, tiring to perform and in the hands of anyone other than a skilled caster, inelegant and crude.

EXCESSIVE DISTANCE CASTING WITH OVERHEAD STYLE RODS - Rod manufacturers have always known that beginners or inexperienced flyfishers will rate their progress on how far they can cast without any reference to their ability to make the correct presentation or line and fish control. Rod salesmen are even more aware of the distance casting sales ploy and will stress this characteristic without reference to presentation or line and fish control.

Many anglers, aided and abetted by rod salesmen, have come to believe that the farther they can cast, the more fish they can catch. Others are convinced that the fish are always on the other side of the river regardless of the fact that there are anglers on the other side of the river casting over to this side. This situation can have amusing results as flies from each side of the river tangle. The thrill of hooking an imaginary fish is usually followed by descriptive references to each angler's lineage. Other happy flyfishers enjoy false casting and excessive, unproductive distance casting to the extent that it appears to be the only reason to be on the river and that catching fish is of secondary importance. These people can easily be identified, standing in deep water to clear their backcast and looking around to see if anyone was privileged to see that last 'out-of-sight' overhead cast.

TO SUM UP...

- Distance casting sells rods.
- Distance casting is good for the ego.

DON'T FORGET...

- Distance casting does not mean more fish.
- Avoid the excessive distance casting syndrome.
- If you must distance cast, join a tournament club.

OVERHEAD CASTING - FULL SUNK LINES - HEAVY FLIES - One other sales technique used by overhead rod salesmen is the ability to sink a heavy fly in fast or deep water without much skill required. Unfortunately the weight of the line or fly makes it difficult to make across stream or upstream casts and restricts the presentation to the all too prevalent downstream presentation hoping that the fly will 'get down'. A clear case of weight being substituted for skill and a brutal method of flyfishing. A much better solution to the 'age old' problem of getting the fly down to the 'required depth' would be to use a floating line, a much lighter fly and an across or upstream presentation, then mending the line to control the sink rate of the fly.

TO SUM UP...

- Get your fly down by skill, not weight.
- Enjoy casting with lighter tackle.
- Save money on medical bills or physiotherapy.
- Learn speyfishing with a true speyrod.

To illustrate the difference between the overhead style and speyfishing, we will examine a typical angling scene found on many rivers. Almost all meandering streams have a beach on one side and a cutbank on the other. Fish will lie in deeper water behind rocks that have rolled out of the bank or near the slower water close to the beach. Sketch 1 shows an overhead caster on the beach and a speycaster on the cutbank side.

THE OVERHEAD CASTER - The overhead caster would be unable to fish on the bank side and has chosen his location to provide backcasting space to enable him to cast to the fish on the other side of the river. Once having located a suitable beach area, he has waded out to clear his back cast and could have disturbed fish that were holding where he is now standing. This can prove embarrassing when a more experienced angler hooks a fish that has moved back to its hold directly behind the distance caster.

Once in position, the overhead caster spends a great deal of time with the fly out of productive water. He has to contend with stripping in line, falsecasting, being hooked in the bushes, retying flies, picking out wind knots and shooting line. He is capable of making enormous overhead casts, however, he will be unable to control the line or the fly due to the excessively long cast. This style of fishing, all too prevalent with inexperienced anglers, could rightly be called 'chuck it and chance it', or perhaps 'sling it and swing it'. The need for distance casting is usually a self-inflicted condition and is very good for the ego, however, the fish are seldom impressed.

THE SPEYCASTER - Another glance at Sketch 1 shows the speycaster standing at the foot of the embankment and speycasting over the same fish that the overhead caster is trying to reach from the other side of the river and has perhaps driven over towards the speycaster. This scene is repeated on many rivers. The speycaster can choose a potential fish-holding location regardless of wind, current or backcasting restrictions, choose the appropriate presentation and line control, and return the fly to the water immediately after it has been fished through to the end

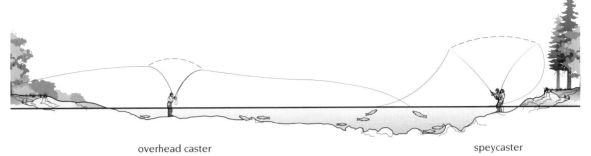

overhead caster   speycaster

of the presentation. It can easily be shown that the speycaster's fly is in

Sketch 1

Overhead versus Spey

productive water at least twice as long as the overhead caster. When demonstrating speyfishing to fishing clubs or other interested groups, the first observation from the more intelligent onlookers is invariably... *"Now I know how to fish that difficult stretch of water on my favourite river."* The next remark is... *"How do I learn speyfishing?"*

How to Choose a Speyrod for Practising

Selecting a speyrod for fishing is thoroughly covered later on, however, at this point we are more concerned with what is the best rod for learning and practising speycasting. Assuming that we are selecting a true speyrod, we must now choose the best length and line size. In order to decide, the following points must be understood...

- As the caster must feel the weight of the line at all times during the cast, heavy lines are better than lighter ones.
- Having chosen the line weight, the timing of the cast depends on the length of the rod.
- Long rods for heavy lines are easier to learn speycasting than short rods for light lines.

THE OPTIMUM LENGTH AND LINE WEIGHT - It has been my experience, after many years of teaching speycasting, that a fifteen foot true speyrod, casting a double taper ten weight floating line is the most successful teaching outfit for all ages and physical characteristics of a student. This advice may come as a shock to prospective speyfishers who have been fishing with a short light-line rod, however, you must bear in mind that you are entering into an entirely different world of fishing and must put aside many of the tackle choice criteria from other methods of fly-fishing. By this time, you are probably saying... *"Does this mean I am going to need more than one rod?"* Just ask yourself how many single-handed rods you own. By the way, the fifteen foot, ten weight rod is my favourite fishing rod and seems to be the natural choice of many other anglers.

FLY LINES FOR PRACTISING - The tapers on heavier fly lines must be extended to prevent 'splash down' and to allow the line and leader to roll out smoothly. This is covered in Chapter Twenty-Seven.

How to Choose Equipment for Fishing

The optimum rod for practising may not be your preferred rod when out on the river fishing. Advice on selecting speyfishing tackle to suit the many different size of fish or type of river is given in Part Five.

Part One ~ Chapter Three
The Controlled Energy Speyrod

THE CHARACTERISTICS OF A TRUE SPEYROD - A well-designed speyrod should provide the following advantages...

- Be powerful enough to make any required presentation regardless of adverse conditions.
- Be limber enough to perform all required line controls.
- Sensitive enough to detect any interested fish.
- Resilient, yet powerful enough to control and land fish quickly and humanely.

It should be realized that not all double-handed rods have all of these desirable characteristics even if their manufacturers say they do. Calling a double-handed rod a speyrod will not make it into one.

THE DEVELOPMENT OF SPEYCASTING - Our old country cousins will know our speyrod as a salmon rod and I hope the 'newfangled' term does not irritate traditionalists. Speycasting (*named for the Scottish river Spey*) was developed to combat the extremes of wind, current, overhanging trees and embankments that inhabit many highland rivers. The object of the sport was to catch fish with a rod and a fly by any legal method. As backcasting was virtually impossible, a form of rollcasting developed. The first objective was to get the fly out to the fish but, more importantly, to keep the fly away from the angler, especially when wearing kilts.

Eventually a method of speycasting developed based on making the final delivery above the water in contrast to the splashy rollcast delivery. After a demonstration of a rollcast, an observant and acid-tongued student was heard to say, *"If that's a rollcast, I don't want to learn"*. His next stage whisper was, *"It makes a wake like a duck landing at high speed"*.

As excessive distance casting was difficult with the heavy limber solid rods, greater emphasis was given to controlling the line and the fly. There are many fine anglers who still prefer to use solid greenheart or split cane double-handers, usually handed down from generation to generation. However, it must be remembered that they have probably been fishing since childhood and are both mentally and physically equipped to use their inherited rods.

DISAPPOINTMENT WITH EARLY TUBULAR RODS - Having learned my speycasting with heavy traditional greenheart and cane rods, it was disappointing to find that fibreglass and later on, graphite rods, made true speycasts difficult and tiring even though they were much lighter. As the ability to make long overhead casts was realized, these rods became lighter and stiffer. This compounded the problem facing the unfortunate speycaster looking for a replacement for his grandfather's old greenheart or cane monster and not wanting to overhead cast.

Having defined the problems of the early tubular rods and knowing the desirable characteristics of a true speyrod, it occurred to me to try and design a graphite rod with all the desirable features of a cane speyrod. As a practising consulting structural engineer, specializing in composite materials and structures, I approached the problem as if it had been presented to me by a rod manufacturer wishing to produce a graphite true speyrod. This approach led me on 'many a wild goose chase' and down many 'wrong roads' for about ten years. The following is a condensed version of my investigations, experiments and solutions.

WHAT WAS SO GOOD ABOUT CANE SPEYRODS? - To watch a skilled speycaster fishing with a well-designed, long heavy limber cane rod is an example of energy conservation. All movements 'appear to be' relaxed with the final forward stroke sending the fly out over the water with a neat loop as if it had been made with an overhead cast. When the fly was finally out on the water, the angler would try and keep it out there as long as possible. 'Hanging the fly' over productive water is very effective, however, it also avoided having to make too many casts with such a heavy rod.

If you picked up one of my heavy old cane rods, you would realize why all casting strokes are very deliberate and slow... the rods are so heavy and limber that there is no other way of doing it. You would soon find out that your attention and your physical efforts are concentrated on getting the rod moving and then stopping it again at the end of the cast. Many an unwary beginner has been toppled over trying to stop an excessively powerful forward stoke due to the self-weight momentum of a long heavy rod. You would also notice that the line would shoot out well above the water in a neat loop if all previous movements of the rod had been performed correctly. Obviously the self-weight momentum of the recoiling rod was doing the job, if you had stopped the rod correctly at the end of the final stroke. Although not entirely true, you would feel that you were casting the very heavy rod, not the relatively weightless line. In other words, when casting with long, heavy cane double-handers, you cast the rod and forget the line. It should be pointed out at this time that this concept is directly opposite to casting with a modern graphite true speyrod where you must cast the line and forget the rod.

ON ROD DESIGN - The process of structural design is largely a clear understanding of the physical properties of the material to be used, the restraints imposed by the method of construction and last, but not least, a clear and unobstructed picture of how you want the final product to perform. If you miss out on any one of these important points, you are doomed to failure or will have to make do with an inferior article and then 'invent' a reason for having produced a rod with that particular power or action. Many rods will eventually reflect the characteristics that the designer or the salesman thinks are the most important.

INNOVATIVE BUT QUESTIONABLE DESIGN - There have been and still are numerous attempts to make a graphite rod 'bend like an old cane rod'. These attempts include the ludicrous idea that all you have to do is weaken the butt. When testing a rod for a friend, without knowing that it had a softened butt design, the blank broke just ahead of the cork grip on a long double spey cast. When analyzing the failure, it appeared that the designer could not perform a double spey and had no concept of the immense bending (*tension and compression*) stresses, coupled with horizontal shear and the resulting principal stresses acting on a tubular composite section under the bending, shear and torsional forces which are present during a double spey cast. It is difficult to understand that there are still designers who believe that weakening the butt makes a speyrod. My advice to these misguided people is not to let a Scottish gillie cast with one of their handicapped rods.

MY FIRST GRAPHITE SPEYROD DESIGNS (1974) - As the objective was to produce a rod similar in action and power to my favourite cane rod, I started by measuring the deflection at numerous points along the rod when loaded with a static weight equal to the dynamic load produced by about sixty feet of the appropriate fly line. These measurements were then expressed as percentages of the maximum tip deflection and sent off to the blank makers for him to duplicate with a graphite rod. The blank was delivered exactly as ordered and quickly made into a rod. It then proved to be a bitter disappointment when trying to cast this rod as I would the cane rod that it was copied from.

After many futile, counter-productive attempts to change the rod, something was still missing. It soon became obvious that the all important punch that shot the line out over the water was missing in the graphite rod. None of the discarded experimental rods were wasted. Some were kept as horrible examples, some became wading staffs and others were given to people I did not particularly like. As the punch was a product of the self-weight momentum of the heavy cane rod, it seemed natural to weight the graphite rod to produce the punch. It is obvious that adding weights to a relatively light rod is not a practical solution. Another method of duplicating the cane rod punch had to be found.

THE POWER PUSH IS DEVELOPED - Some single-handed tournament distance casters use the advanced technique of prematurely turning the rod over during the forward stroke and pushing the tip forward and upwards just like a sword thrust. The object is to bend the tip back, tighten the loop, accelerate the line and increase the length of the stroke. Using the same graphite rod and line outfit as before, it was possible to make a reasonable imitation of my cane rod cast by using a crude push cast. With a few minor changes to the rod and major changes to the push casting technique, I had arrived at a graphite speyrod that allowed me to cast with more precision, delicacy and pleasure than my heavy cane rods. To differentiate this type of rod from all other graphite double-handers, it was given the name 'true speyrod'. It was somewhat 'flattering' when this 'catch phrase' was borrowed by certain creative brochure writers to describe any style of double-hander that bent just a little more than their other stiff overhead casting rods.

ON REPRODUCING AN EXPERIMENT - Scientific experiments are of little value unless the results are carefully recorded and are capable of being interpreted and reproduced by others. Just because it was relatively easy for me to cast and fish with the 'true speyrod', did not mean that other anglers would be able to do so. When searching for a willing student to test out my

Taking a Break
Tom Wilson 'playing dead' after an exhausting day-long session testing my casting and presentation techniques on the Bulkley River back in 1982.

Photography © Maxwell

theories, I was fortunate to meet and secure the assistance of *Tom Wilson*. Tom is a Canadian angler and a professional fisheries and wildlife conservationist, who had the ability to interpret my often confusing instructions to a remarkable degree.

After weeks of painstaking and often frustrating work on the casting pond, it was obvious that my original ideas needed improving. After many more weeks of practice, I was delighted to find that Tom had added additional techniques of his own and had developed into an accomplished speycaster. When testing our new casting methods when fishing on the river, it soon became obvious that our presentation, line control and fish control needed further work, however, it did not take us long to accomplish this.

It is a further requirement of good science that a student is able to reproduce an experiment without supervision. Perhaps the following event will allow you to judge the results...

After perfecting his newfound techniques, Tom was fishing the prestigious Dean River in the coastal mountains of British Columbia, at just about the time of the proliferation of the long stiff magnum overhead double-handers and heavyweight flies. After explaining to other anglers how he was hooking and landing so many large steelhead on dry flies, he was asked why he did not cast as far as they were with their 'vaulting poles' and shooting heads. His taciturn reply was... "*I don't need to*".

Part One ~ Chapter Four
The Energies of Speycasting

UNDERSTANDING CASTING ENERGIES - All bending and moving objects obey the laws of physics and it is essential to understand how this applies to speycasting. In speycasting, we are constantly producing bending energy (*potential*) in the rod, motion energy (*kinetic*) in the line, then concentrating these energies to cast the line in the required direction.

- Hence the term 'controlled energy' speycasting[1].

THE RELATIVE IMPORTANCE OF THE TWO ENERGIES - Having grasped the concept of casting energies, it is helpful to know the relative importance of the bending energy (*potential*) and energy of the moving line (*kinetic*) so that we can divide our attention sensibly when casting.

THE CONTRIBUTION OF THE ROD - Probably the most misleading gem of information that the beginner is faced with is that the rod is a spring and will do the work for you if you bend it enough. This curious statement is repeated over and over by 'hotshot' rod salesmen and untrained casting instructors. To really understand the contribution of the bent speyrod, carry out the following simple experiment...

- Have an accomplished overhead caster false cast 60 feet of line (*measured from the reel*) and estimate the maximum bend in the rod. You will be surprised how little it does bend.
- Now have a helper pull back on the line to produce the same bend - you will also be surprised at the small load required.
- From now on, the caster holds the rod rigidly and makes no attempt to cast.
- When all is ready and the helper releases the line, the rod will recoil, the line will flop forward and fall to the ground without even passing the caster and illustrate the relative lack of spring effect of a fly rod.

THE ROD WILL NOT DO THE WORK - It is obvious by now that the main purpose of the rod is to accelerate and direct the line when casting and that it will not do the work for you. It must also be equally obvious that the contribution of the potential energy of the bent rod is minimal when compared with the kinetic energy of the moving fly line which leads us to the following rule... *when speycasting with a true speyrod, forget the rod and cast the line.*

UNDERSTANDING LINE ENERGY - The term 'generating energy' is not scientifically correct, however, it will be used as a legitimate abbreviation. Throughout this

---

[1] *Mike Maxwell* 1975

book, there will be constant reference to the generation and control of kinetic energy. It is vital that this process is understood as it is the foundation of controlled energy speycasting.

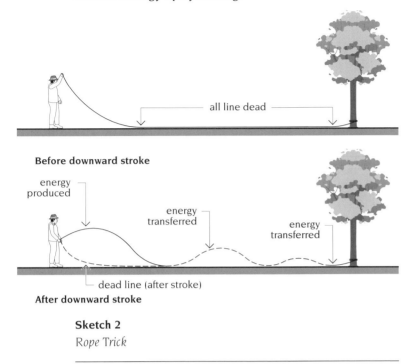

all line dead

Before downward stroke

energy produced

energy transferred

energy transferred

dead line (after stroke)

After downward stroke

Sketch 2
Rope Trick

THE FLUID ENERGY CONCEPT

Any object that is set in motion will take energy from the driving force and continue on until all energy is expended by air drag, gravity or some other external force. Kinetic energy in a flexible object such as a fly line acts in a strange and fascinating way. Energy provided at one end of a moving line can flow down to the other end. To illustrate this important phenomenon, carry out the following experiment, as shown in Sketch 2...

- Tie a heavy rope or extension cord to a fence post or tree and walk back about 40 feet.
- Let the rope lie on the ground, lift the end as high as possible.
- Without pulling back on the rope, make a powerful forward and downward stroke on to the ground in front of you.
- As you make your stroke, you will be generating kinetic energy in the moving loop of the rope.
- As the initial loop falls to the ground, it will lose some of its energy and pass the remaining energy on to the stationary rope in front which will jump up and form another loop and so on until all energy is dissipated by air drag, friction and internal bending forces.

THE IMPORTANCE OF THE FLUID ENERGY CONCEPT - The ability to produce energy at one end of a fly line and let it concentrate or flow down to the other end of the line is a fundamental concept of controlled energy speycasting. When conducting the live rope experiment, it will be obvious that only the moving loop of rope is energized and that the rope laying on the ground is dead.

It must be thoroughly understood that... *only the moving portion of a fly line is energized, all non-moving parts of the line are dead.* We will learn why when discussing line acceleration due to energy concentration.

'CALCULATING' LINE ENERGY (KINETIC) - Kinetic energy can be calculated as follows *(put your slide rules away, you won't need them)*...

$$E = \tfrac{1}{2}Mv^2 \text{ where...}$$

- E = kinetic energy
- M = mass (weight)
- v = velocity (speed)

This law applies to all moving objects from a baseball to the space shuttle, and simply means that to calculate the kinetic energy, you multiply half the weight by the speed and then the speed again ($E = \frac{1}{2}Mv^2$).

THE IMPORTANCE OF LINE VELOCITY - It is obvious that the kinetic energy stored in the moving line will increase by the square of the velocity.

For example…

- A line moving at 20 mph will have 20 x 20 = 400 units of energy.
- A line moving at 40 mph will have 40 x 40 = 1600 units of energy.

This extremely important relationship shows that doubling the speed produces four times the energy. Conversely, halving the speed will only produce a quarter of the energy. This shows that a slight change in line speed produces a major change in line (*kinetic*) energy.

CALCULATING THE SPEED OF THE LINE (VELOCITY) - It is important to know how the speed of the line varies with the amount of energy it receives and the decreasing mass as the loop proceeds.

The kinetic energy equation…

$E = \frac{1}{2}Mv^2$ can be transposed to show that…

$v = \sqrt{E/\frac{1}{2}M}$

By inspecting the equation, it can be seen that the velocity will increase as the mass (*weight*) decreases. This important phenomenon explains why a fly line accelerates towards the end of a well-executed cast. Later on, we will examine the importance of energy concentration and velocity increases when speycasting.

THE OVERHEAD CAST (NOT TAUGHT) - This cast is only included to demonstrate casting energies. It has limited applications and although true spey-rods make outstanding overhead rods, the use of the overhead cast is discouraged. Anglers who cannot resist the urge to 'give it a try' out on the river should make sure that they have an adequate supply of flies. The stages of a well-executed overhead cast are illustrated in Sketch 3. The shaded areas above the line are intended to show the parts of the line that are energized. The thickness of the shaded areas show the intensity of the energy.

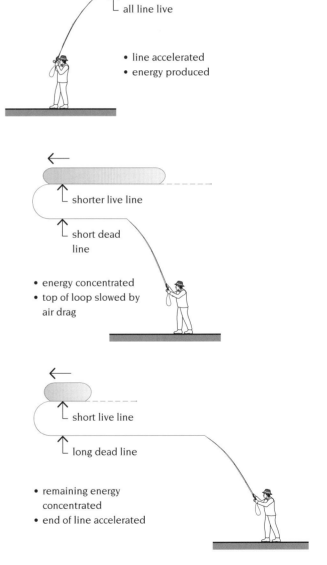

- all line live
- line accelerated
- energy produced

- shorter live line
- short dead line
- energy concentrated
- top of loop slowed by air drag

- short live line
- long dead line
- remaining energy concentrated
- end of line accelerated

Sketch 3
Energies of Overhead Cast

COMBINING THE STAGES OF FLYCASTING - OVERHEAD CASTING - By examining Sketch 3, you can observe that casting a fly line depends on the following sequence of events...

- Generating the energy required for the length of line being cast.
- Allowing the energy to concentrate and accelerate the line.
- And finally, directing the accelerating line in the required direction.

THE PURPOSE OF THE OVERHEAD CAST DISCUSSION - The numerous stages leading up to any speycast can be confusing to a beginner, therefore the overhead cast has been used to demonstrate the process of generating, concentrating and directing line energies. The final delivery of any true speycast will resemble a well-executed forward delivery of an overhead cast as we shall see later on. Do not interpret this discussion as an endorsement of overhead casting with a double-hander.

Part One ~ Chapter Five
Speycasts You Will Learn

THE PRELIMINARIES - Although the intention of this book is to teach you how to cast and fish with a speyrod, there are many important subjects we must discuss before proceeding to the lessons and practices. It is assumed that you have digested Chapter One and are aware of the numerous advantages of casting and fishing with a true speyrod. It will also be necessary to understand how casting energies are generated, concentrated and directed as given in Chapter Four.

WHAT SPEYCASTS WILL YOU LEARN? - The wonderful thing about true speycasting is that there are only two basic casts that you must learn to cover the river under almost any variation of weather, water condition and restricted back casts. There are, of course, exceptions to any rule, therefore we will also learn many other special techniques (*just variations of the two basic casts*) such as casting very short, shooting line and casting with absolutely no room behind you at all... *we all know those rock walls with deep fish holds just in front.* You will find that no matter what special cast you are making, they are all based on the double spey and single spey.

❖ THE DOUBLE SPEY - This wonderful cast is the work horse of the speyfisher. It allows casting in any direction from directly downstream to any angle across stream or directly upstream without the fly coming near or going behind the angler.

DOUBLE SPEYS ON EITHER SIDE OF THE RIVER - Speycasters determine the left and right banks when looking down river.

• THE RIGHT BANK DOUBLE SPEY - This cast is the basic double spey with the final delivery made over the right side of the body, this being the 'natural' casting position for a right-handed caster.

• THE LEFT BANK DOUBLE SPEY - This cast is precisely the same cast as the right bank cast, however, the final delivery is made on the left side of the body.

• NO NEED TO CHANGE HAND POSITIONS - A true speyrod is so light and limber that there is no need to change hands to cast over the left shoulder. A slight twist and lean to the left will send the line over to the left of the body allowing the cast to proceed virtually the same as a right bank cast.

- Double Speys in Upstream Wind - The final delivery of both the right and left bank double speys takes place on the downstream side of the angler. In 'strong' upstream winds, the line can blow onto the angler on the forward stroke or cross over and foul the forward delivery. When this occurs, it is time to start speycasting with the single spey technique.

❖ The Single Spey - Once you have mastered the versatile double spey covering the river to any required angular change of direction, you will find that you will only use the single spey as an emergency cast when a strong wind makes double speying dangerous. Single speys can be made on either side of the river.

Limitations of the Single Spey - The single spey should be limited to a maximum of a 45° change of direction due to the difficulty of placing the line upstream without fouling the line to the rear or having it fall 'dead' on the water behind you.

- The Left Bank Single Spey - This cast is made on the right side of the body and is relatively easy for right-handers. Although the right bank single looks simple, the timing is critical.

- The Right Bank Single Spey - This cast is virtually the same as the left bank single with the final delivery being made on the left side of the body.

The Misconceptions About Speycasting - There are many 'authorities' who cannot or will not speycast over the left side of the body. This could be due to the stiffness of their rods or their lack of skill.

Casting Left-Handed - There are always people who enjoy making things difficult for themselves. Instead of learning the simple technique of placing the line over to the left side of the body, they change the rod over to the other side of the body and cast left-handed. This complicated solution to a simple problem means learning to cast all over again and does not make sense.

Using the Wrong Cast - Probably the most ridiculous 'gems of misinformation' quoted by uninformed 'authorities', unable to place the line over to the other side of the body is that the double spey is only used on the right side of the river because the final delivery is on the right side of the body and that the single spey is only used on the left bank because the final delivery is made over the right shoulder. Don't be a 'right shoulder only' caster. Right shoulder only casters are easily identified by their preference for right bank casting locations. The right shoulder only people will also be found on the sometimes neglected left bank, making inefficient downstream presentations with a single spey even though there is a downstream wind obstructing their casting.

Speycasting is Easy - Fishing with a true speyrod must be the most relaxed, pleasant and effective method of flyfishing. Providing you are taking up the sport for the right reasons, not just distance casting or to use heavy sunk line or flies. If you learn why it works, not just how and are prepared to practise regularly, there is no reason why you should not become an accomplished speyfisher and enjoy the learning experience.

Part One ~ Chapter Six
More About Speycasting Energies

WHAT ARE ALL THOSE STRANGE ROD MOVEMENTS? - When watching an accomplished speycaster, the rod and line seem to be going 'every which way' before finally shooting out over the water with a beautifully controlled forward delivery. Are they necessary? You begin to wonder if all those 'weird' movements really are necessary or is it just having fun waving that big rod around before making that 'classy looking' forward delivery?

PRELIMINARY MOVEMENTS - The truth about all those strange movements is that they are only to take the line from directly downstream and place it in position to make the final delivery. It is obvious that the final delivery is the most important part of speycasting and must be studied in detail.

THE LINE ENERGIES OF THE FINAL DELIVERY - *Sketch* 4, *pages* 22 *and* 23, shows the five stages of the forward delivery of a speycast. This procedure is used on every speycast, double or single, on either side of the river.

The Stages of the Forward Delivery

Once again, the shaded areas above the line show the magnitude and location of the line energy as it is generated, concentrated and directed.

STAGE 1

THE FORWARD STROKE COMMENCES - The caster has rocked back, made an efficient 'backcast' with the line loop high up and live. As no line is fed out, the line is anchored to the reel and to the water in front of the angler. The left hand is tight to the chest, the right hand is tight to the right shoulder. The caster rocks forward and generates a small amount of energy in the accelerating length of the line. The line and fly are anchored in the water.

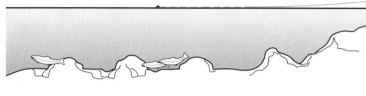

STAGE 2

THE FORWARD STROKE PROCEEDS - The caster continues to rock forward with the rod still held tight to the body. More line is now moving and the energy is building. More energy is concentrated close to the rod tip as it is moving faster. The line is still anchored in the water.

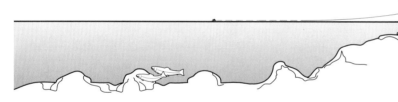

STAGE 3

THE FORWARD STROKE ENDS - The caster continues to rock forward with the rod still held tight to the body. At this point, the maximum line energy has been generated. When the caster stops the forward rock, the rod is still tight to the body. At this point, the rod tip is held back by the line, however, the powerful flexible butt of the true speyrod will recoil ahead and create a compound curve in the recoiling rod. As the rod recoils into a compound curve, the caster pushes the rod upwards and outwards against the pull of the line. This bends the rod tip back even further and directs the line forward in a tight loop.

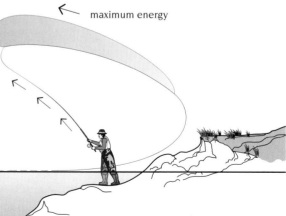

maximum energy

Sketch 4
Energies of Forward Delivery

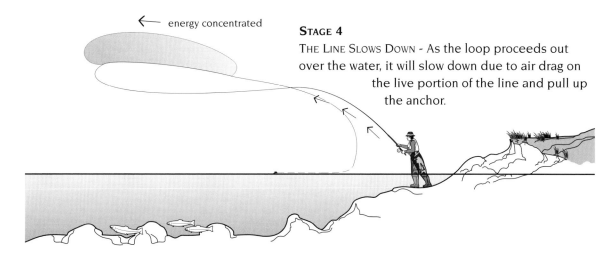

← energy concentrated

STAGE 4

THE LINE SLOWS DOWN - As the loop proceeds out over the water, it will slow down due to air drag on the live portion of the line and pull up the anchor.

STAGE 5

END OF LOOP ACCELERATES - When the water anchor is pulled, the remaining energy concentrates in the short section of live line. The velocity increases due to energy concentration ($v = \sqrt{E/\frac{1}{2}M}$). The end of the loop will straighten well above the water, exactly like a well-executed overhead cast, in direct contrast to a rollcast delivery.

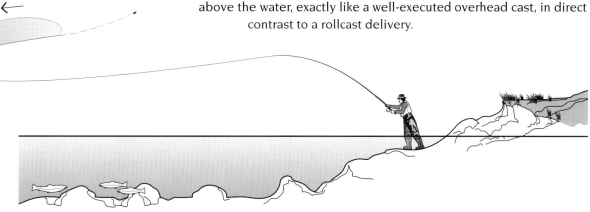

←

HOW MUCH ENERGY IS REQUIRED? - It is obvious that the line will not accelerate or straighten out if insufficient power is used. Too much power will cause the line to bounce back after straightening. Gauging the correct power for the forward delivery of a speycast can only be learned by practice.

TO SUM UP...

The sketches show that the caster has been able to make a forward delivery with a neat loop well above the water exactly like a well-made overhead cast without making a long tree-catching back cast. The cast was made by producing, concentrating and directing kinetic energy.

The Compound Curvature of True Speyrods

A glance at Sketch 5 shows shows that a well-designed speyrod, both limber and powerful, will recoil into a strange double curvature during the final delivery of a well-executed speycast. The importance of this strange behaviour cannot be overlooked and must be discussed in greater detail.

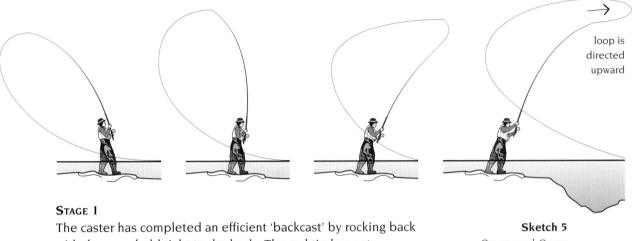

loop is directed upward

Sketch 5
Compound Curve

STAGE 1
The caster has completed an efficient 'backcast' by rocking back with the arms held tight to the body. The rod tip has not travelled very far to the rear.

STAGE 2
The caster then rocks forward with arms still held tight to the body to produce the required kinetic energy in the accelerating line and the potential energy in the bent rod. When the caster feels that sufficient velocity and energies have been produced, the forward power stroke is stopped firmly.

STAGE 3
At this point, the rod tip is still being held back by the line, however, the powerful butt section of the rod will recoil forward, producing the double curvature. As more of the butt sections of the rod recoils, it accelerates the tip section which adds additional velocity to the line. The caster is still rocking forward with the hands close to the body. As the butt recoil continues, the tip section of the rod is bent back even further by the increasing pull on the accelerating line.

STAGE 4
Just before the final rod recoil, the caster continues to rock forward and pushes the rod tip upwards and outwards against the pull of the line. If the body rock and power push are timed correctly, the line will accelerate rapidly and produce a tremendous surge of energy which will shoot the line out over the water in a tight air resistant loop wherever it is aimed. To understand why the power push acceleration is so efficient, it must be remembered that kinetic line energy increases with the square of the velocity ($E = 1/2\,Mv^2$) and means that any increase in velocity produces a real bonus in line energy.

Remember... *Twice the velocity gives four times the energy.*

To Sum Up...

The object is to generate potential energy in the rod, kinetic energy in the line, allow the energies to concentrate and then direct the line out above the water in a tight air resistant loop. Very little strength is required as most of the cast is made with body rock and arm push. It should now be obvious why casting with a powerful limber true speyrod can be called controlled energy speycasting. It should be also be obvious why stiff 'fast-action' overhead style double-hand rods are not suitable for true speycasting.

The Forward Delivery With Stiff Double-Handers

To illustrate the difference between a controlled energy speycast made with a well-designed speyrod and a stiffer overhead-style rod, compare Sketch 6 with the previous sketch.

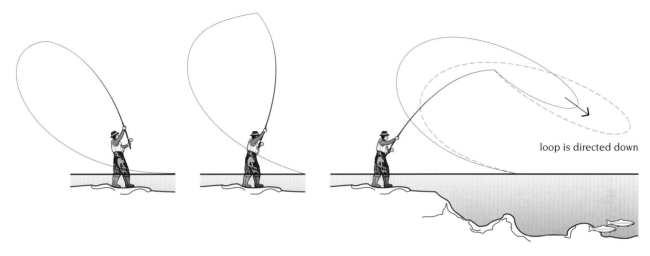

loop is directed down

STAGE 1
The overhead caster has made an efficient back cast with the arms raised and the rod tip well to the rear.

Sketch 6
Stiff Rod Delivery

STAGE 2
The caster then makes a huge forward stroke by rotating the butt of the rod with both arms. As the stroke proceeds, the caster will have difficulty in generating line speed and will instinctively make a power snap at the end of the stroke.

STAGE 3
After the very long stroke and 'power snap' is completed, the rod tip will invariably be travelling in a downward direction which directs the line downwards and degenerates into a standard splashy, fish-disturbing rollcast with no possibility of aerial mending.

TO SUM UP...

The stiff overhead style of rod is based on the mistaken premise that a speyrod is just an overgrown single-hander and that you should cast it the same way. The athletic ability and strength required is beyond most prospective speycasters and has deterred most intelligent anglers. The difficulty of making across stream or upstream presentations with a stiff double-hander is a serious handicap when speyfishing. The further difficulty of making tight, above water line deliveries without the line falling down into a rollcast has discouraged many anglers who are interested in speycasting.

You would not want to rollcast all day with your single-handed rod, so why would you enjoy rollcasting all day with a double-hander?

The Rollcast Delivery

Sketch 7 shows the progression of a true rollcast delivery. This somewhat exaggerated example shows how a downward stroke of the rod tip directs the line onto the water. Rollcasting can be avoided when speyfishing with a true speyrod.

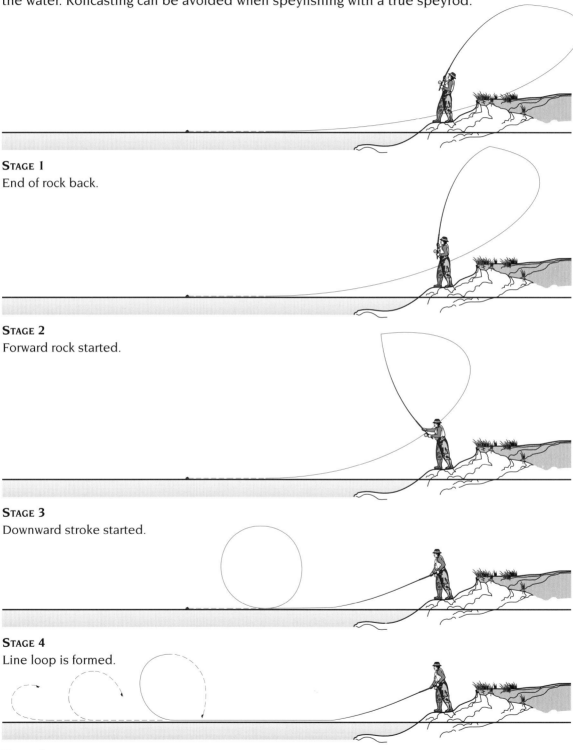

STAGE 1
End of rock back.

STAGE 2
Forward rock started.

STAGE 3
Downward stroke started.

STAGE 4
Line loop is formed.

STAGE 5
Line rolls out on the water.

Sketch 7
Rollcast

Overhead Casting With a True Speyrod

It is often stated that true speyrods make overhead casting difficult or impossible, due to their limber action. This is nonsense! If the caster uses the same body rock and arms close to the body technique used for true speycasting, superb overhead casts can be made. This method was demonstrated by an expert angler and practical-joker friend, who after making a faultless double spey from directly downstream to across stream suddenly lifted the line off the water and commenced to make tight-looped overhead false casts, finally shooting extra line an enormous distance across the river. As you have probably guessed, he was in a casting location that permitted long back casts and was just rattling my cage. Once you have mastered the art of making long relaxed speycasts with very little effort, you will no longer feel the urge to revert to overhead casting even if backcasting conditions allow it.

Part One ~ Chapter Seven
Using the Body and Arms

THE IMPORTANCE OF CORRECT CASTING POSITIONS - We now know that the body weight is used when controlled energy speycasting. The correct use of body weight allows effortless casting, however, it must be studied in detail to fully understand how to utilize it to the best advantage.

THE RIGHT FOOT IS ALWAYS FORWARD - Placing the right foot forward (*for a right-handed caster*) is fundamental to controlled energy speycasting. The primary reason is allowing the major muscles of the legs, body and shoulders to be used equally as the caster turns and rocks when casting; *see* Photo 2A – 2C, *page* 31.

PLACING THE WRONG FOOT FORWARD - So many sports require the left foot to be placed forward that it seems natural to do so when speycasting. Let's take a look at the muscle involvement during a left foot forward cast. As the caster rocks back and turns, the muscles are not 'wound up' very tightly. As the caster reaches the upright position on the forward stroke, the wound up spring effect of the muscles will have already been released. As the caster rocks forward and turns, the muscles will now be wound up again in the wrong direction which will impede the cast, not help it.

TO SUM UP... The right foot forward allows the powerful wound up spring effect of the muscles to be used to advantage on the forward delivery. The left foot forward makes hard work of speycasting as it requires pushing against the spring effect of the body muscles during the forward delivery. By the way, the one sport that requires the right-hander to place the right foot forward is fencing (*the one with swords - not posts and barbed wire*).

HOW YOU GRIP THE ROD - How you hold a true speyrod when casting will seem strange to the single-hander. The first question is... *"What on earth is all that cork for?"* The next question is... *"Where do I put my hands?"*

WHAT ARE ALL THOSE CORKS FOR? - The length of cork grip used in controlled energy casting is relatively short. The extremely long section of cork (*some as long as 30"*) is to provide extra leverage when controlling fish.

HAND GRIPS WHEN CASTING - We have seen that controlled energy speycasting requires the caster to push the rod on the forward delivery. It should also be obvious that the longest push will make the best cast. The longest push can be made with the left hand gripping the butt and the right hand gripping the corks just above the reel. This close-to-the-reel grip is very difficult for a beginner to understand, as once again, it does not seem natural (*whatever that means*).

THE WRONG POSITION OF THE RIGHT HAND - If the right hand is placed at the top of the cork grip, it will seriously reduce the efficiency of the forward delivery for the following reasons... *it will reduce the length of the final stroke and waste the advantages of the power push*. Remember... *generate*, *concentrate* and *direct* line energy. Placing the right hand at the top of the cork grip will inevitably lead to a wide arc by rotating the rod with both hands. This faulty procedure will produce a sloppy forward cast directed down onto the water similar to that shown in Sketch 6, page 25.

WHY IS THIS SO IMPORTANT? - We already know that the caster rocks backwards and forwards with the arms close to the body to produce the line energy when making the final delivery of a true speycast. If the correct hand and arm positions are not maintained the cast will degenerate and become very tiring. If the rod is kept close to the body in the correct position, the entire energy is produced by body movement, not arm movement and allows you to cast all day long with hardly any effort. To impress this important point on an incredulous student, I frequently speycast when holding the rod with only two fingers and a thumb of each hand. What impresses them is that the rod is a fifteen foot true speyrod and that I am speycasting seventy feet of double taper line. This is not trick casting, you will be able to repeat it once you become an accomplished caster.

Hand and Rod Positions

RIGHT SHOULDER CAST

A glance at Photo 1A (*below*), Photos 2A and 2B (*facing page*) shows the correct position of the rod, hands and arms for all movements of speycasting except the final power push.

Photo 1:
CASTING POSITIONS -
FRONT

A - *Right Shoulder*   B - *Left Shoulder*   C - *Left Shoulder*
Cast Correct   *Cast Correct*   *Cast Wrong*

Right shoulder casting position…

- The rod is angled to the side of the caster.
- The left hand is exactly in the centre of the chest.
- The right hand is close to the reel and at the right shoulder.
- The shoulder is turned to the right.

Note… *the rod is hugged close to the body.*
Remember… *the right foot forward.*

LEFT SHOULDER CAST

Now look at the left shoulder casting position, Photo 1B…

- The rod is angled to the left of the caster.
- The body is leaned to the left.
- The right foot is still forward.

It can be seen that all you have to do is lean the body over to place the rod tip and line over to the left side.

LEFT SHOULDER CAST ~ 'THE WRONG WAY'

Take a good look at the casting position shown in 1C, then make a vow never to cast that way unless you have the reactions of a professional tennis player making a bone-crushing backhand stroke or the rubber bones of a contortionist.

- The entire rod is on the wrong side.
- Both arms and hands are on the wrong side.
- It is virtually impossible to make a controlled speycast from the wrong side. What usually happens is a power snap that produces a wild splashy delivery that goes everywhere except where you want it to go.

Photo 2:
CASTING
POSITIONS ~ SIDE

A - *Back Cast*   B - *Forward Lean*   C - *Power Push*

THE IMPORTANCE OF THE LEFT SHOULDER - We have learned that your coverage of the river would be seriously affected if you cannot speycast over the left shoulder, as you will not be able to make the following important casts...

- The single spey on the right bank.
- The double spey on the left bank.

Don't be a right bank only double speycaster or a left bank only single spey-caster.

PRACTISE THE BODY MOVES (WITHOUT LINE) - To familiarize yourself with the limber action of a true speyrod, adopt the standard casting position and swish the rod around in an accelerated figure-eight motion directly above you, keeping the rod close to the body. The rod will take a considerable bend and swishing noise will be noticed. These strange effects are essential to a good speyrod. However, the noise must be eliminated when speycasting as it indicates wasted energy.

ROCKING THE BODY - The object of the body rock is to produce most of the line acceleration and avoid tiring the arms; *see Sketch* 8.

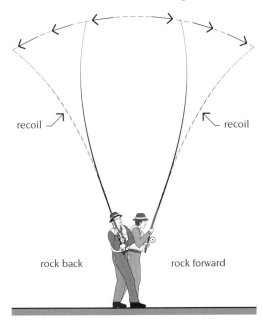

recoil

recoil

rock back   rock forward

Sketch 8
Body Rock (Without Line)

To practise this, proceed as follows...

- Assume the standard casting position.
- The arms and the hands must remain close to the body throughout the practice.
- Resist the tendency to make a casting stroke, similar to your single-hand cast.
- Rock forward and stop suddenly when the rod reaches ten o'clock.
- Now rock back and stop suddenly at two o'clock.
- Repeat the forward and backward rock.
- Observe the considerable bend and recoil of the long limber rod, caused by the body rock alone, without any assistance from the casting stroke or power push.

SUBDUE FORMER CASTING STYLE REACTIONS - Anglers come to controlled energy casting with varied previous experiences. Most are single-handed casters. Many are skilled in the use of cane double-handers or have been using double-handers with the overhead casting style. Each of these previous methods of casting will be imprinted in the angler's memory bank and it is vital that these reactions be modified when learning controlled energy casting.

ARE ALL THOSE BODY MOVEMENTS NECESSARY? - As you become more familiar with true speycasting, you will find that most of the line energies are produced by body movement when rocking or turning to the side or to the rear. This is in direct contrast to the wrist and arm jarring style of casting advocated by stiff rod casters. Take the time to study, learn and practise all body moves; these body moves allow you to make effortless casts, all day long, without producing aching wrists, tennis elbows or dislocated shoulders. Just think how impossible it would be if golfers, tennis players or baseball pitchers did not understand the value of '*body English*'.

THE VALUE OF THE BODY MOVEMENTS - As we have just discussed, most of the casting energies are produced by a circular rocking movement of the shoulders and upper body. When demonstrating this very simple technique to Joan Wulff on the banks of the Yellowstone River, it was disconcerting to hear her say... "S*top, don't you know what you are doing?*"

When one instructor is demonstrating for another equally or better qualified instructor, you have to be ready for criticism. Having steeled myself for a few 'constructive remarks', it came as a complete surprise to see Joan, upstream on a sandbar, performing dance movements that would look more at home in a ballet class than a Montana river. "*You see, Mike, you are dancing.*" Now, this was news to me, however, this simple analogy demonstrated the upper body gyrations of my speycasting. When relating this episode to some of my more 'rigid' students, you can be sure that I do not attempt to imitate Joan's graceful dancing lessons.

GETTING THE MOST OF THE BODY MOVEMENTS - Unless you are content to let your forward delivery degenerate into the water-disturbing rollcast shown in Sketch 6, page 25, the rod must be locked to the body during the entire casting procedure, except of course, the final power push. The body movement and 'locked in' rod procedure produces a smooth, controlled cast and eliminates wearing out the arms and the shoulders. Newcomers are surprised how powerful the correct body rock procedure is and begin to understand how effortless true speycasting is going to be.

KEEP YOUR LEFT HAND ON YOUR CHEST - Throughout the book, there will be constant reference to keeping the left hand on the chest (*don't let it slide down to the belt buckle*). This advice should be written in blood as it is the single-most important procedure in true, controlled energy speycasting, however, it is also the least understood.

Now, a '**GOLDEN RULE**' of true speycasting...

- The left hand must be locked to the chest at all times. Your progress depends on your ability to keep your left hand on your chest - *except when power pushing*.

Part Two ~ Pond Casting

Chapter

Eight	*Forward Spey*
Nine	*Circular Forward Spey*
Ten	*Single Spey*
Eleven	*Double Spey*
Twelve	*Advanced Techniques*
Thirteen	*Speycasting in Wind*

Backcast on the Pond...

Mike Maxwell demonstrating controlled energy speycasting on a practice pond. A well-timed backcast forms a graceful curve in the line as Mike prepares for the next stage... the forward rock and power push.

Part Two ~ Chapter Eight
Forward Spey - Pond

Learn on a Casting Pond - Having acquired an adequate speycasting outfit, the beginner will want to rush down to the river and have a go. This often produces hilarious results, varying from imitating a helicopter taking off, to knitting a giant sweater. It makes sense to learn and practise on a casting pond before taking on the river. As most of the casting procedure is independent of water current, it is preferable to use a casting pond without the distractions of moving water and the need for waders, etc. Casting ponds are more available than rivers and often provide shelter from high winds. Still water also allows inspecting the cast, before the line is swept away by moving water. Although it is commonly supposed that speycasting on still water is extremely difficult or impossible for a beginner, the advantages easily outweigh the disadvantages. There are many ways of simulating the desirable effects of moving water without the use of the river.

Equal Time for Each Shoulder - A casting pond allows casting from each shoulder to simulate the right and left banks of a river... *without moving the casting location.* Practising on moving water requires crossing over to the other side and usually results in neglecting the left or the right shoulder casts.

Slow Water Out on the River - When casting on the moving water of a river, the current will automatically tighten the line during the dip and lift stages of the cast. However, if your line drifts into very slow or dead water, you will have real problems if you have not mastered the dip and lift technique on the still waters of the casting pond. Many anglers will lift the line and start the next cast well before it swings into the difficult slow water. The paradox is, fish will often hold in the current seam between fast and slow water, or in backwaters. Take your time with the dip and lift technique, it will improve your moving water casting and allow you to fish those productive areas that the poorly trained speycaster avoids.

Standard Forward Spey

All speycasts finish with a forward spey. It is essential you are able to perform this procedure (*on either side of the body*) before moving on to any other subject.

ADVANTAGES OF LEARNING THE FORWARD SPEY - This training cast is ideal for learning and practising the following procedures...

- Getting the feel of the cast and seeing what the line is doing.
- Timing each stage of the cast.
- Getting used to the right foot forward stance, together with arm and rod positions.
- Judging the power required for each phase of the cast.
- Imprinting the body rock, shoulder turn and power push techniques.
- Simulating the line tightening effect of moving water on still water.
- Learning speycasting on either side of the body.

REVIEW OF BODY ROCK AND POWER PUSH - Anglers coming from other styles of fly-casting often have difficulty with the body and arm movements required for controlled energy speycasting, therefore it should be reviewed before proceeding. Each of the five stages are equally important. Do not expect to make any progress if either of the stages are not understood or are performed incorrectly.

DON'T USE FLIES - Always use a two inch length of bright coloured fluorescent yarn when practising (*tie it on with an improved clinch knot*). Hooks are extremely dangerous even with the point and bend cut off.

IMPROVED TAPER LINES - The end tapers are inadequate on heavier double taper lines and must be improved to allow the line and leader to roll out correctly. You will be pleasantly surprised how your speycasting improves when practising or fishing with a correctly designed improved taper; *see Sketch 42, page* 208.

HANDLING LINE BEFORE PRACTISING - It is vitally important that you use the correct length of line for practising (*and fishing*). Most faults can be traced back to either too long or too short a line.

MARK YOUR LINE - You should not fall into the trap of using the wrong line length if you mark your lines with a waterproof felt pen; *see Sketch 44, page* 210.

A - *Forward lean, dip*   B - *Forward lean, lift*   C - *Rock, backcast, right*

GETTING OUT LINE - There is a natural tendency to make short tree-hooking back casts when getting out line before casting. This also applies when fishing and can be avoided with the following procedure...

- Pull out about one rod length of line through the guides and let it anchor in the water.
- Strip the additional required length of line off the reel and let it fall to the ground.
- Now swish the rod from side to side feeding the line through the guides as the water drag pulls it out onto the water.
- Finally, get the line out straight and the rod tip dipped, ready for the first lift (*anyway you can for the first lesson*).

HOLDING THE LINE WHEN CASTING - When speycasting with a well-maintained reel, with a light drag, additional unwanted line can be pulled off the reel with each cast. To avoid this cast disturbing effect, trap the line under the right hand just above the reel. Get used to this 'line hold' and use it on every cast when practising and fishing.

PREREQUISITES - It is assumed that you have a suitable speyrod and floating line combination. Don't forget the improved taper. See Chapter Twenty-Five on rod selection. Check the security of your rod joints; *see page* 200.

Standard Forward Spey - Right Shoulder - Pond

GETTING SET TO CAST - Study the casting positions shown in sequences Photo 3, facing page and below. Also refer to Sketch 9, pages 40 and 41. Begin with four rod lengths of line measured from the reel.

Photo 3:
STANDARD
FORWARD RIGHT
SHOULDER - POND

D - *Forward rock, power push*   E - *Forward lean, dip*

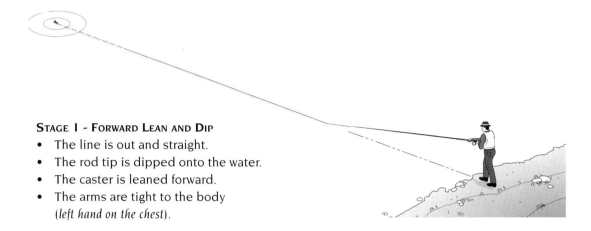

Stage 1 - Forward Lean and Dip

- The line is out and straight.
- The rod tip is dipped onto the water.
- The caster is leaned forward.
- The arms are tight to the body
  (*left hand on the chest*).

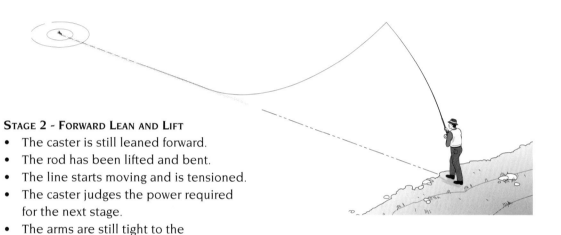

Stage 2 - Forward Lean and Lift

- The caster is still leaned forward.
- The rod has been lifted and bent.
- The line starts moving and is tensioned.
- The caster judges the power required
  for the next stage.
- The arms are still tight to the
  body (*left hand on the chest*).

Stage 3 - Rock Backcast

- The caster has rocked back and
  turned to form the rear loop.
- The turn allows inspecting the
  loop and placing the shoulder
  ready for the next stage.
- The rear loop is live.
- The end of the line is still
  anchored in the water.
- The arms are still tight to the
  body (*left hand on the chest*).

Sketch 9
*Standard Forward Right Shoulder
Pond - Stages 1, 2 and 3*

STAGE 4 - FORWARD ROCK AND POWER PUSH

- The caster has rocked forward and pushed the shoulder forward to generate line energy.
- The arms are still tight to the body (*left hand on the chest*).
- Just before the forward rock is completed, the caster pushes the tip of the rod against the pull of the line.
- The rod tip is pushed upwards and outwards in a straight line.
- The caster is still leaned forward and the arms are fully extended.
- The accelerating line will flow forward and start to lift the anchor.

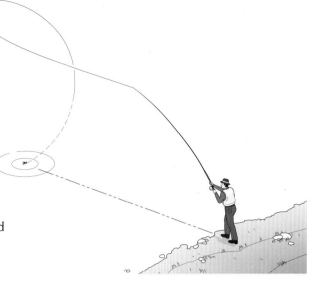

STAGE 5 - FINAL DELIVERY

- The anchor is pulled.
- The line unrolls well above the water.
- The end of the line will accelerate due to energy concentration.

STAGE 6 - FORWARD LEAN AND DIP

- The line will straighten and fall to the water.
- The rod is dipped as the line falls.
- The caster is still leaned forward with the arms extended.

Sketch 9
*Standard Forward Right Shoulder
Pond - Stages 4, 5 and 6*

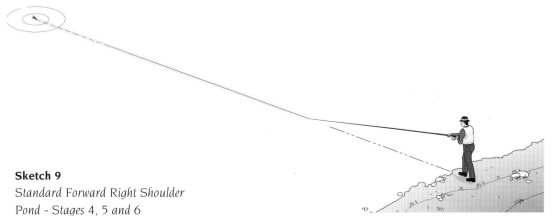

Preparing for the Next Cast - Before commencing the next cast, it's essential that...

- The line is out straight.
- The rod is dipped with no slack line.
- The caster is leaned forward.
- The arms are tight to the body (*left hand on the chest*).

Watch Out for These Common Faults

- Not dipping the rod before the lift.
- Not maintaining the forward lean during the lift.
- Not rocking correctly.
- Not using the shoulder turn.

The Worst Faults

- Feet position wrong way around.
- Feet not far enough apart.
- Arms not held close when body rocking (*left hand on the chest*).
- Arm not fully extended when pushing.
- Not dipping the rod at the end of the cast.

The Absolute Worst Faults

- Going all out for distance with excessive power.
- Trying to cast a limber speyrod as you would a stiffer single-hander.
- Right hand away from the reel.
- Making a rollcast not a speycast delivery.
- Wrong length of line.

A Word of Encouragement - Don't worry if your first practice sessions look like knitting a giant sweater. No speycaster makes a perfect cast every time.

A - *Forward lean, dip*   B - *Forward lean, lift*   C - *Twist, rock, backcast, lift*

Standard Forward Spey - Left Shoulder - Pond

GETTING SET TO CAST - Study the casting positions shown in sequences Photo 4, facing page and below. Also refer to Sketch 10, pages 44 and 45. Begin with four rod lengths of line measured from the reel.

The left shoulder spey is the same as the right shoulder spey, with the line passing to the left of the caster. By comparing Sketch 9 and Sketch 10, you will see that the only difference is in STAGES 3 and 4.

THE LEFT SHOULDER ROCK BACK - The technique of making the loop form to the left requires special consideration as it is the foundation of all left shoulder spey-casts. The problem is to make the line go to the left without placing the whole rod and arms over to the left side of the body.

THE BODY TWIST - Instead of rocking back and turning the shoulder slowly as for the right shoulder cast, twist the body firmly to the left, returning to face forward immediately. If the body twist is made correctly, the line loop will form behind without placing the rod and arm over to the left side.

TO SUM UP...

- Lean left, rod tip to the left.
- Arms tight to the body.
- Rock back and twist to the left, untwist immediately.
- Keep the arms tight to the body.

A WORD OF ENCOURAGEMENT - Don't worry if you do not perform the body twist exactly as described, many of my students have gone on and developed their own techniques for this tricky procedure.

Photo 4:
STANDARD
FORWARD LEFT
SHOULDER - POND

D - *Forward rock, power push*   E - *Forward lean, dip*

STAGE 1 - FORWARD LEAN AND DIP

- The line is out and straight.
- The rod tip is dipped onto the water.
- The caster is leaned forward.
- The arms are tight to the body (*left hand on the chest*).

STAGE 2 - FORWARD LEAN AND LIFT

- The caster is still leaned forward.
- The rod has been lifted and bent.
- The line starts moving and is tensioned.
- The caster judges the power required for the next stage.
- The arms are still tight to the body (*left hand on the chest*).

STAGE 3 - TWIST AND ROCK BACKCAST

- The caster has leaned to the left, twisted and rocked back to form the loop and untwisted immediately to face forward again.
- The rear loop is live.
- The arms are still tight to the body (*left hand on the chest*).
- The end of the line is still anchored.

Sketch 10
*Standard Forward Left Shoulder
Pond - Stages 1, 2 and 3*

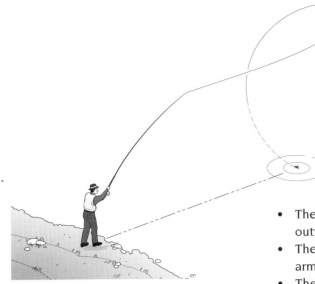

STAGE 4 - FORWARD ROCK AND POWER PUSH

- The caster has rocked forward and pushed the shoulder forward to generate line energy.
- The arms are still tight to the body (*left hand on the chest*).
- Just before the forward rock is completed, the caster pushes the tip of the rod against the pull of the line.
- The rod tip is pushed upwards and outwards in a straight line.
- The caster is still leaned forward and the arms are fully extended.
- The accelerating line will flow forward and start to lift the anchor.

STAGE 5 - FINAL DELIVERY

- The anchor is pulled.
- The line unrolls well above the water.
- The end of the line will accelerate due to energy concentration.

STAGE 6 - FORWARD LEAN AND DIP

- The line will straighten and fall to the water.
- The rod is dipped as the line falls.
- The caster is still leaned forward with the arms extended.

Sketch 10
*Standard Forward Left Shoulder
Pond - Stages 4, 5 and 6*

PREPARING FOR THE NEXT CAST - Before commencing the next cast, it's essential that...

- The line is out straight.
- The rod is dipped with no slack line.
- The caster is leaned forward.
- The arms are tight to the body (*left hand on the chest*).

COMMON FAULTS

- Feet wrong.
- Arms not tight to the body, when required (*left hand on the chest*).
- Rocking back prematurely.
- Not making the body twist.
- Not maintaining the sidecast position.
- Letting the rear loop die.
- Not dipping at the end of the cast.
- Wrong length of line.

WORST FAULTS

- Placing the rod and hands to the left of the body.
- The right hand away from the reel.
- Making a rollcast not a speycast delivery.
- Using excessive power.

PRACTICE... Standard Forward Spey - Both Shoulders - Pond
Four rod lengths of line - measured from the reel...

THE OBJECT OF THE PRACTICE - How you practise is even more important than what you practise. Forward speys from each side of the body must be imprinted into your long term memory.

EQUAL TIME - Once again, casting on the right side of the body may seem 'natural' at this stage of your training, however, you must give equal time to casting on the left side unless you are content to be a 'right bank preferred speycaster'.

CHANGING THE DIRECTION OF THE CAST - If you examine the sketches of the forward speys. You will see that the forward delivery is always made to the side of the pick-up point to avoid fouling the line. If a number of casts are made on the same side of the body, you would not be able to make the forward push in the right direction because your feet and body are pointing in the wrong direction.

CHANGING THE DIRECTION OF THE FEET - To avoid falling over or making a feeble power push, simply turn in the direction of the next delivery and change the position of the feet to make a full forward rock and power push.

IMPORTANCE OF THE DIRECTION OF THE FEET - By now, you will know how important the body moves and power push are when controlled energy speycasting. You will also have learned that speycasting allows casting to any required angle out on the river. Failure to reposition the feet could result in a cold surprise if you rock and push sideways.

Uninformed 'critics' ask... *how can you stand with your feet apart, rocking the body and power pushing while you are up to your armpits in a swift river with a slippery bottom?* The answer is, of course, that as a speycaster you would not need to cast from such a potentially dangerous position. Make sure that repositioning the feet becomes a part of every practice cast from now on and is firmly imprinted in your long term memory. Failing to change the feet is a prime cause of sloppy casts.

Choosing a Target - Pull out four rod lengths of line from the reel. Adopt all the correct casting positions and cast the line out onto the water. It is a good idea to choose an imaginary target such as an object on the other side of the pond and cast slightly to the side of it as you make each additional practice cast in either direction.

Mime the Cast Through in Your Mind - Before making any speycast, mime the cast through in your mind. This valuable technique allows your brain to 'access' your long term memory bank and release all the correct reactions stored there. Some of us have sticky brains that require a little nudging now and then.

Isolate Your Problems - Not even skilled casters make perfect speycasts every time. Identify and correct each problem as it shows up. Don't just bash away hoping to luck out and suddenly cast better.

Timing the Movements - Don't worry about the timing of the cast until you are satisfied with each separate stage of the cast.

When reasonably satisfied with your progress, make three casts from the right side - moving to the left, then three casts from the left side moving to the right. This procedure gives equal time to each side of the body and brings you back to the original starting position.

Keep repeating the three sets of casts in each direction until you are satisfied with your performance and are ready to move on to the next lesson.

Preparation and Faults - Pay particular attention to all recognizable faults.

Watch Out for These Common Faults

- Not dipping the rod before the lift.
- Not maintaining the forward lean during the lift.
- Not rocking correctly.
- Not using the shoulder turn or twist.

The Worst Faults

- Feet position wrong way around.
- Feet not far enough apart.
- Arms not held close when body rocking.
- Right hand away from the reel.
- Arm not fully extended when pushing.
- Not dipping the rod at the end of the cast.
- Using excessive power.

The Absolute Worst Faults

- Going all out for distance.
- Trying to cast a limber speyrod as you would a stiffer single-hander.
- Right hand away from the reel.
- Making a rollcast, not a speycast delivery.
- Wrong length of line.

A Word of Encouragement - Don't worry if your first practice sessions look like knitting a giant sweater. No speycaster in the world makes a perfect cast every time.

Value of Faults - Don't feel bad about making faults. Identifying and solving problems is a valuable teaching aid and a rewarding experience when practising and fishing.

IMPORTANCE OF THE STANDARD FORWARD SPEY - The forward spey training aid must be taken seriously as it teaches the value of the hand and arm positions - the correct feet placement - the body movements - the power push and the timing of the final delivery.

WHAT COMES NEXT? - Now that we have imprinted the standard forward spey, it is time to move one step closer to a true speycast with the circular forward spey.

Power Push...
The line shoots out, pulling the anchor.

Part Two ~ Chapter Nine
Circular Forward Spey - Pond

THE OBJECT OF THE CAST - Having learned the essential casting positions, body movements and power push of the standard forward spey, it is time to explore another important training aid, *the circular forward spey.*

ALL SPEYCASTS FINISH WITH A CIRCULAR FORWARD SPEY - As previously discussed in Chapter Six, all those strange rod and line movements leading up to a single or double spey are only required to place the line in the correct position for the final stages of the cast. When learning the standard forward spey, we were allowing the line to pass close to the body and making the forward delivery with the rod tip tilted slightly sideways, to practise the body movements and the power push without having to concentrate on anything else.

When observing the final delivery of a double or single spey, you will see that the rod and line are swung around, well to the side as the caster rocks backwards and forwards to make the final delivery. This procedure helps to keep the line away from the angler to avoid getting pierced by the fly on a windy day or a poorly-made cast. As the rod tip swings backward and forward, almost like a side cast, it makes a wide circular movement and becomes the circular forward spey.

PRIME IMPORTANCE OF THE CIRCULAR FORWARD SPEY - As every speycast, single or double, from either side of the body, finishes with a form of circular forward spey, it is probably the most important procedure in controlled energy speycasting.

DIFFICULTY WITH STIFF RODS - Once again, the wide circular movements of the rod tip are difficult or impossible to make with a stiff rod. It is the powerful limber action of a well-designed true speyrod that prevents excessive movement of the arms or overpowering the cast. The rod tip is moved by body power, not arm power.

A - Forward lean, dip   B - Forward lean, lift   C - Twist, rock, backcast, right

Circular Forward Spey - Right Shoulder - Pond

GETTING SET TO CAST - Study the casting positions shown in sequences Photo 5, facing page and below. Also refer to Sketch 11, pages 52 and 53. Begin with four rod lengths of line measured from the reel.

COMMON FAULTS

- Feet positions wrong.
- Arms not tight to the body, when required (*left hand on the chest*).
- Rocking back before completing the lift.
- Not maintaining the side cast positions.
- Not keeping the rear loop live.
- Arms not extended when power pushing.
- Not dipping the rod at the end of the cast.
- Wrong length of line.

THE WORST FAULTS

- Trying to cast a limber speyrod as you would a stiff single-hander.
- The right hand away from the reel.
- Making a rollcast not a speycast delivery.
- Using excessive power.

ISOLATE YOUR FAULTS - Work on each problem as it occurs, pay particular attention to the circular side cast procedure and the timing of each stage of the cast.

Photo 5:
CIRCULAR FORWARD
RIGHT SHOULDER -
POND

D - *Forward rock, power push*   E - *Forward lean, dip*

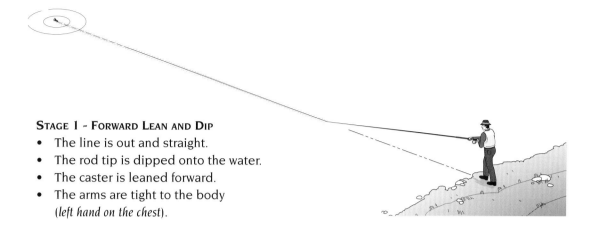

STAGE 1 - FORWARD LEAN AND DIP

- The line is out and straight.
- The rod tip is dipped onto the water.
- The caster is leaned forward.
- The arms are tight to the body
  (*left hand on the chest*).

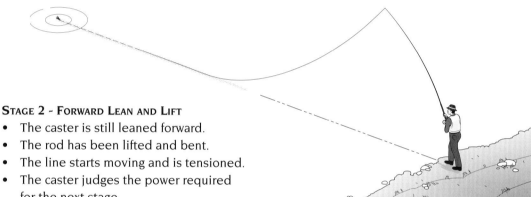

STAGE 2 - FORWARD LEAN AND LIFT

- The caster is still leaned forward.
- The rod has been lifted and bent.
- The line starts moving and is tensioned.
- The caster judges the power required
  for the next stage.
- The arms are still tight to the body
  (*left hand on the chest*).

STAGE 3 - ROCK BACK CIRCULAR BACKCAST (SIDE CAST)

- The caster rocks back and turns
  with the arms close to the body
  making a circular side cast to
  the right.
- The rod tip moves downwards
  and upwards again to form a
  live loop behind the caster.
- The caster is still turned to
  inspect the backcast.
- The arms are still tight to the
  body (*left hand on the chest*).
- The caster is still rocked back.
- The rod is still in the side cast
  position.

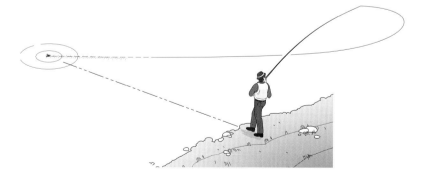

Sketch 11
*Circular Forward Right Shoulder
Pond - Stages 1, 2 and 3*

STAGE 4 - FORWARD ROCK AND POWER PUSH (SIDE CAST)

- The caster has maintained the side cast rod position, rocked forward and pushed the shoulder to generate line energy.
- The rod is still held in the side cast position.
- Just before the forward rock is completed, the rod is pushed upwards and outwards against the pull of the line.
- The caster is leaned forward, the arms are fully extended.

STAGE 5 - FINAL DELIVERY

- The anchor is pulled.
- The line unrolls well above the water and is directed towards the target.

STAGE 6 - FORWARD LEAN AND DIP

- Line acceleration due to energy concentration occurs.
- The rod is dipped as the line falls to the water, ready for the next cast.

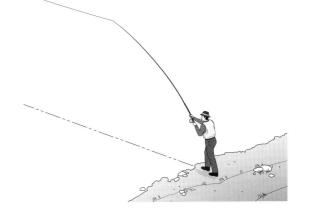

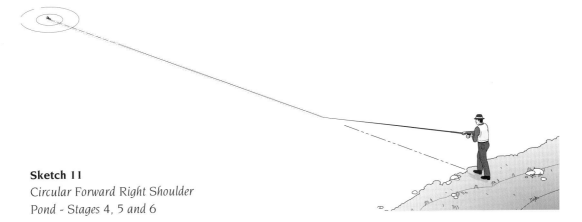

Sketch 11

Circular Forward Right Shoulder
Pond - Stages 4, 5 and 6

PREPARING FOR THE NEXT CAST - Before commencing the next cast, it's essential that...

- The line is straight.
- The rod is dipped.
- The caster is leaned forward.
- The arms are tight to the body (*left hand on the chest*).

A - Forward lean, dip   *B - Forward lean, lift*   *C - Twist, rock, backcast, left*

Circular Forward Spey - Left Shoulder - Pond

GETTING SET TO CAST - Study the casting positions shown in sequences Photo 6, facing page and below. Also refer to Sketch 12, pages 56 and 57. Begin with four rod lengths of line measured from the reel.

THE BODY TWIST SIDE CAST - Once again the line is placed over to the left side of the caster by leaning to the left and making a twisting movement of the body. The only new procedure is maintaining a side cast position of the rod.

COMMON FAULTS

- Feet positions wrong.
- Arms not tight to the body, when required (*left hand on the chest*).
- Rocking back before completing the lift.
- Not making the body twist.
- Not maintaining the side cast positions.
- Not keeping the rear loop live.
- Arms not extended when power pushing.
- Not dipping the rod at the end of the cast.
- Wrong length of line.

THE WORST FAULTS

- Trying to cast a limber speyrod as you would a stiff single-hander.
- Placing the rod and arms to the left of the body.
- Right hand away from the reel.
- Making a rollcast not a speycast delivery.
- Using excessive power.

Photo 6:
CIRCULAR FORWARD
LEFT SHOULDER -
POND

D - *Forward rock, power push*   E - *Forward lean, dip*

STAGE 1 - FORWARD LEAN AND DIP

- The line is out and straight.
- The rod tip is dipped onto the water.
- The caster is leaned forward.
- The arms are tight to the body
  (*left hand on the chest*).

STAGE 2 - FORWARD LEAN AND LIFT

- The caster is still leaned forward.
- The rod has been lifted and bent.
- The line starts moving and is tensioned.
- The caster judges the power required
  for the next stage.
- The arms are still tight to the body (*left
  hand on the chest*).

STAGE 3 - ROCK BACK CIRCULAR
BACKCAST (SIDE CAST)

- The caster leans to the left with the
  arms tight to the body and makes a
  circular side cast to the left by twisting
  the body.
- The rod tip moves downwards and
  upwards again to make a neat live loop
  behind the caster.
- The arms are still tight to the body (*left
  hand on the chest*).
- The caster is still rocked back.
- The rod is till in the side cast position.

Sketch 12
*Circular Forward Left Shoulder
Pond - Stages 1, 2 and 3*

STAGE 4 - FORWARD ROCK AND POWER PUSH (SIDE CAST)

- The caster has rocked forward and pushed the shoulder forward to generate line energy.
- The arms are still tight to the body.
- Just before the forward rock is completed, the caster pushes the tip of the rod against the pull of the line.
- The rod tip is pushed upwards and outwards in a straight line.
- The caster is still leaned forward and the arms are fully extended.
- The accelerating line will flow forward and start to lift the anchor.

STAGE 5 - FINAL DELIVERY

- The anchor is pulled.
- The line unrolls well above the water.
- The end of the line will accelerate due to energy concentration.

STAGE 6 - FORWARD LEAN AND DIP

- The line will straighten and fall to the water.
- The rod is dipped as the line falls.
- The caster is still leaned forward with the arms extended.

Sketch 12
Circular Forward Left Shoulder
Pond - Stages 4, 5 and 6

PREPARING FOR THE NEXT CAST - Before commencing the next cast, it's essential that...

- The line is out straight.
- The rod is dipped with no slack line.
- The caster is leaned forward.
- The arms are tight to the body (*left hand on the chest*).

PRACTICE... Combined Right and Left Shoulder - Pond
Four rod lengths of line - measured from the reel...

When reasonably satisfied with your progress, make three casts from the right side, moving to the left, then three casts from the left side moving to the right. This procedure gives equal time to each side of the body and brings you back to the original starting position. Keep repeating the three sets of casts in each direction until you are satisfied with your performance and are ready to move on to the next lesson.

ISOLATE YOUR FAULTS - Work on each problem as it occurs. Pay particular attention to the circular side cast procedure and the timing of each stage of the cast.

EQUAL TIME - Don't forget to practise both the right and left shoulder casts. Give each side equal time, don't be a right shoulder only caster.

CHANGE THE DIRECTION OF THE CAST - Make sure that your cast is aimed and pushed in the right direction by changing your feet position each time you make the next cast.

CHOOSE AN IMAGINARY TARGET - Before starting to cast, select a target on the other side of the pond as a starting point. This will prevent your practice casts from wandering around all over the pond.

MIMING THE CAST IN YOUR MIND - Activate your long term memory bank by miming each cast through your head, before starting the cast. Many skilled casters follow this procedure out on the river.

ISOLATE YOUR PROBLEM - Work on each problem as you recognize it. Don't just go ahead and hope to suddenly 'cast better'.

TIMING THE CAST - You will notice that the circular forward spey requires particular attention to keeping the rear loop live during the circular side cast. Don't let the rear loop fall down and mess up your forward delivery.

FAULTS - Pay particular attention to all the faults. Don't feel bad about making faults. Identifying and solving problems is an essential and valuable self-teaching aid and can be very rewarding when practising and fishing.

IMPORTANCE OF THE CIRCULAR FORWARD SPEY - This cast is the business end of all speycasts. Do not proceed until you can make satisfactory casts from each shoulder and have imprinted this important procedure into your long term memory bank.

WHAT COMES NEXT? - Having absorbed the circular forward spey teaching aid, we will proceed to our first actual fishing cast... *the single spey.*

Part Two ~ Chapter Ten
Single Spey - Pond

***

THE OBJECT OF THE CAST - The single spey is our first actual fishing cast and is a useful tool when making small angle changes of direction or for very short casts, however, its principal advantage is in keeping the fly and the line away from you in strong upstream winds... *remember our Scottish friend in the kilt.*

DISADVANTAGES OF THE SINGLE SPEY - This cast is limited to very small angular changes of direction, makes across stream casts difficult and upstream casts impossible. Inexperienced anglers can often be seen beating the water to a froth as they make a series of single speys to make an upstream presentation. It was disconcerting to be told that this was called a 'triple spey', perhaps one more repetition would be a 'fourple spey'.

EMERGENCY WIND CASTING ONLY - The single spey looks easy when performed by a skilled caster, however, placing the anchor upstream of the caster is critical and difficult unless the wind is blowing in the upstream direction, therefore the single spey should only be used as an emergency cast in strong upstream winds.

MISUSE OF THE SINGLE SPEY - Many anglers have restricted themselves to excessive and unnecessary use of the single spey for the following reasons...

- THE WRONG ROD - Many fine rod companies produce double-handed rods principally and intentionally designed for the overhead style of cast. These rods are sometimes wrongly called speyrods to distinguish them from single-handed rods (*using a tennis racket with both hands does not make it a golf club*). These rods make double speys difficult and tiring to perform. A form of single spey can be made. If you are only able to make a single spey, could it be your rod?

- DID NOT LEARN TO DOUBLE SPEY - Many anglers are quite happy to use the single spey exclusively, never having learned the double spey. This is their choice, however, the more enlightened, having seen the grace, simplicity and advantages of the double spey, will want to learn.

- DID NOT LEARN THE LEFT SHOULDER CAST - Some anglers are restricted to a double spey on the right bank, over the right shoulder and a single spey on the left bank, over the right shoulder. Limiting your casting to single speys on the left bank will definitely reduce your river coverage, the pleasure of speycasting and your success in hooking fish.

SIMILAR TO CIRCULAR FORWARD SPEY - The single spey looks just like a circular forward spey with one very important and critical difference.

PLACING THE ANCHOR - When learning the forward speys (*training aids*), we were lifting the line off the water directly in front and casting it out with very small changes of feet position or cast direction. With the single spey, we must lift the line off the water from well to the side of the line of cast, make a large angular change and drop the fly to the other side of the line of cast (*out of harm's way*). It is obvious that the caster must be pointed in the direction of the cast, before the pick-up, in order to take full advantage of the power push or avoid falling into the water.

SINGLE SPEYS FROM EITHER SHOULDER - As previously discussed the wind will most certainly start to blow the moment you pick up your speyrod, no matter what side of the river you are on. Stronger upstream winds will blow the line onto you when double speying and make for miserable and sometimes dangerous fishing. Make sure you learn to single spey on each side of the body so that you can fish on either side of the river in strong upstream winds.

PLACING THE ANCHOR - It is possible that placing the anchor correctly is the most important and most difficult procedure in both the single and double speycasts.

PLACING THE ANCHOR INCORRECTLY - There are three main errors in placing the anchor...

- Placing the anchor too close to the edge of the water could cause the fly to flip up into your face on a poorly timed cast.
- Placing the anchor so that the final delivery crosses and tangles with the anchored line.
- Placing too much anchor line will make it impossible to pull it out of the water again on the forward delivery.

60

A - *Sideways lean, dip*   B - *Forward lean, lift*   C - *Rock back, circular side cast, right*

PLACING THE ANCHOR CORRECTLY - The first concern is to place the anchor out of harms way, however, there is one common sense and often neglected procedure that makes longer casts more attainable with very little extra effort.

ANCHOR ON OPPOSITE SIDE - Before proceeding, it is vital you understand that when single speying, *the anchor is always placed on the opposite side to the pick-up.*

- Pick-up on right - anchor on left.
- Pick-up on left - anchor on right.

THE FORWARD REACH ANCHOR PLACEMENT - Others observing my 'seemingly' effortless long distance speycasts are amazed how easily the anchor is picked up allowing the line to proceed out over the water in a smooth narrow loop. The secret was placing the anchor as far out towards the target as possible. Think of it this way...

- The closer the anchor is to you, the longer the length of line to be lifted and the more power required.
- Conversely, the closer the anchor is to the target, the shorter the length of line to be lifted and the less power required.

When demonstrating (*not fishing*) my more powerful rods, it is relatively easy to make casts of over one hundred feet by leaning forward and placing the anchor as close to the target as possible which makes a much shorter length of line to be lifted on the final delivery. Always place the anchor out of harm's way and as close to the target as possible.

Single Spey - Right Shoulder - Pond

GETTING SET TO CAST - Study the casting positions shown in sequences Photo 7, facing page and below. Also refer to Sketch 13, pages 62 and 63. Begin with four rod lengths of line measured from the reel.

Photo 7:
SINGLE RIGHT
SHOULDER - POND

D - *Forward rock, power push*   E - *Forward lean, dip*

This cast is used as an emergency cast when strong upstream winds blow the line on to you when double speying on the left bank of the river.

PREREQUISITES - Make sure that you are able to perform the right shoulder circular forward spey before proceeding.

STAGE 1 - SIDEWAYS LEAN AND DIP

- Choose a target directly out from the bank and place the line at 30° to the left of the cast line (*use a circular single spey*).
- The rod should be dipped and the line straight.

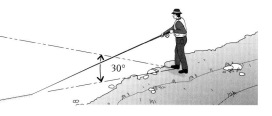

- The body should be leaned to the left.
- The arms should be tight to the body (*left hand on the chest*).
- The feet should then be placed to face the target.

STAGE 2 - FORWARD LEAN AND LIFT

- The caster has leaned forward.
- The rod has been lifted and bent.
- The line is moving and tensioned.
- The power for the next stage is judged.
- The arms are still tight to the body (*left hand on the chest*).

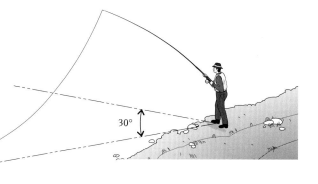

STAGE 3 - ROCK BACK CIRCULAR SIDE CAST

- The caster rocks back with the arms close to the body, making a circular side cast to the right.
- The anchor has been placed well to the right of the cast line.
- The arms are still tight to the body (*left hand on the chest*).
- The rod is still in the side cast position.

Sketch 13
Single Right Shoulder
Pond - Stages 1, 2 and 3

STAGE 4 - FORWARD ROCK AND POWER PUSH (SIDE CAST)

- The caster has maintained the side cast rod position, rocked forward and pushed the shoulder to generate line energy.
- The rod is still held in the side cast position.
- Just before the forward rock is completed, the rod is pushed upwards and outwards against the pull of the line.
- The caster is leaned forward, the arms are fully extended.

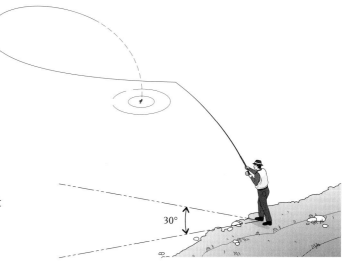

STAGE 5 - FINAL DELIVERY

- The anchor is pulled.
- The line unrolls well above the water and is directed towards the target.
- Line acceleration due to energy concentration occurs.

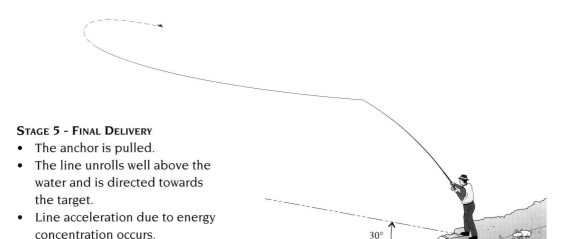

STAGE 6 - FORWARD LEAN AND DIP

- The rod is dipped as the line falls to the water, ready for the next cast.

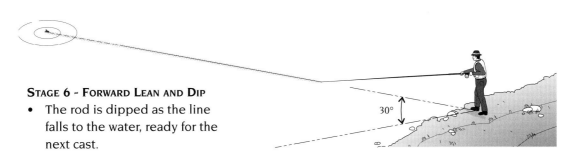

Sketch 13
*Single Right Shoulder
Pond - Stages 4, 5 and 6*

Preparing for the Next Cast - Before commencing the next cast, it's essential that...

- The line is straight and 30° to the left of the cast line.
- The rod is dipped.
- The caster is leaned forward.
- The arms are tight to the body (*left hand on the chest*).

Common Faults

- Feet positions wrong.
- Arms not tight to the body, when required (*left hand on the chest*).
- Rocking back before completing the lift.
- Not maintaining the side cast positions.
- Not keeping the rear loop live.
- Arms not extended when power pushing.
- Not dipping the rod at the end of the cast.

The Worst Faults

- Trying to cast a limber speyrod as you would a stiff single-hander.
- The right hand away from the reel.
- Fouling the forward delivery due to incorrect anchor placement.
- Making a rollcast not a speycast delivery.
- Using excessive power.
- Using too much line.

Isolate Your Faults - Work on each problem as it occurs. Pay particular attention to the circular side cast procedure and the timing of each stage of the cast.

A - Sideways lean, dip   *B - Forward lean, lift*   *C - Rock back, circular side cast, left*

Single Spey - Left Shoulder - Pond

GETTING SET TO CAST - Study the casting positions shown in sequences Photo 8, facing page and below. Also refer to Sketch 14, pages 66 and 67. Begin with four rod lengths of line measured from the reel.

This is an emergency cast if strong upstream winds blow the line onto you when making a double spey on the right bank of the river.

PREREQUISITES - Make sure that you can perform the left shoulder circular forward spey before proceeding.

Photo 8:
SINGLE LEFT
SHOULDER - POND

D - *Forward rock, power push*   E - *Forward lean, dip*

STAGE 1 - SIDEWAYS LEAN AND DIP

- Choose a target directly out from the bank and place the line at 30° to the right of the cast line (*use a circular single spey*).
- The rod should be dipped.
- The body should be leaned to the right.
- The arms should be tight to the body (*left hand on the chest*).
- The feet should then be placed to face the target.

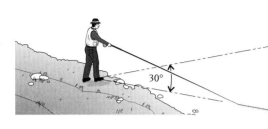

STAGE 2 - FORWARD LEAN AND LIFT

- The caster has leaned forward.
- The rod has been lifted and bent.
- The line is moving and tensioned.
- The power for the next stage is judged.
- The arms are still tight to the body (*left hand on the chest*).

STAGE 3 - ROCK BACK CIRCULAR SIDE CAST

- The caster rocks back with the arms close to the body making a circular side cast to the left with a body twist.
- The anchor has been placed well to the left of the cast line.
- The arms are till tight to the body (*left hand on the chest*).
- The rod is still in the side cast position.

Sketch 14
Single Left Shoulder
Pond - Stages 1, 2 and 3

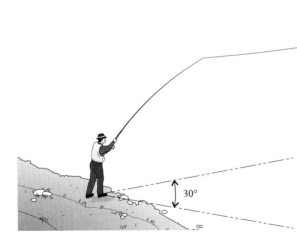

STAGE 4 - FORWARD ROCK AND POWER PUSH (SIDE CAST)

- The caster has maintained the side cast rod position, rocked forward and pushed the shoulder to generate line energy.
- The rod is still held in the side cast position.
- Just before the forward rock is completed, the rod is pushed upwards and outwards against the pull of the line.
- The caster is leaned forward, the arms are fully extended.

STAGE 5 - FINAL DELIVERY

- The anchor is pulled.
- The line unrolls well above the water and is directed towards the target.
- Line acceleration due to energy concentration occurs.

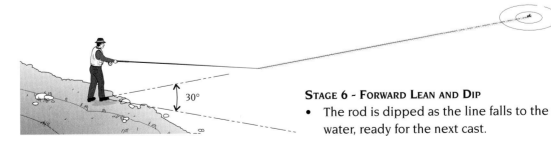

STAGE 6 - FORWARD LEAN AND DIP

- The rod is dipped as the line falls to the water, ready for the next cast.

Sketch 14
Single Left Shoulder
Pond - Stages 4, 5 and 6

PREPARING FOR THE NEXT CAST - Before commencing the next cast, it's essential that...

- The line is straight and 30° to the right of the cast line.
- The rod is dipped.
- The caster is leaned forward.
- The arms are tight to the body (*left hand on the chest*).

COMMON FAULTS

- Feet positions wrong.
- Arms not tight to the body, when required (*left hand on the chest*).
- Rocking back before completing the lift.
- Not maintaining the side cast positions.
- Not keeping the rear loop live.
- Arms not extended when power pushing.
- Not dipping the rod at the end of the cast.

THE WORST FAULTS

- Trying to cast a limber speyrod as you would a stiff single-hander.
- The right hand away from the reel.
- Making a rollcast not a speycast delivery.
- Using excessive power.

ISOLATE YOUR FAULTS - Work on each problem as it occurs, pay particular attention to the circular side cast procedure and the timing of each stage of the cast.

EQUAL TIME - Don't forget to practise both the right and left shoulder casts. Give each side equal time, don't be a right shoulder only caster.

CHANGE THE DIRECTION OF THE CAST - Make sure that your cast is aimed and pushed in the right direction by changing your feet position each time you make the next cast.

CHOOSE AN IMAGINARY TARGET - Before starting to cast, select a target on the other side of the pond as a starting point. This will prevent your practice casts from wandering around all over the pond.

MIMING THE CAST IN YOUR MIND - Activate your long term memory bank by miming each cast through your head, before starting the cast. Many skilled casters follow this procedure out on the river.

ISOLATE YOUR PROBLEM - Work on each problem as you recognize it. Don't just go ahead and hope to suddenly cast better.

TIMING THE CAST - You will notice that the circular forward spey requires particular attention to keeping the rear loop live during the circular side cast. Don't let the rear loop fall down and mess up your forward delivery.

PRACTICE... Combined Right and Left Shoulder ~ Pond
Four rod lengths of line - measured from the reel...

When reasonably satisfied with your progress, make two casts from the right shoulder, moving to the left, then two casts from the left shoulder, moving to the right. This procedure gives equal time to each side of the body and brings you back to the original starting position. Keep repeating the two sets of casts in each direction until you are satisfied with your performance and are ready to move on to the next lesson.

FAULTS - Pay particular attention to all the faults. Don't feel bad about making faults. Identifying and solving problems is an essential and valuable self-teaching aid and can be very rewarding when practising and fishing.

IMPORTANCE OF THE SINGLE SPEY - This cast will enable you to carry on fishing when less skilled speycasters are beaten by strong winds, however, it must be remembered that the single spey is limited to small angular changes of direction and cannot be used for across stream or upstream casts.

WHAT NEXT? - When you are reasonable proficient with the single spey, it is time to move on to the wonderful, controlled energy double spey, the work horse of true speyfishing.

Acceleration...

The anchor pulled, the line picks up speed.

Part Two ~ Chapter Eleven
Double Spey - Pond

THE OBJECT OF THE CAST - The double spey is the most useful and effective cast in speyfishing. It is also the most graceful and elegant style of flycasting known to man or woman.

EFFECTIVE AND SAFE - The double spey is the answer to a flyfisher's dreams. There is virtually no part of any stream or river that cannot be effectively and safely fished having mastered the double spey on each side of the river. Speaking of safety... *an Australian student now speycasts when fishing on saltwater marshes, hosting man-eating saltwater Asian crocodiles, with nowhere to make a back cast.*

USE ANY PRESENTATION YOU WANT TO - Anglers who have learned their fishing on constricted rivers will invariably make a down and across presentation and will continue to do so even when backcasting is possible. These unfortunate people seem unaware of the advantages of the across or upstream presentation which allows sinking a fly by skill, not weight and presenting it to a fish in a more appetizing way. Those of you who fish surface or dry fly will already know the advantages of the long controlled downstream drifts possible with across or upstream presentation.

DOUBLE SPEY - CIRCULAR FORWARD SPEY - Those of you have taken the time to learn and practise the circular forward spey with the side cast delivery, will be pleased to know that you are already three quarters of the way to the double spey. All that remains is the correct placement of the anchor.

PLACING THE ANCHOR - As previously discussed the strange preliminary rod movements when double speying are only required to place the line and the anchor out of harms way before making the final circular side cast, forward delivery. The one consolation of the double spey is that placing the anchor correctly is much easier than for the single spey.

WHAT LENGTH OF ANCHOR? - The correct length of anchor is critical in all speycasts, however, it can only be found by trial and error. As a general rule, leave enough line on the water to prevent pulling it out during the preliminary procedures and not too long to prevent the forward delivery.

ANCHOR ON THE SAME SIDE - Unlike the single spey, the anchor is always placed on the same side as the pick-up.

THE FORWARD REACH ANCHOR PLACEMENT - Others observing my 'seemingly' effortless long distance speycasts are amazed how easily the anchor is picked up allowing the line to proceed out over the water in a smooth narrow loop. The secret was placing the anchor as far out towards the target as possible.

Think of it this way…

• The closer the anchor is to you, the longer the length of line to be lifted and the more power required.

• Conversely, the closer the anchor is to the target, the shorter the length of line to be lifted and the less power required.

A - Sideways lean, dip   *B - Forward lean, lift*   *C - Forward lean, side cast, left*

MAKE DOUBLE SPEYS FROM EITHER SHOULDER - Unfortunately there are many, otherwise skilled anglers who have not learned to make the forward delivery on the left side of the body. There are even books implying that it can't be done and that you should use a single spey over the right shoulder when fishing on the left side of a river. Following this misleading advice would seriously handicap you when attempting to make an upstream presentation on the left bank of the river.

Double Spey ~ Right Shoulder ~ Pond

GETTING SET TO CAST - Study the casting positions shown in sequences Photo 9, facing page and below. Also refer to Sketch 15, pages 74 and 75. Begin with four rod lengths of line measured from the reel.

The object of the cast is to cover all angles of presentation on the right bank of a river, from downstream to across stream and upstream.

Photo 9:
DOUBLE RIGHT
SHOULDER - POND

PREREQUISITES - Make sure that you are proficient with the forward reach anchor placement and the right shoulder circular forward spey before proceeding.

D - *Rock back, circular side cast, right*   E - *Forward rock, power push*   F - *Forward lean, dip*

STAGE 1 - SIDEWAYS LEAN AND DIP

- Choose a target directly out from the bank.
- Place the line 60° to the right of the cast line.
- The body is leaned forward and to the right.
- The rod should be dipped and the line straight.
- The arms are tight to the body (*left hand on the chest*).
- The feet are placed to face the target.

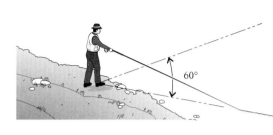

STAGE 2 - FORWARD LEAN AND LIFT

- The caster leans forward and lifts the rod.
- The line is moving and tensioned.
- The power for the next stage is judged.
- The forward and sideways lean is maintained.
- The arms are still tight to the body (*left hand on the chest*).

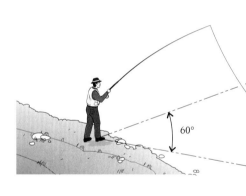

STAGE 3 - FORWARD LEAN SIDE CAST

- The caster rocks to the left with the arms close to the body, making a side cast to the left.
- The anchor is placed out and to the right.
- The caster is still leaned forward and left.
- The line does not go behind the caster.
- The power for the next stage is judged.

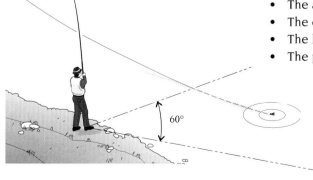

Sketch 15
Double Right Shoulder
Pond - Stages 1, 2 and 3

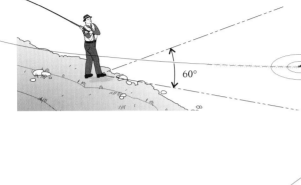

STAGE 4 - ROCK BACK CIRCULAR BACKCAST (SIDE CAST)

- The caster rocks to the right and to the rear with the arms tight to the body, making a circular side cast to the rear.
- The rear loop is high and live.
- The anchor is still in place.
- The arms are still tight to the body (*left hand on the chest*).
- The power for the next stage is judged.

STAGE 5 - FORWARD ROCK AND POWER PUSH (SIDE CAST)

- The caster has maintained the side cast position and rocked forward with the arms still tight to the body and pushed the shoulder to generate line energy.
- Just before the forward rock is completed the rod is pushed upwards and outwards against the pull of the line.
- The caster is still leaned forward, the arms are fully extended.
- The moving line is pulling on the anchor.
- The line proceeds out well above the water.
- Line acceleration due to energy concentration occurs.

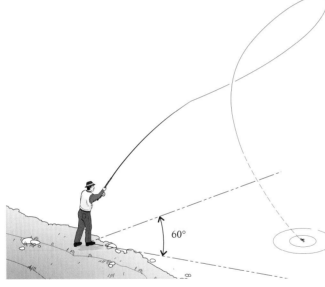

STAGE 6 - FORWARD LEAN AND DIP

- The line straightens above the water.
- The caster leans forward as the line falls gently to the water.

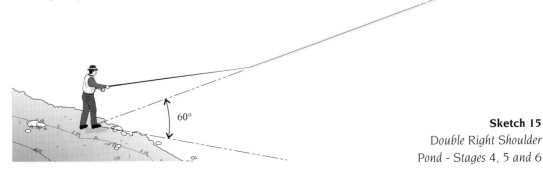

Sketch 15
Double Right Shoulder
Pond - Stages 4, 5 and 6

PREPARING FOR THE NEXT CAST - As the double spey (*pond practice*) requires a large change of direction, the line must be placed back to the starting point for each cast. *Make a few single speys to get you back to the 60° start point.*

COMMON FAULTS

- Not dipping before and after casting.
- Feet not placed to push towards the target.
- Rod not held tight to the body when required (*left hand on the chest*).
- Body and shoulder movements not used.
- Not timing the push correctly.
- Not aiming the push upwards and outwards.
- Arms not extended fully when power pushing.
- Not dipping the rod at the end of the cast.

THE WORST FAULTS

- Casting a speyrod as you would a stiff rod.
- Right hand away from the reel.
- Fouling the forward delivery due to an incorrectly placed anchor.
- Making a rollcast delivery.
- Using too much line.
- Using excessive power.

ISOLATE YOUR FAULTS - Work on each stage of the cast separately. Pay particular attention to placing the anchor, the circular backcast and power push.

A - Sideways lean, dip　　　　　　*B - Forward lean, lift*　　　　　　*C - Forward lean, side cast, right*

IMPROVING YOUR TIMING - Don't worry about your timing until you have mastered all the separate stages of the cast. When you are finally confident with each procedure, link them all together keeping the following guidelines in mind...

- Keep the line moving and live at all stages.
- Concentrate on the line, forget the rod.
- Separate each stage to waltz time...

> DIP - *one, two, three...*
> LIFT - *one, two, three...*
> SIDECAST - *one, two, three...*
> CIRCULAR BACKCAST - *one, two, three...*
> FORWARD ROCK AND POWER PUSH - *one, two, three...*
> LINE ROLL OUT AND DIP - *one, two, three...*

Double Spey - Left Shoulder - Pond

GETTING SET TO CAST - Study the casting positions shown in sequences Photo 10, facing page and below. Also refer to Sketch 16, pages 78 and 79. Begin with four rod lengths of line measured from the reel.

Although the left shoulder double spey seems complicated, it is only a left shoulder circular spey with a different way of placing the anchor during the cast. The curious thing about this cast is that it will finally become your favourite cast. When asked to demonstrate the double spey out on the river, I will always choose the left bank as it is my best cast. The object of the cast is to cover all angles of presentation when fishing on the left bank of the river from downstream to across stream and upstream.

Photo 10:
DOUBLE LEFT
SHOULDER - POND

PREREQUISITES - Make sure that you can perform the forward reach anchor placement procedure and the left shoulder circular forward spey before proceeding.

D - *Rock back, circular side
     cast, left*

E - *Forward rock, power push*

F - *Forward lean, dip*

STAGE 1 - SIDEWAYS LEAN AND DIP
- Choose a target directly out from the bank.
- Place the line 60° to the left of the cast line.
- The body leaned forward and to the left.
- The rod should be dipped and the line straight.
- The arms are tight to the body (*left hand on the chest*).
- The feet are placed to face the target.

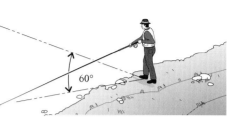

STAGE 2 - FORWARD LEAN AND LIFT
- The caster leans forward and lifts the rod.
- The line is moving and tensioned.
- The power for the next stage is judged.
- The forward and sideways lean is maintained.
- The arms are still tight to the body (*left hand on the chest*).

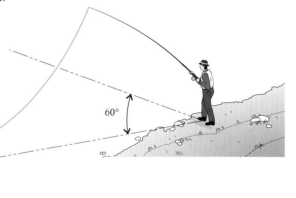

STAGE 3 - FORWARD LEAN SIDE CAST
- The caster rocks to the right with the arms close to the body, making a side cast to the right.
- The anchor is placed out and to the left.
- The caster is still leaned forward and right.
- The line does not go behind the caster.
- The power for the next stage is judged.

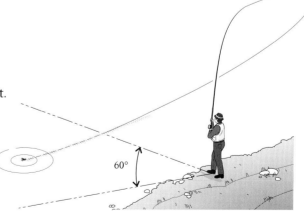

Sketch 16
Double Left Shoulder
Pond - Stages 1, 2 and 3

STAGE 4 - ROCK BACK CIRCULAR BACKCAST (SIDE CAST)

- The caster rocks to the left and to the rear with the arms tight to the body, making a circular side cast to the rear with a body twist.
- The rear loop is high and live.
- The anchor is still in place.
- The arms are still tight to the body (*left hand on the chest*).
- The power for the next stage is judged.

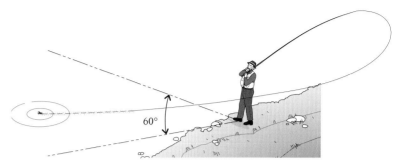

STAGE 5 - FORWARD ROCK AND POWER PUSH (SIDE CAST)

- The caster has maintained the side cast position and rocked forward with the arms still tight to the body and pushed the shoulder to generate line energy.
- Just before the forward rock is completed the rod is pushed upwards and outwards against the pull of the line.
- The caster is still leaned forwards, the arms are fully extended and the rod is still in the side cast position.
- The moving line is pulling on the anchor.
- The line proceeds out well above the water.
- Line acceleration due to energy concentration occurs.

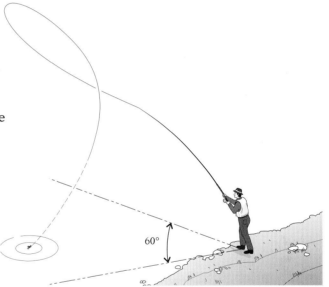

STAGE 6 - FORWARD LEAN AND DIP

- The line straightens above the water.
- The caster leans forward as the line falls gently to the water.

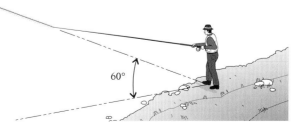

Sketch 16
Double Left Shoulder
Pond - Stages 4, 5 and 6

PREPARING FOR THE NEXT CAST - As the double spey (*pond practice*) requires a large change of direction, the line must be placed back to the starting point for each cast. *Make a few single speys to get you back to the 60° start point.*

COMMON FAULTS

- Not dipping before and after casting.
- Feet not placed to push towards the target.
- Rod not held tight to the body when required (*left hand on the chest*).
- Body and shoulder twist movements not used.
- Not timing the push correctly.
- Not aiming the push upwards and outwards.
- Arms not extended fully when power pushing.
- Not dipping the rod at the end of the cast.

THE WORST FAULTS

- Casting a speyrod as you would a stiff rod.
- Right hand away from the reel.
- Fouling the forward delivery due to an incorrectly placed anchor.
- Making a roll cast delivery.
- Using too much line.
- Using excessive power.

ISOLATE YOUR FAULTS - Work on each stage of the cast separately. Pay particular attention to placing the anchor, the circular backcast and power push.

IMPROVING YOUR TIMING - Don't worry about your timing until you have mastered all the separate stages of the cast. When you are finally confident with each procedure, link them all together keeping the following guidelines in mind...

- Keep the line moving and live at all stages.
- Concentrate on the line, forget the rod.
- Separate each stage to waltz time...

DIP - *one, two, three...*
LIFT - *one, two, three...*
SIDECAST - *one, two, three...*
CIRCULAR BACKCAST - *one, two, three...*
FORWARD ROCK AND POWER PUSH - *one, two, three...*
LINE ROLL OUT AND DIP - *one, two, three...*

The speed of the waltz will depend on the length of rod you are using and on keeping the line live.

PRACTICE... Combined Right and Left Shoulder - Pond
Four rod lengths of line - measured from the reel...

When satisfied with your double speys over each shoulder, make a right shoulder cast, then a left, then a right, etc. This useful procedure gives equal time to each shoulder and avoids wandering all over the pond when practising.

FAULTS - Work on all errors, however, remember that absolutely nobody makes a perfect speycast every time. Keep up your practice... *analyze your problems intelligently and sooner or later you will make that elusive perfect cast you have been looking for.*

THE IMPORTANCE OF THE DOUBLE SPEY - This wonderful cast will allow you to fish undisturbed water denied to non-speycasters. You will be able to make any presentation you select instead of the one you are forced into by wind, current or restricted backcasting. It will also keep you out of dangerous water and avoids wading around like a hungry bull moose.

WHAT'S NEXT? - Now that we can make double speys with a direction change of 60°, we must practise casting at 45°, 90° and 135° cast line changes.

Photography © Kelly Fisher

Final Delivery...

A well executed cast forms a tight loop in the line.

Part Two ~ Chapter Twelve
Advanced Techniques - Pond

DOUBLE SPEYS TO DIFFERENT ANGLES - The presentation you select will dictate the direction of your cast. After your line has drifted directly downstream (*when out on the river*), it can be placed back out onto the water again with a 45° downstream cast, a 90° across stream cast and a 45° upstream cast (135° *from downstream*). Each of these presentations require closer study if you are to make them correctly without tying yourself in a knot or falling into the pond.

DIRECTION OF THE CAST - Placing the feet to take full advantage of the body rock and power push is vital to controlled energy speycasting. It is important for small angle direction changes and critical on large changes. Just imagine making a double spey from downstream and power pushing 45° upstream with the feet pointing downstream. Anyone foolish enough to try this should wear a life jacket.

PLACING THE ANCHOR - Placing the anchor correctly is the key to all speycasting and it is obvious that the location of the anchor will vary with each change of casting angle. As we have seen the anchor must be placed away from the cast line and far enough out to assist in the final delivery.

PROBLEMS WITH ANCHOR PLACEMENT - Surprisingly, placing the anchor correctly with small angle changes is more difficult than larger angles. The most frequent error is placing the anchor past the cast line and fouling the forward delivery.

Double Speys - Different Angles - Pond

Unless you are content to handicap your double spey casting to a 45° angular change (*many anglers do*), you must imprint the reactions necessary for other angles of presentation by regular and intelligent practice; guidelines for double speys through 45°, 90° and 135° direction changes follow.

PRACTICE... Double Spey 45° Direction Change - Both Shoulders - Pond
Four rod lengths of line - measured from the reel...

- Choose an aiming mark on the other side of the pond and another one 45° to the left.
- Starting at the right side marker, make a right shoulder double spey towards the left marker.
- Now make a left shoulder double spey towards the right marker.
- Keep repeating the progress until you are able to make small angular changes without fouling the line on the forward delivery.
- Check all standard positions and movements.
- Use the correct length of line.
- Don't forget to change the feet each time.
- Keep the power down, go for style.

IMPORTANCE OF THE 45° CAST - Many speycasters are unable to make delicate, small angle double speys due to the difficulty of placing the anchor and have to make do with a single spey. The ability to make controlled small angle, double speys is a trademark of an accomplished speycaster.

PRACTICE... Double Spey 90° Direction Change - Both Shoulders - Pond
Four rod lengths of line - measured from the reel...

- Choose an aiming mark on the other side of the pond and another one 90° to the left.
- Starting at the right side marker, make a right shoulder double spey towards the left marker.
- Now make a left shoulder double spey towards the right marker.
- Keep repeating the progress until you are able to make 90° angular changes without fouling the line on the forward delivery.

REMINDERS...

- Check all standard positions and movements.
- Use the correct length of line.
- Don't forget to change the feet each time.
- Keep the power down, go for style.

IMPORTANCE OF THE 90° CAST - As you become a more proficient speyfisher, you will not be content with the often inappropriate down and across presentation and will be making much wider angle of cast presentations. This may be to allow a relatively light weight wet fly to sink to a downstream fish or increase the length of the downstream drift of a surface or dry fly. The across stream 90° cast eventually becomes the speyfishers most used technique. Practise it regularly, it will really pay off when Murphy's Law is in effect.

PRACTICE... Double Spey 135° Direction Change - Both Shoulders - Pond
Four rod lengths of line - measured from the reel...

- Choose an aiming mark on the other side of the pond and another one 135° to the left.
- Starting at the right side marker, make a right shoulder double spey towards the left marker.
- Now make a left shoulder double spey towards the right marker.
- Keep repeating the progress until you are able to make 135° angular changes without fouling the line on the forward delivery.

REMINDERS...

- Check all standard positions and movements.
- Use the correct length of line.
- Don't forget to change the feet each time.
- Keep the power down, go for style.

IMPORTANCE OF THE 135° CAST (45° UPSTREAM) - The value of an upstream presentation cannot be overestimated, however, it seems to be the nemesis of many speycasters. Could this be due to the use of stiff rods, lack of training or being totally unaware that an upstream presentation was possible? Putting the fly upstream allows sinking a wet fly or nymph to the required depth as it drifts down to the fish in deep or fast water without using half a pound of lead core line. It also allows surface or dry flies to be controlled as they make extremely long downstream drifts.

The upstream double speycast, coupled with the aerial mend technique, is the most effective procedure when speyfishing and a true indication of a master speyfisher.

Short Line Double Speys - Pond

There will be many situations when fish are very close to the bank if they have not already been chased away by clumsy overhead casters searching for that perfect backcast location. The following 'improbable' incident illustrates this point...

Improbable
Mike Maxwell, shortly before landing his 'improbable' steelhead when guiding Trey Combs on the Bulkley River.

When fishing with Trey Combs on the Bulkley River, travelling in a jet boat, we pulled into the beach to park the boat, at the least likely place to hold a fish. Trey was fishing a few yards downstream covering a known fish hold. I, of course, was exercising the rights of being English and sitting in the boat enjoying a cup of tea. Not knowing how dangerous it could be to disturb this time-honoured tradition, he insisted that I get out my fifteen foot, ten weight speyrod and 'get fishing'. As I had not finished the last drop of my tea, I whiled away the time by stringing up my rod and tying on a size four Telkwa Stone dry fly. Now here comes the 'improbable' part of the incident.

When standing in the jet boat moored to the bank and not wanting to get out and fish just yet, I 'flipped' out about five feet of line and leader, which of course landed in a heap. Now bear in mind that the jet boat had been churning up the water in this exact spot some fifteen minutes earlier. On making a second leader-straightening cast, a large summer steelhead stuck its head out of the water and 'inhaled' the fly, not more than fifteen feet from the boat. It was difficult to say who was the most surprised... Trey, me or the fish.

USING THE LIMBER ACTION OF A TRUE SPEYROD - So far we have been making relatively long casts using the concept of neglecting the rod and casting the line. When short line casting with a light weight length of line, we must forget the line and use the self-weight momentum of the rod to make the cast.

STIFF RODS - It must be obvious that the stiffer the rod, the more difficult it will be to utilize its self-weight momentum.

BODY MOVEMENTS NOT NECESSARY - When short line double-speying by using the momentum of the rod, everything happens so quickly that there would not be time to make any rocking movements or power push.

THE ROD POSITION - As the rod tip does not have to travel very far to cast such a short line, it does not have to be swung back to the rear and can remain out over the water in a low lift position.

THE HAND POSITION - To utilize the limber action of the rod, keep the left hand against the body. The right hand must be close to the reel and pointing forwards out over the river.

THE FEET POSITION - Don't forget to place the feet correctly when changing the cast direction.

THE SIDE ARM DELIVERY - Making a short, quick side arm delivery will keep the line live during the crucial forward delivery.

CASTING ANGLE - CHANGES - Short line double speys can be made to any angle allowing you to use the exact cast line and presentation you select.

SMALL BRUSHY STREAMS - There are many small streams and side channels of larger rivers that have overhanging bushes or trees with deep shadowy fish holding water close to the bank. Careful wading and the short line technique, will allow you to make a side arm delivery close to the water under the overhanging trees and reach the hiding fish.

PRACTICE... Short Line Double Spey - Pond
Two rod lengths of line - measured from the reel...

- Start with a right shoulder cast and make several casts to the left, vary your angles.
- Now make several left shoulder casts back towards your starting point, once again vary your angles.

KEEP PRACTISING - Short line casts happen so quickly that you can make a lot of casts in a very short time. Take advantage of this and practise them regularly. Those unfortunate people who still believe that speycasting is just for excessive distance casting are not usually impressed with short line casting. To paraphrase Jim Green's advice on casting, there are going to be many situations where you can cast only half as far and catch twice as many fish.

THE IMPORTANCE OF SHORT LINE CASTING - The ability to make delicate controlled short line speycasts will enable you to cover those productive fish holds close to the bank that 'lesser mortals are denied'. Practise your single spey short line casts as well so that you are prepared for those nasty upstream winds.

REMINDERS...

- Use the self-weight momentum of the rod.
- Keep the left hand close to the body (*left hand on the chest*).
- Lean forward - keep the rod tip low.
- Make a side arm presentation.
- Adjust your timing - keep the line live.
- Keep the power down.

Restricted Backcasts

There are many tempting fish holds located directly in front of casting stations that have embankments, canyon walls or bush that will not allow the normal back-casting movements of a speycast. This often happens in high water situations.

CHECK THE BACKCAST CLEARANCE - As a general rule, if you can touch any obstacle to the side, above or behind with the rod and arms extended, you could foul your cast or break your rod, therefore you will have to use the restricted backcast technique.

LENGTH OF CAST - Although extremely long casts are possible with the restricted backcast technique, they are rarely necessary as fish are usually undisturbed and close to the side of the river in these protected locations.

BODY MOVEMENTS - As it is impossible for the rod to go behind the caster, the body rock can't be used in that direction, however, the sideways rock movements are critical.

ROD AND ARM POSITION - In order to take advantage of the very short but necessary backcast stroke, the caster leans forward and stays forward with the arms fully extended and the right hand close to the reel during the entire cast.

FEET POSITIONS - It is often difficult to maintain the correct stance when perched on a narrow ledge below a canyon wall, however, do the best you can without practising your 'underwater speycasting'.

MORE ABOUT STIFF RODS - Stiffer rods, principally designed for long distance overhead and rollcasting, are virtually useless in a restricted backcast situation, as they are not flexible enough to make the huge bends required for this technique. The stiffer the rod, the more difficult it will be to use under these circumstances.

PRACTICE... Restricted Backcast Double Spey - Pond
Three rod lengths of line - measured from the reel...

- Start with a right shoulder cast to the left.
- Now make a left shoulder cast to the right, back to where you started.

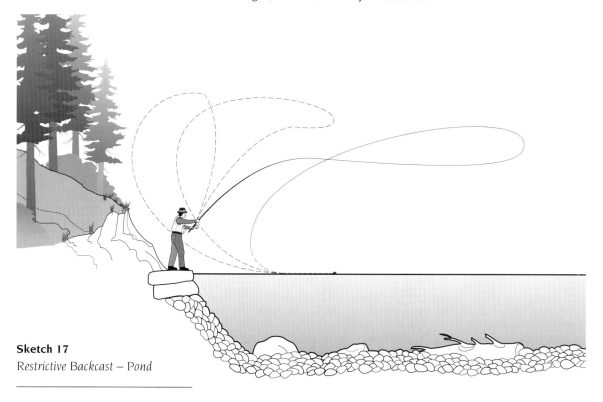

Sketch 17
Restrictive Backcast – Pond

VARY YOUR ANGLES - Make sure that you practise all casting directions from each side of the body.

SINGLE SPEYS - Don't forget your single speys to beat those upstream winds.

REMINDERS...

- Your optimum cast length will be reduced.
- You must use a limber speyrod.
- Lean forward, keep the rod tip low.
- Keep the arms extended.
- Make a side arm presentation.
- Adjust your timing, keep the line live.
- Be careful with the extra power required for this technique.

IMPORTANCE OF THE RESTRICTED BACKCAST TECHNIQUE - If you take the time to master this amazing technique, you will be able to fish those difficult waters that others can 'only dream about'.

ONE LAST THOUGHT - Nearly all casting ponds have that annoying tree close to the water. Go and stand in front of it to practice.

Shooting Line

Although the cleanliness of a fly line is important in all flyfishing, it is critical when shooting line. Don't even try and shoot line unless your line is slick and squeaky clean.

Sooner or later every accomplished speycaster will instinctively know what length of line he enjoys casting. This 'optimum' distance will vary according to the casters ability and the length and power of the rod. It will also vary with wind, current flow or depth of wading. Shooting extra line allows anglers to make longer casts without exceeding their optimum length of line during the preliminary stages of the cast.

USING TOO MUCH LINE - As we've already discussed, the efficiency of a speycast depends on the line energy generated when it reaches the required speed (*velocity*) and that this will vary according to the 'square of its velocity' ($E = \frac{1}{2}Mv^2$).

Remember the rules...

- Double the speed - get four times the energy.
- Half the speed - get only one quarter of the line energy.

The significance of this is, that when trying to cast more line than your optimum length of line, it will slow down and dump the presentation well short of the intended distance. Trying to aerialize more line than your optimum cast is counter-productive.

HOW MUCH LINE CAN YOU SHOOT? - Once again this will vary according to the caster's ability and the local casting conditions (*wind, etc.*).

- As a general rule, don't try and shoot more than ten percent of your optimum length of cast.
- The length of shoot will vary with the efficiency of your speycast.

WHEN IS THE LINE RELEASED? - To understand the correct time to release the shooting line, re-examine the energies of the forward spey; *refer to Sketch 4, pages 22 and 23.* It must be obvious that the shooting line is released as the line proceeds out over the water in Stage 5, after the anchor is pulled. Important... *releasing the line prematurely will prevent line energy concentration and destroy the cast.*

HOW DO YOU KNOW 'WHEN'? - The exact moment to release the shooting line will only be learned by constant practice, however, when you find that 'magic moment', you will rarely forget it.

AIM UP WHEN SHOOTING - Just as when throwing a ball, aim up if you want to get extra distance.

PRACTICE... Shooting Line - Pond
Four rod lengths of line - measured from the reel...

- Make circular forward speys to start with.
- Practise casting over each shoulder
- Strip off ten percent more shooting line and trap it with the right hand; *see Photo 15B, page 144*, similar to feeding line.
- Let the shooting line hang down.
- Cast and shoot the line.

CHECK FOR

- Did your cast deteriorate?
- Did you reach your target?
- Was all your shooting line pulled out?

COMMON FAULTS

- Speycast too slow - low energy.
- Releasing line - *too soon - too late.*
- Not aiming high enough.
- Too much power.

IMPORTANCE OF SHOOTING LINE - The ability to shoot line allows you to cast to those fish holding areas just out of reach of your optimum cast. Experienced spey-fishers will invariably keep their cast short and shoot line on every presentation when fishing. A clear case of using skill, not just muscle.

Line Control During Casting - Pond

It could be said that the prime advantage of a true limber speyrod is the ability to present the fly to the fish in the most natural and appetizing way, by controlling the line after casting without wearing yourself out doing it.

WHAT IS LINE CONTROL? - Line control is the art of making the line and fly do what you want it to do instead of being swept around by the current. This is vital when fishing a dry fly as a living insect or getting a sunk fly down to the required depth without the use of heavy-weight lines and leaded flies. The prime concern in speyfishing is that the fly must go down the river ahead of the leader, which must be ahead of the line. These techniques are accomplished by skilful mending.

MORE LINE CONTROL THAN CASTING - As the fly is returned to the water immediately when speycasting (*no false casting required*) and then kept out on the water for a considerable time by line control, you will begin to realize that you will spend more time line controlling than you are speycasting. It follows that stiff rods designed for distance casting, make line control tiring.

THE GOLDEN RULES OF LINE CONTROL - All other things being equal, the number of fish you hook is directly proportional to your ability to control line. As a corollary to this, your ability to control line will be proportional to how close your rod is to a well-designed flexible speyrod. When considering the golden rules, it should be remembered that speycasting originated in Scotland, where 'thrifty and canny' Atlantic salmon anglers were more interested in hooking fish by superb line and fly control, than wasting their limited time on an expensive beat, showing off their distance casting skills.

MENDING LINE - This misleading medieval term was originally used to indicate changing anything that was 'not to your liking' even if it was not broken. In flyfishing terminology, 'mending line' means reshaping the line before it falls to the water by 'aerial mending' and after it falls to the water by 'water mending'.

PRACTICE ON STILL WATER - Although we will be fishing on moving water out on the river, we will be better prepared if we practise line mending on the pond before proceeding. Once again, we must simulate the effect of moving water.

Aerial Mending

As its name implies, this is the process of reshaping the line in the air before it falls to the water. There are two useful styles of aerial mending when speycasting... *serpentine and reach cast.*

THE SERPENTINE AERIAL MEND - It will often occur that a fish will show itself well downstream and close in when you are casting 'way out' there in front from your safe and comfortable casting location. The serpentine mend allows the fly to travel straight downstream without being dragged unnaturally by the line.

PRACTICE... Serpentine Aerial Line Control - Pond
Four rod lengths of line - measured from the reel...

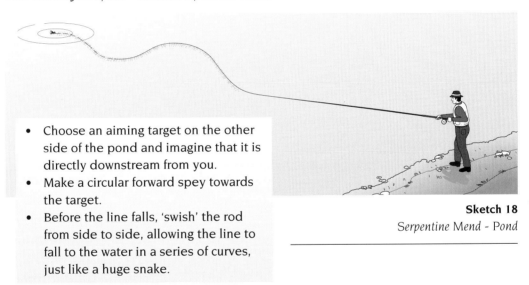

- Choose an aiming target on the other side of the pond and imagine that it is directly downstream from you.
- Make a circular forward spey towards the target.
- Before the line falls, 'swish' the rod from side to side, allowing the line to fall to the water in a series of curves, just like a huge snake.

Sketch 18
Serpentine Mend - Pond

COMMON FAULTS

- The fly is not aimed towards the target.
- The curves are too small or too large.
- The line was not aimed high enough to allow the curves to form before falling to the water.

PRACTISE ON BOTH SHOULDERS - Don't forget to practise your serpentine cast from each side of the body.

IMPORTANCE OF THE SERPENTINE CAST - It is often thought, by 'uninformed' anglers that the fish holding directly downstream is the most difficult to hook. This is true if you just swing the fly across its narrow field of view with a down and swing presentation, giving the fish a momentary glimpse as it zips past. A downstream fish will be much more interested and motivated by a fly coming directly downstream towards it and remaining in its field of view for a considerable length of time.

THE REACH CAST AERIAL MEND - As its name implies, this procedure (*popularized by angling author and educator Doug Swisher*) allows the line to be reshaped in the air by 'reaching' the rod upstream before the line falls to the water.

THE OBJECT OF THE REACH CAST MEND - The first few seconds that the fly is on the water is often the most productive part of the presentation. Unfortunately, the leader often lands upstream of the line and the current starts to distort the line. This drags the fly unnaturally, therefore it must then be water mended to get the leader ahead. All of this can be avoided by aerial mending. The line falls to the water already mended.

PRACTICE... Reach Cast Aerial Line Control - Pond
Four rod lengths of line - measured from the reel...

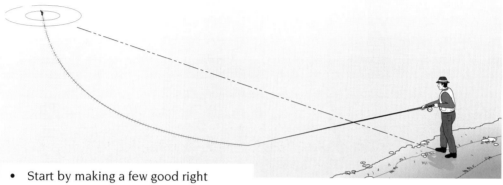

Sketch 19
Reach Mend - Pond

- Start by making a few good right shoulder double speys towards your aiming marks.
- Make sure your line rolls out well above the water before falling.
- Don't forget that the right shoulder cast simulates casting on the right bank with the river flowing to the right.
- Make a good high line delivery and swing the rod to the left before the line falls to the water.
- If all goes well, the line will fall to the water in a reasonably straight line between the rod tip and the fly.
- Now repeat the practice on the left shoulder, reach to the right.

COMMON FAULTS

- Not aiming high enough to allow the reach cast before the line falls.
- Pulling the line back short of the target.
- Missing the target completely.

IMPORTANCE OF THE REACH CAST - The reach cast mend avoids that annoying, fly disturbing 'first mend' required on moving water. Although Doug Swisher developed the reach cast using a single-handed rod, just imagine how effective a long limber speyrod is. An accomplished speyfisher makes an aerial reach cast mend on every double or single speycast.

Water Mending

Water mending allows the line to be reshaped after it has fallen to the water to combat the drag effect of moving water. No matter how well you performed the aerial mend, the current will eventually distort the line and drag the fly unnaturally. This is true for all styles of fishing from dry fly to sunk fly. By skilful water mending, drag can be reduced to a minimum.

PRACTICE... Water Mending - Pond

Even before you start practising, it must be realized that water mending on the still water of a pond will not provide the moving water drag effect, however, we must practise it.

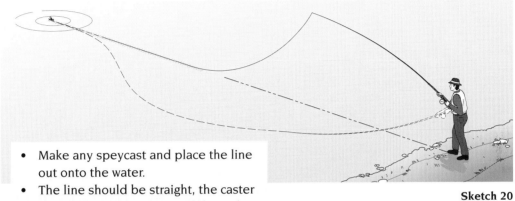

Sketch 20
Water Mend - Pond

- Make any speycast and place the line out onto the water.
- The line should be straight, the caster leaned forward and the rod dipped.
- Lift the rod tip and gently swing the rod to the side, throwing a loop of line on to the water.
- The object of the practice is to mend as much line as you can without pulling the fly back.
- Don't worry if your water mending is not too successful on still water.

COMMON FAULTS

- Not raising the rod high enough.
- Not swinging the rod far enough.
- Swinging the rod too much.
- Too much power.

IMPORTANCE OF WATER MENDING - The secret of successful speyfishing is in making the fly do 'What you want it to do' instead of being swept around by the current. To counter the continuously varying fly disturbing effect of moving current, the line must be mended frequently to keep the fly 'on track'. Once again, it can be seen that an experienced speyfisher will be water mending line for a much longer time than casting and that a long limber speyrod will allow this with the least fatigue.

Conclusion to Advanced Techniques

It is human nature to practise your best cast and down play the more difficult or recently learned procedures. Don't fall into this ever present trap or you will pay for it out on the river when you are forced into making the only presentation you are capable of and knowing that there is a much better way, which you are incapable of performing. Practise your advanced procedures every time you go out to the pond. Use it as a 'cool down' session.

Part Two ~ Chapter Thirteen
Speycasting in Wind - Pond

WIND IS UNPREDICTABLE - The moment you pick up your rod on the river, the wind will start to blow, suddenly change direction, change in velocity and seem to blow from all directions at the same time. This can be dangerous and frustrating for the less experienced angler, however, it should not deter the skilled speycaster. It is useful to deal with the wind from four principal directions (*things will not be so simple out on the river*). Being able to outsmart the wind is part of the pleasure of speycasting.

PRINCIPAL DIRECTIONS OF THE WIND - Wind can blow from four principal directions. We will examine each direction separately. They are...

- from the front
- from the rear
- downstream
- upstream

❖ WIND FROM THE FRONT - Wind decreases in velocity the closer it is to the water, due to the drag effect of the choppy water produced by the wind. It makes sense to try and get your delivery down into the slower air when casting directly into a wind. There are two methods available...

- METHOD 1 - LOWER SIDECAST - DOUBLE SPEY - Instead of making the normal side cast delivery, drop the rod tip almost to the water and see how well you can cast under the wind. Don't worry about disturbing the water, it will already have been chopped up by the wind.

- METHOD 2 - ROLLCAST DELIVERY - This cast is useful in medium strength head winds, however, it has the disadvantage of a wind catching, high rod and line position during the initial stages of the forward stroke; *see Sketch 7, page 26*. It can be seen that the roll cast is the same as a forward spey except that the forward delivery is directed down on to the water instead of above.

❖ WIND FROM THE REAR - This is no problem for the speyfisher when there is an obstruction behind to break the wind. Wind from the rear will make the formation of the rear loop difficult, however, it will do wonders for your forward delivery.

❖ DOWNSTREAM WINDS - This is no problem for the speycaster. Use the double spey. The upstream side cast will require a little more effort as it will be against the wind. Large angular changes are more difficult with higher wind speeds. Single speys should not be attempted during downstream winds as the final delivery (*made upstream of the caster*) will tangle.

❖ UPSTREAM WINDS - Double speys should not be attempted in strong upstream wind (*use the single spey*) as the line and fly will attack you when forming you rear loop. Double speys in lighter upstream wind can be made by leaving the anchor farther downstream and then make a 'lower side cast delivery'.

PRACTICE... Wind Casting - Pond
Three rod lengths of line - measured from the reel...

Before starting out, it must be remembered that the wind blows on each side of the river, practise your wind casting on both sides of the body.

PRACTISING WITHOUT WIND - Practise your wind casting from each direction and from each side of the body even if the wind is not blowing.

❖ WIND FROM THE FRONT

- DOUBLE SPEY - BOTH SHOULDERS

  - Choose an aiming point.
  - Start with a standard side cast delivery.
  - Gradually lower the side cast positions on each successive cast.
  - Try and get your forward delivery as low as possible with the line straightening out before falling.
  - Now repeat the practice over the left side of the body.
  - Don't forget to lean well over to the left.

- ROLL CASTING - BOTH SHOULDERS

  - Choose an aiming point.
  - Roll cast the line down on to the water.
  - Try to get the line down onto the water as close as you can (*under the wind*).
  - Make sure your line is fully extended as it finally rolls out.

❖ DOWNSTREAM WIND - Although downstream winds keep the line and fly away from you when double speying, they can blow your presentation too far downstream if you are not careful.

- Practise your 135° casts regularly.
- Don't forget to practise on both sides of the body.

❖ UPSTREAM WIND - Heavy upstream wind will dictate using the single spey, however, lighter winds can be tackled with the double spey and downstream anchor and low side cast technique.

- Practise placing your anchor well to the side before the forward delivery.
- Don't forget the left shoulder practice.

REMINDERS...

- Aim at your target. There is no point in casting in wind if your fly does not go where you aimed it.
- Your optimum cast length will reduce in proportion to the wind speed.
- Try and use the wind, don't fight it.
- Practise on both sides of the body.
- Above all, remember... speycasting was originated by Scotsmen who did not want the wind to blow a big heavy triple hook fly up the back of their kilts.
- One final reminder on safety... always wear head and eye protection, particularly when wind casting.
- Even practice flies and leaders can cut you.

THE IMPORTANCE OF WIND CASTING TECHNIQUES - Once again, pick up your speyrod on the river, the wind starts to blow. All your beautiful calm wind casting will be useless, unless you have practised all the wind casting techniques from both sides of the body on the casting pond.

Effective Practice ~ Pond

How you practise is just as important as what you practise. The ideal practice session will imprint the correct techniques and procedures into you long term memory so that it becomes a reflex action instead of a conscious effort.

Remember... *Olympic athletes earn their medals on the practice field, not at the games.*

DON'T JUST PRACTISE YOUR BEST CAST - It is human nature to dwell on things that give us pleasure, however, this procedure will leave you seriously handicapped when things don't go right on the river.

DON'T PRACTISE YOUR FAULTS - Many speycasters are fully aware that there is something wrong with the cast they are practising and keep going without analyzing and correcting the fault. This is just getting better and better at doing it wrong. Don't proceed until you at least understand what is wrong.

A TYPICAL SHORT PRACTICE SESSION - Always follow the same program when practising. Start with the forward speys to reinforce stance, rod hold and body moves and finish with wind casting. Don't wear yourself out.

PRACTISE IN PAIRS - It is very difficult for a speycaster to see everything that is happening to the rod and line. It is even more difficult to detect mistakes in procedure or timing. A second speycaster will get a much larger and more detailed view of the whole process and can alert the caster. When working with six students at a club speycasting course, we were able to use three identical rods with two casters taking turns on each rod. This system worked well, however, it was a complete surprise when the observing students, having seen the faults of the others, cast so much better when their turn came around again. Practise in pairs, it really pays off.

A FEW LAST REMINDERS...

- Don't just go for distance.
- Give equal time to each shoulder.
- Don't forget your line shooting.
- Practise line control.
- Practise your wind casting.

Above all, remember… speycasting can be an effortless, elegant and satisfying method of fishing providing you have worked through all the lessons and practices.

PRACTISE ON THE POND BEFORE GOING FISHING - Why waste your valuable fishing time trying to get your casting 'back together' out on the river. A few minutes 'tuning up' on the pond can prevent hours of frustration on the river.

Part Three ~ River Casting

Chapter

Fourteen   *Speycasting on Moving Water*

Fifteen   *Speycasting on the Right Bank*

Sixteen   *Speycasting on the Left Bank*

Seventeen   *Special Casting Techniques*

Photography © Joe Kambietz

CANYON RUN, VARZINA RIVER...

To *be successful at catching Atlantic salmon in Russia you must be able to first deceive and then motivate the fish to strike your fly... there is no more important aspect to this than total line control.*

Above:

Joe Kambietz in canyon on Upper Varzina.

Part Three ~ Chapter Fourteen
Speycasting on Moving Water - River

PREREQUISITES - It is assumed that you have successfully completed all pond casting lessons and practices, and are using a true speyrod with the correct line, leader and yarn fly. Real flies can be dangerous when practising, even with the hook cut off.

WIND WHEN PRACTISING - Although we will be wind casting later on, it is impossible to practise many of the required casts in adverse wind. Try and find a wind sheltered location for your first few practice sessions.

THE TRANSITION TO MOVING WATER - Before speycasting on moving water, it is important to know that there are many additional problems not encountered on the casting pond. Being able to recognize these potential difficulties is vital to your success as a speyfisher.

VARIABLES AFFECTING RIVER SPEYCASTING - It is useful to divide the many variables into three groups. They are...

- Equipment
- River conditions
- Caster's ability

When problems occur, find the cause. Is it your equipment, your inadequate casting or something to do with your casting location?

Equipment Variables

Selecting your speycasting tackle can be a frustrating and expensive experience if you don't really know what you are looking for. Take the time to do your homework and most of all, beware of the 'recent expert' (*they seem to be behind every rock*).

- SPEYRODS - The number one requirement is using a true speyrod of the correct length and power for your physical characteristics, the size of the river and the weight of the fish you will be catching later on. Don't make the mistake of using the shortest speyrod you can find.

   Remember... *longer rods are easier to cast than short rods and make much better line and fish controllers.*

- REELS FOR SPEYFISHING - Reels should be capable of holding the makers suggested backing and line with plenty of clearance between the wound on line and the frame. Rim control is advisable and mechanical drag optional. Leave your anti-reverse reels for saltwater as they are not suited for fast catch and release procedures unless the drag is over tightened, which usually means a 'lost' fish. There must be some relationship between the size of the rod and the weight of the reel. Reels for larger lines come in many sizes, always use the smallest for your line weight.

- LINES FOR SPEYCASTING - Lines 'must' be double tapered to allow smooth energy concentration when casting and controlling line. Sinking lines are not required and sink tips should not be used for practising. As the end tapers on line weights of nine and above are not long enough, they have to be improved by adding a short length of a lighter line; *see Improved Taper in Chapter Twenty-Seven.* Those who neglect this advice should not be surprised if their beautiful forward delivery slaps down on the water or does not reach the target or project the leader forward.

  Beware of the plethora of 'sure fire' spey lines available today. Many of these 'new and improved' tapers were invented back in the old silk line days and failed to impress the intelligent angler or survive the test of time. The designers of these 'wonder lines' seem to concentrate on how much farther you can cast with little or no reference to their line control capabilities. Once again, it is the old sales ploy of 'distance sells' and seems to be well received by the 'chuck it and chance it brigade'.

- LEADERS FOR SPEYCASTING - Leaders used on spey lines require special consideration. The butt section must be heavy enough to accept the jolt of energy from the fly line and taper down in relation to the reducing energy.

  Remember... there is no point casting the line if your leader and fly do not roll out ahead.

River Variables

Before you start practising, there are a number of important items you must check. These include the depth and speed of the current, the proximity of any casting obstacles behind you and the direction and intensity of the wind.

- RESTRICTED BACKCASTS - Always check your casting clearances to avoid wasting time retrieving or retying flies or worse still, damaging your rod. You will not foul up on any object that you can't touch with your arm and rod extended. Check to the rear then above and to each side.

- DEPTH OF WADING - The depth of the water you are standing in, will affect the efficiency of your speycasting due to the difficulty of lifting the line and keeping it live and out of the water before the final delivery. Let's assume that you are wading knee deep and have established your optimum controllable length of cast. As often happens, a fish shows itself a few feet farther out. The obvious solution is to wade out a little farther, however, this takes you into deeper water which restricts your cast and you are still well short of your target. As a general rule, every foot of extra wading depth will reduce your cast by five feet. Wading deeper to reach a distant target is often counter-productive.

- SECURITY OF FOOTING - Before casting make sure that your feet are correctly positioned and firmly planted. Many faults can be traced back to a bad stance. If your casting gets rough, check your feet. If you can't stand firmly, you are in the wrong place.

It is sometimes difficult to judge whether or not you are in the wrong place as the following, amusing (*for others*) incident will emphasize...

When guiding my clients on the Bulkley River, it just so happened that Trey Combs was speycasting directly opposite to me on the other side of the river. He was doing a creditable job of casting a heavy sink tip line and making superb line controls to sink his fly to the bottom of a very deep pool close to his side of the river.

It was beautiful... a warm, sunny, Indian summer, fall day with a slight downstream breeze. Somehow or other, I just could not resist the temptation to cast over to his side of the river and pick up a fish, right under his nose. Having placed my feet firmly on a section of 'flat' bedrock, I was having a 'good old time' distance casting over into Trey's water. After showing off for a while, it became obvious that neither the fish or Trey were impressed with my 'beautiful casting'.

When attempting to reel in my line to move to another location, I pulled back my right foot to stand upright again, not realizing that my 'flat' bedrock was in fact tilted slightly forward and quite slippery. Without any warning my feet slowly slid forward from under me and I gracefully sat down on the bottom of the river up to my armpits in water. A clear case of 'pride goethe before a fall'. Check your casting location carefully.

Silent Sentry...
Arthur J. Lingren, avid speyfisher, author and flyfishing historian, on the Dean River.

- SPEED OF THE CURRENT - When pond casting, we were constantly having to simulate the line tightening effect of moving water. On the river, the line is straightened by the current and is ready for the 'dip and lift', the moment it swings directly downstream. During the lift, the line is pulled by the flow enabling the caster to judge the power required for the next stage of the cast. It follows that the faster the current, the longer the length of line you can speycast. Watch out for your line swinging into very slow or dead water. This should be no trouble for those who have learned their speycasting on a casting pond.

- PRACTISE YOUR LINE CONTROL AFTER EACH CAST - When practising in slow current, your line will 'take forever' to swing downstream before it is in position for the next cast. Don't waste this time, practise your water mending.

The Caster's Ability

As your speycasting improves, you will be covering more water, making all necessary line controls and choosing any direction of cast. Make sure that you give equal time to the left bank casts. Don't forget all your special procedures.

- TIMING AND POWER - It would become immediately apparent that the standard forward spey (*training aid*) will not work when standing in water as the rear loop will anchor in the water behind you and destroy the forward cast. The unwanted rear anchor effect will occur an any speycast unless the timing of the cast is adjusted. The golden rule of timing... *keep the anchor in the water and the remainder of the line live.*

Don't worry if you have trouble adjusting to the timing out on the river. It takes me some time to fine tune my timing again, after demonstrating and teaching on still water.

ADJUSTING FOR ALL VARIABLES - Casting and fishing with a speyrod is an intellectual sport with the most important item of equipment located above the shoulders. The ability to make the presentation you select when adjusting to all the constantly changing variables makes true speyfishing into an art form.

ALWAYS CHECK YOUR RIVER VARIABLES - Get into the habit of checking all river variables every time you move to a new casting location. You will be surprised how quickly trees can grow behind you. Watch out for those slippery rocks and those very slow or backwater current flows that will affect your line pick-up.

PRE-PRACTICE REMINDERS...

- Give equal time to each side of the river.
- Don't just practise your favourite cast.
- Give equal time to the advanced techniques.
- Don't practise in the strong wind (*unless you are practising wind casting*).
- Check your river variables.
- Don't wade above your ankles when practising.
- Choose aiming marks to define your casting angles.
- Place your feet to push towards the target.
- Shake out the line, let it float downstream.
- Visualize the cast through in your head for a few casts before proceeding.
- Remember how critical the anchor placement is.
- Place your anchor upstream for single speys.
- Place your anchor downstream for double speys.

Pulling the Anchor...
Mike Maxwell
on the Bulkley
River, B.C.

Part Three ~ Chapter Fifteen
Speycasting on the Right Bank - River

IN THIS CHAPTER WE WILL PUT OUR MANY SKILLS learned on the casting pond into practice on moving water. Many students are pleasantly surprised how easy it is to cast on a river. As we already know, this is due to the line tensioning effect of the current flow.

CASTING ON BOTH SIDES OF THE BODY - We will start with the right bank double spey which is made on the right side of the body, then the right bank single spey which allows us to practise the left shoulder speycast procedure.

A - *Sideways lean, dip*   B - *Forward lean, lift*   C - *Forward lean, side cast, left*

Right Bank - Double Spey 90° Across - Right Shoulder - River

GETTING SET TO CAST - Study the casting positions shown in sequences Photo 11, facing page and below. Also refer to Sketch 21, pages 108 and 109. Begin with four rod lengths of line measured from the reel. Cast on the right side of the body.

Photo 11:
DOUBLE RIGHT
BANK, RIGHT
SHOULDER - RIVER

PREREQUISITES - Make sure that you have practised this cast on the casting pond recently. The across stream presentation is the easiest cast as it is relatively simple to place the anchor correctly.

D - *Rock back, circular side
cast, right*

E - *Forward rock, power push*

F - *Forward lean, dip*

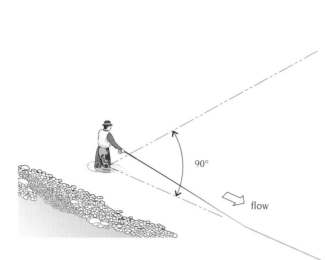

STAGE 1 - SIDEWAYS LEAN AND DIP

- Choose an aiming point at 90° to the flow.
- The line should be directly downstream.
- Place the feet towards the target.
- The body leaned forward and sideways downstream.
- The rod should be dipped.
- The arms are tight to the body (*left hand on the chest*).
- The current pull can be felt.

STAGE 2 - FORWARD LEAN AND LIFT

- The caster leans forward and lifts the rod.
- The current tensions the line and bends the rod.
- The caster judges the power for the next stage.
- The arms are still tight to the body (left hand on the chest).

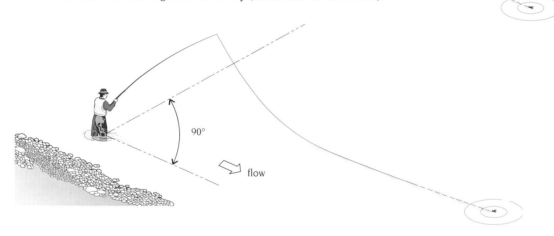

STAGE 3 - FORWARD LEAN AND UPSTREAM SIDE CAST

- The caster rocks to the left and makes an upstream side cast.
- The anchor is placed downstream and out into the flow.
- The loop is high and live.
- The loop does not go behind.
- The power for the next stage is judged.
- The arms are still tight to the body (*left hand on the chest*).

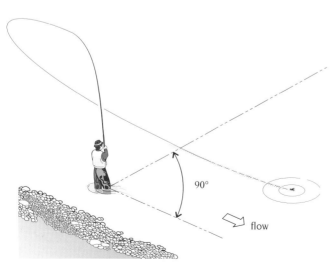

Sketch 21
*Double Right Bank, Right Shoulder
River - Stages 1, 2 and 3*

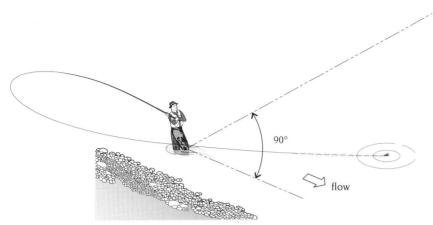

Stage 4 - Rock Back Circular Backcast (Side Cast)

- The caster has rocked back with a circular side cast.
- The loop is high and live.
- The rod tip is still in the side cast position.
- The anchor is still in place.
- The power for the next stage is judged.
- The arms are still tight to the body (*left hand on the chest*).

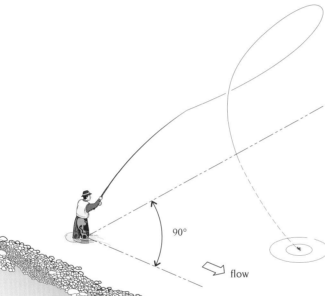

Stage 5 - Forward Rock and Power Push

- The caster has leaned forward with the arms tight to the body and pushed the shoulder to generate most of the line energy.
- Just before the forward rock is completed, the rod is pushed upwards and outwards towards the target against the pull of the line.
- The caster is still leaned forward with the arms fully extended.
- The moving line pulls up the anchor.

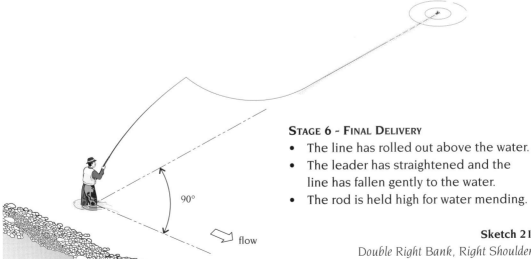

Stage 6 - Final Delivery

- The line has rolled out above the water.
- The leader has straightened and the line has fallen gently to the water.
- The rod is held high for water mending.

Sketch 21
*Double Right Bank, Right Shoulder
River - Stages 4, 5 and 6*

COMMON FAULTS

- Feet out of position.
- Incorrect hand grip.
- Incorrect anchor placement.
- Pulling the anchor prematurely, the fly goes behind you.
- Incorrect body and shoulder moves.
- Not pushing upwards and outwards.
- Not aiming at the target.

WORST FAULTS

- Too much line.
- Too much power.
- Degenerating into a rollcast.

CHECK YOUR TIMING - As this is your first practice when standing in moving water, you must be careful not to allow your rear loop to anchor in the water behind you and destroy your final delivery. Don't forget your waltz time counts, however, speed up the movements if necessary.

A WORD OF ENCOURAGEMENT - Unless you are extremely talented, your first few casts could be a disaster. Many of my most successful students were crushed when shown videos of their first attempts.

PRACTISE THE OTHER ANGLES - The double spey allows the all-too-popular 45° downstream presentation and the very effective 45° upstream cast. As each of these casts have relatively difficult anchor placement procedures, they must be practised regularly.

PRACTICE... Right Bank - Double Spey 45° Downstream - Right Shoulder - River
Cast on the right side of the body...

- Choose an aiming point 45° downstream.
- Place the feet towards the target.
- Drop the anchor well downstream.
- Keep your rear loop out of the water.
- Don't let the forward loop cross your cast line.
- Keep your power low.

TIMING - The 45° downstream cast will require a lot of practice to get the timing right and usually requires a faster casting procedure.

FAULTS

- Incorrect anchor placement, too far upstream.
- Pulling the anchor prematurely, the fly goes behind you.
- Crossing the cast line.
- Incorrect timing.
- Not aiming at the target.
- Too much power.
- Too much line.
- Degenerating into a rollcast.

PRACTICE... Right Bank - Double Spey 45° Upstream - Right Shoulder - River
Cast on the right side of the body...

- Choose an aiming point 45° upstream.
- Place the feet towards the target.
- Bring the anchor well upstream.
- Place the anchor well out into the flow.

TIMING - The 45° upstream cast appears to move at a leisurely pace due to the long pick up and upstream side cast procedure, however, all stages should be timed to produce the required velocity and line energy.

FAULTS

- Placing the anchor too far downstream.
- Crossing the cast line, anchor too far upstream.
- Pulling the anchor prematurely, the fly goes behind.
- Too much power.
- Not enough power.
- Not aiming at the target.
- Too much line.
- Crashing down with a rollcast.

A - Sideways lean, dip   B - Forward lean, lift   C - Rock back, circular side
                                                                                         cast, left

Right Bank - Single Spey 45° Downstream - Left Shoulder - River

GETTING SET TO CAST - Study the casting positions shown in sequences Photo 12, facing page and below. Also refer to Sketch 22, pages 114 and 115. Begin with four rod lengths of line measured from the reel. Cast on the left side of the body.

- Choose an aiming point 45° downstream.
- Aim the feet towards the target.
- Place the anchor correctly.

TIMING - Single speys require meticulous attention to timing. Keeping the anchor upstream and in the water during the cast can only be learned by constant practice. The timing is quite fast when compared to the double spey.

Photo 12:
SINGLE RIGHT
BANK, LEFT
SHOULDER - RIVER

D - *Forward rock, power push*　　　　　　E - *Forward lean, dip*

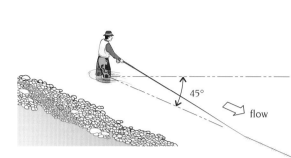

STAGE 1 - SIDEWAYS LEAN AND DIP

- The line should be downstream.
- The rod should be dipped.
- The body should be leaned to the right.
- The arms should be tight to the body (*left hand on the chest*).
- The feet should then be placed to face the target.

STAGE 2 - FORWARD LEAN AND LIFT

- The caster has leaned forward.
- The rod has been lifted and bent.
- The line is moving and tensioned.
- The power for the next stage is judged.
- The arms are still tight to the body (*left hand on the chest*).

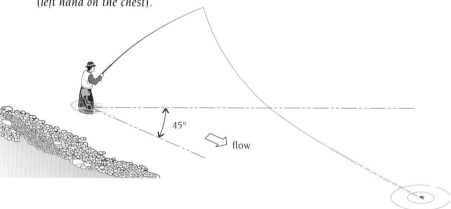

STAGE 3 - ROCK BACK CIRCULAR SIDE CAST

- The caster rocks back with the arms close to the body making a circular side cast to the left - with a body twist.
- The anchor has been placed well to the left of the cast line.
- The arms are still tight to the body (*left hand on the chest*).
- The rod is still in the side cast position.

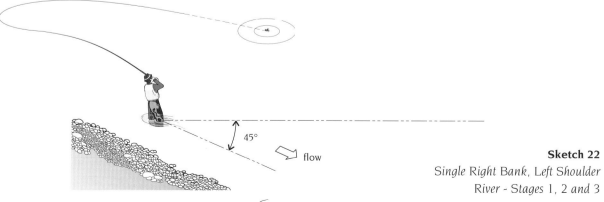

Sketch 22
Single Right Bank, Left Shoulder
River - Stages 1, 2 and 3

STAGE 4 - FORWARD ROCK AND POWER PUSH (SIDE CAST)

- The caster has maintained the side cast rod position - rocked forward and pushed the shoulder to generate line energy.
- The rod is still held in the side cast position.
- Just before the forward rock is completed, the rod is pushed upwards and outwards against the pull of the line.
- The caster is leaned forward, the arms are fully extended.

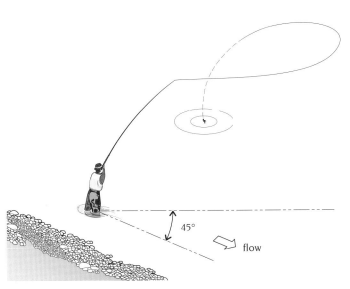

STAGE 5 - FINAL DELIVERY

- The anchor is pulled.
- The line unrolls well above the water and is directed towards the target.
- Line acceleration due to energy concentration occurs.

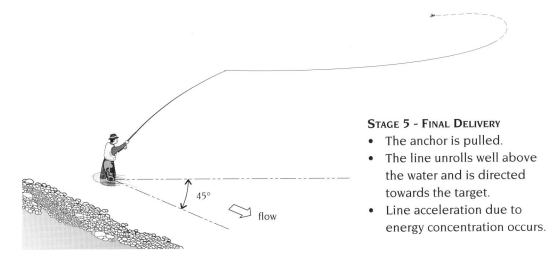

STAGE 6 - FORWARD LEAN AND DIP

- The leader has straightened and the line has fallen gently to the water.
- The rod is held high for water mending.

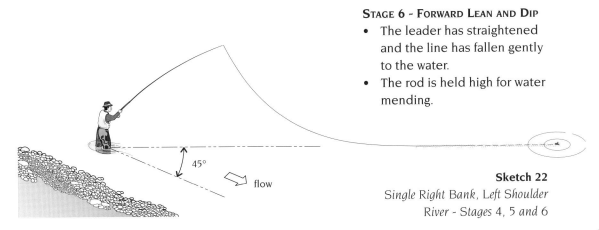

Sketch 22
Single Right Bank, Left Shoulder
River - Stages 4, 5 and 6

FAULTS

- Anchor not placed correctly.
- Crossing the cast line.
- Throwing the fly behind (*in the bushes*).
- Not keeping the line live.
- Timing too slow, the cast degenerates.
- Timing too fast, you will be wearing the line.

PREPARATION FOR THE LEFT BANK - Practise the single spey over the left side of the body. It is good practise for the double spey on the left bank which is also made over the left shoulder.

PRACTICE... Standard Speycasts - Right Bank

Establish your optimum cast length - adjust your length according to the variable conditions...

An intelligent practice session will allow you to imprint all the required reactions for all of the different casting angles and for both right and left shoulder deliveries, give equal time to each. Stay on the right bank until you are making adequate casts more times than not.

LENGTH OF PRACTICE SESSION - Don't tire yourself out, your body moves and reactions will go to pieces if you do. Don't spend more than ten minutes on each cast without a rest. Use the break period to analyze your progress.

THE SCHEDULE - RIGHT BANK

- Start with the 45° downstream double.
- Move to the 90° across stream double.
- Now make 45° upstream double.

When reasonably satisfied with each direction of cast:

- Practise the 45° downstream single.
- Don't forget this is good practice for the left bank double spey.

PRACTICE COOL DOWN - If you are not satisfied with any of your other casts - build up your confidence again by having fun with your favourite speycast.

Photography © Maxwell

The 'Other Half'…

Upstream side cast commences.

Part Three ~ Chapter Sixteen
Speycasting on the Left Bank - River

THE ABILITY TO DOUBLE SPEY OVER THE LEFT SIDE of the body will allow you to make any presentation you select and to any angular change of direction. You will be able to make presentations to 45° downstream and right around to 45° upstream. If you do not master the left bank double, you will have to be content with the left bank single spey which will restrict your left bank fishing to a downstream presentation.

CASTING ON BOTH SIDES OF THE BODY - Start with the left bank double spey over the left side of the body, then the left bank single on the right side of the body.

A - *Sideways lean, dip*   B - *Forward lean, lift*   C - *Forward lean, side cast, right*

Left Bank ~ Double Spey 90° Across ~ Left Shoulder ~ River

GETTING SET TO CAST - Study the casting positions shown in sequences Photo 13, facing page and below. Also refer to Sketch 23, pages 120 and 121. Begin with four rod lengths of line measured from the reel. Cast on the left side of the body.

PREREQUISITES - If you have recently practised your left shoulder single on moving water on the other side of the river, you will be prepared for the left shoulder double on this side of the river. Always start with the across stream cast when practising on moving water. Placing the anchor is more tolerant of mistakes. It will also allow you to adjust your timing before moving onto the somewhat more difficult downstream and upstream presentation.

Photo 13:
DOUBLE LEFT
BANK, LEFT
SHOULDER ~ RIVER

A WORD OF ENCOURAGEMENT - Don't be intimidated by 'lesser speycasters' who have not learned the left shoulder technique or who advise you to change your rod grip and cast left-handed. You will find that with effective practices, your left bank double spey will be your best and favourite cast.

D - *Rock back, circular side cast, left*

E - *Forward rock, power push*

F - *Forward lean, dip*

Stage 1 - Sideways Lean and Dip

- Choose an aiming point at 90° to the flow.
- The line should be directly downstream.
- Place the feet towards the target.
- The body leaned forward and sideways downstream.
- The rod should be dipped.
- The arms are tight to the body (*left hand on the chest*).
- The current pull can be felt.

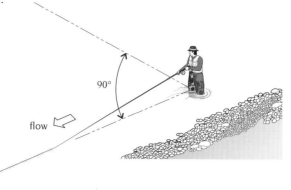

Stage 2 - Forward Lean and Lift

- The caster leans forward and lifts the rod.
- The current tensions the line and bends the rod.
- The caster judges the power for the next stage.
- The arms are still tight to the body (*left hand on the chest*).

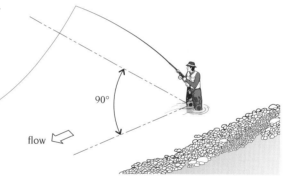

Stage 3 - Forward Lean and Upstream Side Cast

- The caster rocks to the right and makes an upstream side cast.
- The anchor is placed downstream and out into the flow.
- The loop is high and live.
- The loop does not go behind.
- The power for the next stage is judged.
- The arms are still tight to the body (*left hand on the chest*).

Sketch 23
*Double Left Bank, Left Shoulder
River - Stages 1, 2 and 3*

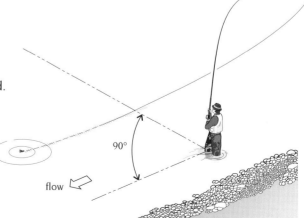

Stage 4 - Rock Back Circular Backcast (Side Cast)

- The caster has rocked back with a circular side cast.
- The loop is high and live.
- The rod tip is still in the side cast position.
- The anchor is still in place.
- The power for the next stage is judged.
- The arms are still close to the body (*left hand on the chest*).

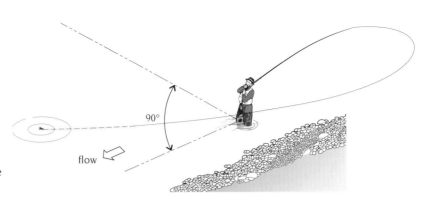

Stage 5 - Forward Rock and Power Push

- The caster has leaned forward with the arms tight to the body and pushed the shoulder to generate most of the line energy.
- Just before the forward rock is completed, the rod is pushed upwards and outwards towards the target against the pull of the line.
- The caster is still leaned forward with the arms fully extended.
- The moving line pulls up the anchor.

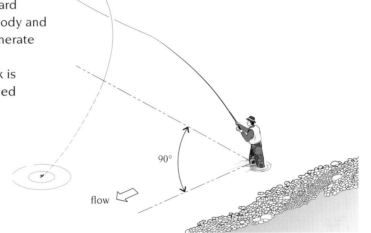

Stage 6 - Final Delivery

- The line has rolled out above the water.
- The leader has straightened and the line has fallen gently to the water.
- The rod is held high for water mending.

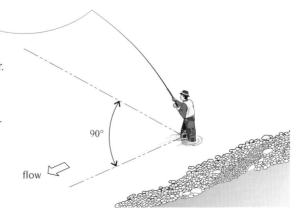

Sketch 23
Double Left Bank, Left Shoulder
River - Stages 4, 5 and 6

Common Faults

- Feet out of position.
- Incorrect hand grip.
- Incorrect anchor placement.
- Pulling the anchor prematurely, the fly goes behind you.
- Incorrect body and shoulder moves.
- Not pushing upwards and outwards.
- Not aiming at the target.

Worst Faults

- Too much line.
- Too much power.
- Degenerating into a rollcast.

Check Your Timing - When standing in moving water, you must be careful not to allow your rear loop to anchor in the water behind you and destroy your final delivery. Don't forget your waltz time counts, however, speed up the movements if necessary.

Practise the Other Angles - The double spey allows the 45° downstream presentation and the very effective 45° upstream cast. As each of these casts have relatively difficult anchor placement procedures, they must be practised regularly.

Practice... Left Bank - Double Spey 45° Downstream - Left Shoulder - River
Begin with four rod lengths of line measured from the reel - cast on the left side of the body...

- Choose an aiming point 45° downstream.
- Place the feet towards the target.
- Drop the anchor well downstream.
- Keep your rear loop out of the water.
- Don't let the forward loop cross your cast line.
- Keep your power down.

Timing - The 45° downstream cast will require a lot of practice to get the timing right and usually requires a faster casting procedure.

Faults

- Incorrect anchor placement, too far upstream.
- Pulling the anchor prematurely, the fly goes behind you.
- Crossing the cast line.
- Incorrect timing.
- Not aiming at the target.
- Too much power.
- Too much line.
- Degenerating into a rollcast.

PRACTICE... Left Bank - Double Spey 45° Upstream - Left Shoulder - River
Cast on the right side of the body...

- Choose an aiming point 45° upstream.
- Place the feet towards the target.
- Bring the anchor well upstream.
- Place the anchor well out into the flow.

TIMING - The 45° upstream cast appears to move at a leisurely pace due to the long pick up and upstream side cast procedure, however, all stages should be timed to produce the required velocity and line energy.

FAULTS

- Placing the anchor too far downstream.
- Crossing the cast line, anchor too far upstream.
- Pulling the anchor prematurely, the fly goes behind.
- Too much power.
- Not enough power.
- Not aiming at the target.
- Too much line.
- Crashing down with a rollcast.

A - Sideways lean, dip   B - Forward lean, lift   C - Rock back, circular side cast, right

Left Bank - Single Spey - Right Shoulder - River

GETTING SET TO CAST - Study the casting positions shown in sequences Photo 14, facing page and below. Also refer to Sketch 24, pages 126 and 127. Begin with four rod lengths of line measured from the reel. Cast on the right side of the body.

- This cast is made with the line delivered on the right side of the body.
- The single spey is an emergency cast in strong upstream wind.
- Don't attempt to make more than a 45° downstream presentation.

THE CAST - LEFT BANK SINGLE SPEY

- Choose an aiming point 45° downstream.
- Aim the feet towards the target.
- Place the anchor well upstream.

TIMING - Single speys require meticulous attention to timing. Keeping the anchor upstream and in the water during the cast can only be learned by constant practice. The timing is quite fast when compared to the double spey.

Photo 14:
SINGLE LEFT BANK,
RIGHT SHOULDER -
RIVER

D - *Forward rock, power push*   E - *Forward lean, dip*

Stage 1 - Sideways Lean and Dip

- The rod should be dipped and the line straight.
- The body should be leaned to the left.
- The arms should be tight to the body (*left hand on the chest*).
- The feet should then be placed to face the target.

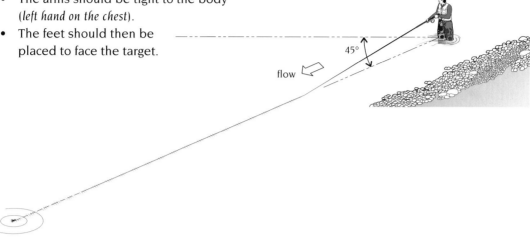

Stage 2 - Forward Lean and Lift

- The caster has leaned forward.
- The rod has been lifted and bent.
- The line is moving and tensioned.
- The power for the next stage is judged.
- The arms are still tight to the body (*left hand on the chest*).

Stage 3 - Rock Back Circular Side Cast

- The caster rocks back with the arms close to the body - making a circular side cast to the right.
- The anchor has been placed well to the right of the cast line.
- The arms are still tight to the body (*left hand on the chest*).
- The rod is still in the side cast position.

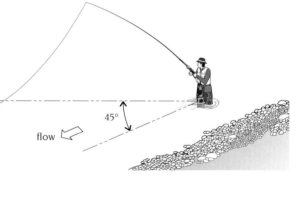

Sketch 24
Single Left Bank, Right Shoulder
River - Stages 1, 2 and 3

Stage 4 ~ Forward Rock and Power Push (Side Cast)

- The caster has maintained the side cast rod position, rocked forward and pushed the shoulder to generate line energy.
- The rod is still held in the side cast position.
- Just before the forward rock is completed, the rod is pushed upwards and outwards against the pull of the line.
- The caster is leaned forward - the arms are fully extended.

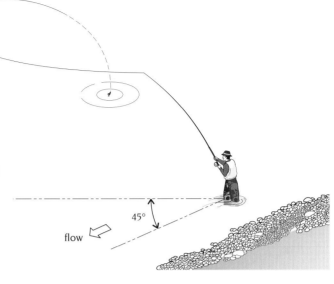

Stage 5 ~ Final Delivery

- The anchor is pulled.
- The line unrolls well above the water and is directed towards the target.
- Line acceleration due to energy concentration occurs.

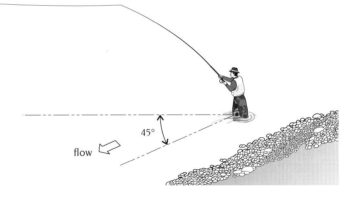

Stage 6 ~ Forward Lean and Dip

- The leader has straightened and the line has fallen gently to the water.
- The rod is held high for water mending.

Sketch 24

Single Left Bank, Right Shoulder River - Stages 4, 5 and 6

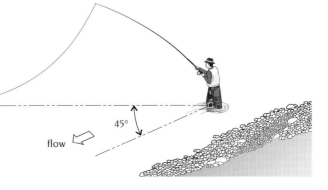

FAULTS

- Anchor not placed upstream.
- Crossing the cast line.
- Throwing the fly behind (*in the bushes*).
- Not keeping the line live.
- Timing too slow, the cast degenerates.
- Timing too fast, you will be wearing the line.

PREPARATION FOR THE RIGHT BANK - Practise the single spey over the right side of the body. It is good practice for the double spey on the right bank which is also made over the right shoulder.

PRACTICE... Standard Speycasts - Left Bank - River
Establish your optimum cast length - adjust your length according to the variable conditions...

THE OBJECT - An intelligent practice session will allow you to imprint all the required reactions for all of the different casting angles and for both right and left shoulder deliveries, give equal time to each. Stay on the right bank until you are making adequate casts more times than not. Don't tire yourself out, your body moves and reactions will go to pieces if you do. Don't spend more than ten minutes on each cast without a rest. Use the break period to analyze your progress.

THE SCHEDULE - LEFT BANK

- Start with the 45° downstream double.
- Move to the 90° across stream double.
- Now make 45° upstream double.

When reasonably satisfied with each direction of cast...

- Practise the 45° downstream single.
- Don't forget this is good practice for the right bank double spey.

PRACTICE COOL DOWN - If you are not satisfied with any of your other casts - build up your confidence again by having fun with your favourite speycast.

Part Three ~ Chapter Seventeen
Special Casting Techniques - River

CASTING AND FISHING CONDITIONS can be difficult and frustrating out on the river. An accomplished speycaster using a true speyrod can handle just about every awkward situation, cast from anywhere to anywhere, regardless of wind, water or casting obstructions. One of the principal advantages of speycasting is staying away from dangerous wading. A thorough knowledge of the special casting techniques should enable you to fish effectively, comfortably and safely.

SHORT LINE CASTING - It is good form to fish the water you are going to wade out to. Many an angler has been seen standing where they should be casting to. This is particularly true in unclear or high water conditions. Fish sometimes hold very close in, adjacent to drop offs or submerged gravel bars, etc. Short line casting restricts the area of water being covered, however, the ability to make very efficient line controls more than makes up for any disadvantage. Graphite speyrods are relatively light however, when making short casts their self-weight momentum can be used to advantage. This technique will be more difficult the stiffer the rod is. (*Make sure your rod is a true speyrod*).

EFFECTIVENESS OF SHORT LINE CASTING - To emphasize the value of the short line technique, let me relate the following 'fishing story'...

When guiding on the Bulkley River, going after summer steelhead, one of my clients was probably the worst single-handed flycaster ever. However, my other client was one of the best and could not resist wading out up to his arm pits and showing off his distance casting, no matter how I tried to restrain him. Luckily the poor flycaster was a very able and successful steelheader when using light baitcasting tackle and a float on other rivers where this method is legal.

The success of this technique depends on drifting the float straight down the river for a considerable distance close to the bank, then extending the length of cast to cover other fishable water farther out. This method of fishing is extremely effective and obviously relies on controlling the float and presenting the bait to the fish coming straight downstream towards it.

In desperation, the former float fisher was handed a speyrod and told to pretend that the fly line was his float and to get it out there anyway he could and make up for his lack of speycasting skill by better line control and more attention to reading the water at which he was an expert.

The irony of the situation was that within minutes this 'duffer' had a sixteen pound steelhead to the beach, directly behind his deep wading friend. This 'beginner's luck' continued all week and was a perfect example of the effectiveness of short line casting plus line control.

PRACTICE... Short Line Casting - River
Two lengths of line measured from the reel...

Make sure that you are capable of all short line casting techniques on the pond before taking on the river. This includes short line double and single speys on each side of the body.

REVIEW OF THE CASTING TECHNIQUE

- Place the feet towards the aiming point.
- Lean forward and downstream, arms extended.
- Stay leaned forward, make your lift.
- Make short delicate casts - with the tip of the rod.
- Use the body weight and self-weight momentum of the rod.
- Don't worry if the anchor is pulled prematurely.

PRACTICE SCHEDULE

RIGHT BANK

- Double speys to all angles of cast.
- Single speys, small angle change.

LEFT BANK

- Double speys to all angles.
- Single speys, small angle changes.

SHORT LINE CASTING ON BRUSHY RIVERS - Fish holding in shadowy protected locations close to the bank can often be covered by casting to them with the short line technique and a side arm delivery.

REMINDERS...

- Adjust your timing for the shorter line.
- Keep your line live.
- Don't use too much line.
- Keep your power down.
- Make side arm presentation.
- Don't slap the line down.

IMPORTANCE OF SHORT LINE PRACTICE - As your speyfishing skills increase you will find that you will spend more time 'fishing short'. A fifty foot cast to where the fish are, is better than a one hundred foot to where 'they ain't'.

Restricted Backcast Clearance - River
See Sketch 17, page 88...

Although the fly does not go behind the angler when speycasting, the short backcast requires space to prevent fouling the line. You will not foul the line on any object that you can't touch with the rod and arms extended. This applies to objects on either side, above and behind. Many sections of prime water are almost unfishable due to rock walls, hedges, etc. and do not provide even the minimum clearance. By varying the casting technique these difficult situations can be covered. The restricted clearance technique also restricts the casting distance, however, it does not interfere with line control. This coupled with undisturbed water is a winning combination.

The cast is somewhat similar to the short line casting technique with a longer length of line. The entire cast takes place in front of the angler, however, the line does not go behind. One sure way to find out if the line goes behind when casting is to find a tree or preferably an embankment and cast. You may have to shorten the line until comfortable with the technique. Single speys should also be practised.

PRACTICE... Restricted Backcast
Three rod lengths of line measured from the reel...

Don't attempt the restricted back cast technique unless you are capable of making accurate, controlled short line casts.

- On each side of the river.
- With double speys.
- And single speys.

CASTING LOCATION - The prime object of the practice is to cast with absolutely no line going behind you, however, this is very difficult to check when casting. Go out and find a rock wall or overhanging tree and find out how close you can get without fouling your line or damaging your speyrod.

WHAT LENGTH OF LINE? - Start your practice with three rod lengths and gradually increase to your optimum length. Don't expect to make perfect presentations every time.

REMINDERS...

- Adjust your timing, usually faster.
- Keep leaning forward.
- Don't let the line go behind you.
- Keep the anchor well out in the river.
- Make side arm movements.
- Don't use too much line.
- Don't overpower the cast.

IMPORTANCE OF RESTRICTED BACKCAST PRACTICE - We all know those 'fishy looking' locations on our favourite rivers with trees, canyon walls, embankments, etc. where backcasting with a single hand rod is impossible. We also know those rivers where the single-handers have to 'take a number' to get into the 'line-up' to fish through the best backcasting areas. Practise your restricted backcast technique, it will really pay off.

Shooting Line - River

There are going to be many times when you can't get your fly out to that interesting spot out on the river with your optimum cast length. We already know that wading out farther or adding too much line is counter-productive. When fish are holding beyond your optimum speycast, they can often be reached by shooting line. In order to shoot line, sufficient energy must be generated during the cast by increasing the acceleration of the rod tip during the forward stroke. The power push must be aimed upwards to give the line sufficient elevation to prevent it falling to the water prematurely. Do not attempt to shoot more than ten per cent of your optimum cast length until you become more proficient. Do not even try to shoot into a head wind.

PRACTICE... Shooting Line
Four rod lengths of line measured from the reel - start shorter and gradually increase...

It is assumed that you have practised shooting line on the pond. Don't attempt to shoot line unless your speycast deliveries roll out well above the water before falling. You can't shoot extra line if your cast slaps down into the water before the shooting line has been pulled out.

HOW MUCH LINE CAN YOU SHOOT? - Assuming that your speycasting is adequate, there are numerous other factors including depth of wading, current speed, wind direction and intensity, however, the most important factors are your ability to produce the additional energy to straighten the shooting line and your line has recently been dressed; *see Chapter Twenty-Seven*.

REMINDERS...

- Adjust your timing, don't rush it.
- Add additional power.
- Place the anchor well forward.
- Check your line markings.
- Use your optimum cast length.
- Gradually add shooting line.
- Find your best shooting length.

RELEASING THE SHOOT - The casting line is trapped under the right hand - just above the reel; *refer to Photo* 15B, *page* 144. The shooting line is pulled off the reel and allowed to fall to the water. The shooting line is released just before the anchor is pulled.

COMMON FAULTS

- Not enough line speed.
- Too much shooting line.
- Not enough elevation.
- Line does not straighten.

IMPORTANCE OF SHOOTING PRACTICE - You will find that you will be aerializing less and shooting more line as your speyfishing skills increase. The ability to shoot a little line now and then will increase your effective fishing area and decrease the effort required.

Line Control (Mending) - River

Line control is the art of making the line do what you want instead of it being swept around by the current. This allows dry flies to be fished as living insects or in getting a sunk fly down to the required depth without the use of heavy weight lines and leaded flies. The prime concern during the presentation is making the fly go down the river ahead of the leader and the leader ahead of the line.

There are two styles of mending... *aerial mending* – before the line falls to the water, and *water mending* – after the line is on the water.

Remember... *Success in fishing is directly proportional to the ability to control line.*

TRUE SPEYRODS ARE IDEAL MENDERS - True speyrods with their long, limber, powerful action make mending line a pleasure. The flexibility of the rod allows long delicate mends by using the self-weight momentum of the rod instead of the arms. Many inexperienced anglers will not attempt or will 'give up' line mending due to the fatigue of using an overstiff rod.

Aerial Mending

The first few seconds that the fly is on the water is often very productive. Unfortunately the leader often lands upstream of the line and the line is nearly always swept around by the current and drags the fly unnaturally. Any attempt to correct these situations will result in dunking your dry fly or pulling your wet fly off course. All of these problems can be avoided if the line is shaped in the air, so that it falls to the water already mended. We will practise the serpentine cast and the reach cast.

THE SERPENTINE CAST - As we have already learned, a fish holding directly downstream is difficult to motivate unless the fly is presented in a natural way. Slapping the line down close to the fish's hold or swinging the fly across its narrow forward field of view is not very effective. We, of course, are going to use the serpentine aerial mend having practised it so diligently on the casting pond. This time we will have the current to complete the presentation.

PRACTICE... **Serpentine Mending**
Four rod lengths of line measured from the reel...

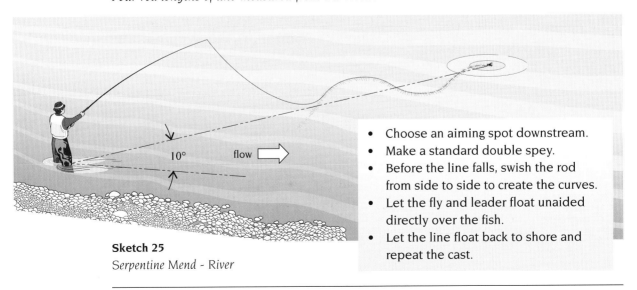

10°   flow

- Choose an aiming spot downstream.
- Make a standard double spey.
- Before the line falls, swish the rod from side to side to create the curves.
- Let the fly and leader float unaided directly over the fish.
- Let the line float back to shore and repeat the cast.

Sketch 25
Serpentine Mend - River

COMMON FAULTS

- Badly shaped curves.
- Not aiming towards target.
- Pulling fly or line when 'swishing'.
- Fly does not cover target.
- Fly lands directly on target.

DON'T FRIGHTEN FISH - There are two major mistakes when using the downstream serpentine presentation. They are...

- Disturbing the natural float of the fly by water mending after the line is on the water.
- Starting the next cast before the line has swung well clear of the fish hold.

IMPORTANCE OF THE SERPENTINE CAST - Fish have an annoying habit of showing themselves close in, directly downstream just as you are all set to cast far out upstream. The serpentine cast will allow you to cover these awkward fish without wading down river and spooking them. Don't forget to practise on both sides of the river.

THE REACH CAST - Without aerial mending, the leader often lands upstream of the line and the current will distort the line, dragging the fly unnaturally. To compensate, the line must then be water mended to get the leader downstream of the line. Most of this can be avoided by reach casting so that the line falls to the water already mended. We will use the reach cast aerial mend practised on the casting pond, this time with the current completing the presentation.

PRACTICE... Reach Cast Mending
Four rod lengths of line measured from the reel...

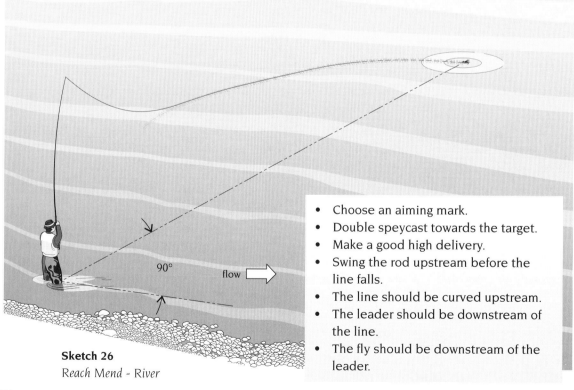

90°   flow ⟹

- Choose an aiming mark.
- Double speycast towards the target.
- Make a good high delivery.
- Swing the rod upstream before the line falls.
- The line should be curved upstream.
- The leader should be downstream of the line.
- The fly should be downstream of the leader.

Sketch 26
Reach Mend - River

COMMON FAULTS

- Not aiming towards the target.
- Pulling the line back, short of the target.
- Not sufficient reach.
- Not enough elevation to allow the mend to form before the line falls.

IMPORTANCE OF THE REACH CAST - The reach cast mend made with a true speyrod is so easy that you should use it on every practice cast from now on.

DON'T FORGET... *Practise your reach casts on each side of the river.*

Water Mending

No matter how well you performed the aerial mend, the river current will eventually distort the line and drag the fly unnaturally. This is true for all styles of speyfishing from dry fly to sunk fly. By skilful water mending, drag can be reduced to a minimum, allowing the fly to drift 'drag free' in the current to fish you are wanting to motivate into taking your fly.

When practising on the casting pond, we did not have the line-straightening advantage of moving water. You will find that water mending on the river is much easier. The following sketches illustrate the difference water mending will make in your presentation... without water mending, *see Sketch 27A below*, and with water mending, *see 27B on page 136.*

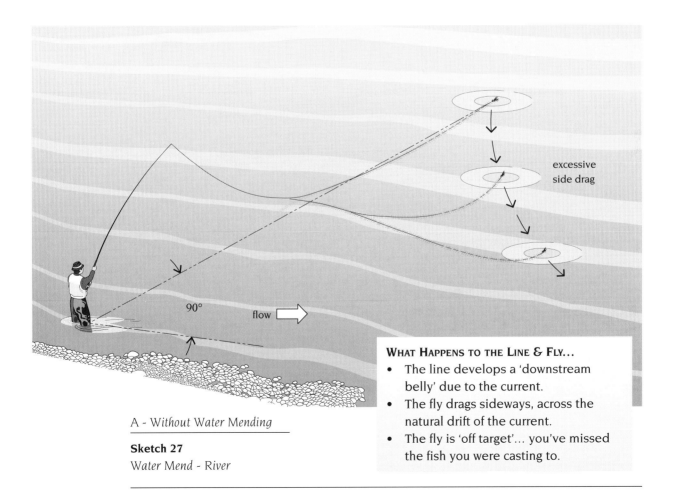

excessive
side drag

90°

flow

WHAT HAPPENS TO THE LINE & FLY...
- The line develops a 'downstream belly' due to the current.
- The fly drags sideways, across the natural drift of the current.
- The fly is 'off target'... you've missed the fish you were casting to.

A - Without Water Mending

Sketch 27
Water Mend - River

PRACTICE... Water Mending
Four rod lengths of line measured from the reel...

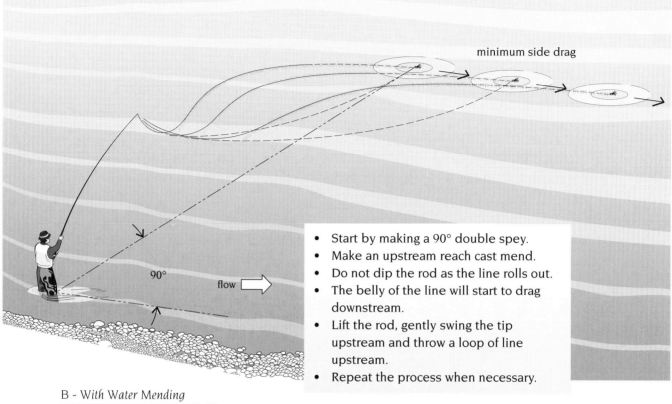

minimum side drag

90°

flow

B - With Water Mending

Sketch 27
Water Mend - River, cont'd

- Start by making a 90° double spey.
- Make an upstream reach cast mend.
- Do not dip the rod as the line rolls out.
- The belly of the line will start to drag downstream.
- Lift the rod, gently swing the tip upstream and throw a loop of line upstream.
- Repeat the process when necessary.

COMMON FAULTS

- Not raising the rod when mending.
- Dragging the fly when mending.
- Too much power.

IMPORTANCE OF WATER MENDING - The secret of successful speyfishing is in making the fly do *'what you want it to do'* instead of being swept around by the current. To counter the continuously varying fly-disturbing effect of moving current, the line must be mended frequently to keep the fly 'on track'. Once again, it can be seen that an experienced speyfisher will be water mending line for a much longer time than casting and that a long limber speyrod will allow this with the least angler fatigue.

MENDING AND FEEDING - To increase the drag free float distance, feed a little line during each mend. Strip the feed line off the reel before you cast.

Casting in the Wind

The ability to cope with all the variations and combinations of wind encountered out on the river is one of the many reasons for becoming a speyfisher. There will be times when you will begin to believe that the intensity of the wind will increase in proportion to the number of fish in the river. Being able to make the correct 'wind-cheating' presentation will allow you to carry on in relative safety. Knowledge of all the many nasty habits of the wind is essential to the accomplished speyfisher.

VARIATION IN INTENSITY - A wind of two hundred miles an hour at twenty thousand feet could be slowed down to twenty miles an hour at twenty feet above the water due to the drag effect of the local terrain and vegetation. Wind blowing across open water will cause ripples. These ripples will produce a drag effect on the wind and slow it down again. The water drag on the surface can sometimes produce a vortex effect with relatively still air a few feet or inches above the water. When head winds are troublesome, make your delivery as close to the water as possible. Wind does not blow continuously and comes in intermittent gusts and lulls. Wind gusts can be seen travelling along the water making a disturbance similar to a low flying helicopter. This disturbance is usually followed by a calm period (*make sure you judge the calm period correctly*). While making a cast during a misjudged calm period, one hundred feet of line slowly did the 'Indian rope trick' and went straight up in the air, finally landing like limp spaghetti twenty feet out. Definitely not your average classic speycast and very difficult to convince onlookers that it was the presentation intended.

Wind conditions encountered while on the river will require different approaches in speycasting to overcome a 'problem' that might just spoil the day's fishing. The adjustments you will need to make in your speycasting for the noted wind conditions are...

- DOWNSTREAM WIND - Use the double spey. The upstream side cast will require a little more effort as it is made against the wind. Large angular changes become more difficult as the downstream velocity increases. Single speys should not be attempted during downstream winds, its the wrong tool as the final delivery is made on the windward side of the caster.

- UPSTREAM WIND - Light, upstream winds are easy with the double spey. Leave the anchor farther downstream and use the side arm technique to keep the fly away from you. Stronger upstream wind will require the single spey.

- WIND FROM THE REAR - This is no problem for the accomplished speycaster as the casting location usually has an obstruction to the rear (*to break the wind*). Wind from the rear will make the back cast difficult, however, it will enhance your forward cast. Cast up into the wind on your forward delivery and 'hang on to your socks'.

- WIND FROM THE FRONT - This situation is the most difficult. A knowledge of the 'wind behaviour' is essential, judging the gusts and lulls is critical. Do not expect to make long casts, or perfect aerial mends. The general rules are... *Don't let the wind pull your anchor on the back cast and keep the forward delivery low.* When all else fails, use the rollcast (*the wind will already have disturbed the water*).

PROTECT YOURSELF - Don't forget to wear head, neck and eye protection, even when practising with a wool fly. When speyfishing on the beautiful Patagonia rivers of Argentina decades ago, wind was a real problem, due to my inability to understand what was happening and how to fish under those conditions. By the end of the trip, my face was so leader-slashed that it resembled the much-prized duelling scars of a nineteenth century Prussian army officer.

LEARNING TO USE THE WIND - Once the wind starts to blow, 'neither your profanity nor piety' will calm the waters. So you might as well accept the situation and make the best of it. *Use it, don't fight it.*

PRACTICE... Wind Casting - Double Spey
Four rod lengths of line measured from the reel...

It is obvious that we can't work to a fixed schedule to practise all wind casts. Wind is so contrary that probably won't blow when you intend to practise your wind casting techniques. Just carry on with your normal or special techniques and practise your wind techniques for what direction it finally does blow. It is assumed that you have studied and practised wind casting out on the casting pond, and are reasonably accomplished at speycasting on moving water.

HEAD WINDS

- Keep your forward delivery as low as possible, under the wind.
- Use a side cast technique.
- Don't expect to make long casts.
- Don't let the wind blow your rear loop into the bushes.

FOLLOWING WINDS

- Keep your rear loop as low as possible.
- Use a side cast to keep your rear loop under the wind.
- Make a high forward delivery to let the wind carry the line out.

DOWNSTREAM WINDS

- Your upstream side cast will need more power.
- Make sure that the wind does not disturb your anchor placement.
- You will have difficulty with upstream deliveries.

UPSTREAM WIND - LIGHT

- Drop your anchor well downstream.
- Make a side cast rear loop under the wind.
- Get the forward delivery under the wind.

UPSTREAM WIND - HEAVY

- Use a single spey.
- Make sure your anchor is well downstream.
- Don't let the wind blow your rear loop into the bushes.
- Don't expect to make downstream presentations.

WIND CANNOT MAKE UP ITS MIND

- Check where most of the gusts are coming from.
- Watch the pressure waves for calm periods.
- Be ready for sudden direction changes.
- Abort any dangerous looking casts.
- When all else fails, move to a more sheltered location.

THE IMPORTANCE OF DEALING WITH WIND - Wind is a fact of life when speyfishing. As Mark Twain said... *"Everybody complains about the weather, but nobody does anything about it."* There is nothing you can do to stop the wind, however, you can do something about being able to speycast in it. The ability to carry on in adverse wind is an absolute necessity for your success as a speyfisher. Being able to analyze the direction and velocity of the wind, making the appropriate cast and using the wind where possible, is one more asset that makes speycasting so fascinating and rewarding.

It Pays to Practise...

Dr. Brumwell of Vancouver with the steelhead that 'ruined' his practice session.

Effective Practising on the River

It often happens that sane and logical students go to pieces and develop buck fever the moment they see a river which holds fish. The larger the potential fish, the more acute the fever. All thoughts of practising mysteriously disappear, leaving the unfortunate 'would be' speyfisher, attempting to cover the river without the skills to make the correct presentation, deal with all the awkward casting situations such as wind and restricted back casts, and worst of all, not being able to control the line or the fly.

There is one overriding problem that seems to affect all newcomers to speyfishing and it is the main cause of failure to hook fish. As you have probably guessed, it is the 'old bogy' of excessive distance casting. It is human nature to practise the things you are 'good at' and neglect all those boring special procedures that you are having trouble with. Fish will not be impressed with the length of your cast. However, they will be highly motivated by your ability to feed the fly to them in an appetizing way.

Keep practising and 'tidying up' your procedures even when you are fishing. The following illustrates just one of the benefits of practising on the river...

My good friend, Dr. Charles Brumwell, a founding member of the Steelhead Society of British Columbia, recently having 'seen the light' and 'converted' to speyfishing, was fishing on the mighty Thompson River which hosts enormous and powerful summer steelhead. Not wanting to join the deep wading, distance casting anglers on the popular beach side of the river, he crossed over the bridge to the steep embankment on the other side. His intention was to practise his limited backcast clearance technique at the foot of the embankment and line control with a surface fly. Although Charlie is a very accomplished angler (his speycasting 'still leaves a lot to be desired'), he does not cast more than sixty feet and makes up for this by concentrating on line control. Much to his surprise and annoyance a sixteen pound steelhead ruined his practice session by taking his fly.

If you concentrate on all casting and line control procedures even when fishing, you will find that they will eventually be imprinted into your long term memory allowing you to finally concentrate on fishing not just casting.

DON'T EXPECT MIRACLES - Unless there is something lacking with your genetic makeup, your adrenal glands will go into overdrive the moment you step into river water, your latent 'hunter-gatherer' instincts will take over and fill your mind with fish. All your recently acquired speycasting skills will be temporarily subdued, don't worry, you are quite normal, however, you must remember that there are many new techniques that must be absorbed before you are able to catch fish intelligently when speyfishing. Some anglers, who have successfully completed the pond exercises are disappointed with their performance out on the river and can't understand why they are not hooking fish immediately. Others put the thoughts of fish out of their minds and concentrate on all the new procedures and techniques required for successful speyfishing.

This approach was recently demonstrated by fellow engineer, *Frank Neunemann* of Germany, who attended our speyfishing course on the Bulkley River. Those not familiar with German engineering techniques should know that it relies on meticulous training and fanatical attention to detail. When it was explained to Frank that there were not too many fish around at that time of the year, his reaction was, *"Good, now I can concentrate on my casting and line control, this is the first year of my apprenticeship."* Not all of us have Frank's dedication, however, it should be an example to those misguided anglers who are expecting miracles.

'Apprentice'... *Frank Neunemann with a Bulkley River steelhead caught on the second year of his 'apprentice-ship'.*

PART FOUR ~ SPEYFISHING

CHAPTER

Eighteen   *On Speyfishing*

Nineteen   *About Fish Behaviour*

Twenty   *Know Your Fish and Your River*

Twenty-One   *Think Before You Fish*

Twenty-Two   *Angling Techniques*

Twenty-Three   *Hooking, Controlling and Landing Fish*

SAMURAI STEELIE...

Hiro Imai of Japan, accomplished speycaster, with a fine steelhead just prior to its release on the beautiful Bulkley River in British Columbia. Hiro's dedication and enthusiasm to the sport of speyfishing is infectious.

Part Four ~ Chapter Eighteen
On Speyfishing

CONFUSING SPEYCASTING WITH SPEYFISHING - There are many intelligent anglers who have invested their time and money in learning 'all there is to know' about speycasting and are capable of making any presentation required. Unfortunately some will go to their favourite pool on their local river where they had previously been fishing with a single-hander or an overhead double-hander, then wade out (*and disturb fish*) and start speycasting with their 'usual' down and across presentation. To put it bluntly, they have wasted their time and effort in learning speycasting, having only changed their previous style of rod for a speyrod and carried on fishing in the same place and the same style as they did with their previous rods.

Many misguided beginner speyfishers are disappointed that they are not any more successful in catching fish than they were with their single-handers. If you were able to read their minds, you would find that they are saying to themselves, *"How come I am not catching any more fish than with my other rod, after all, I am using a nice big fly and casting way farther than before?"* Is this a 'Freudian slip'? Was this really the reason that they bought their double-handers or is this the excessive distance casting 'ogre' raising its ugly head again? To summarize, a speyrod is no better than any other style of rod unless it is used intelligently and for the purpose for which it was designed, and that is speyfishing.

It took years for me to understand why accomplished speycasters would restrict themselves to the popular beach locations when they are quite capable of covering all those undisturbed waters, too difficult for the overhead caster. Then suddenly, the light went on. They could not read the other water and had no idea where fish were holding. There are many reasons why some anglers are not able to locate fish on unfamiliar water, however, the most probable reason is that they have always fished on pools where every inch of the water had been fished in exactly the same way for donkey's years. Many known pools have named features such as Joe's rock or Fred's riffle and don't require reading. Unskilled anglers will even choose their fishing location by reading the parking lot, not the river. This must be a good spot today, just look at all those cars.

READ THE RIVER AS A SPEYFISHER - Before we can catch fish, we must know where they are and why they are there. We must also know how to present the correct fly in the most natural way to motivate the fish to take it. In order to present the fly in the most appealing way, we must know something about the properties of light underwater and the amazing characteristics of a fishes eyesight. When armed with our speycasting skills and knowledge of the river and its fish, we will be able to read the river as a speyfisher and fish anywhere we want to, comfortably, safely, successfully and elegantly.

Handling the Rod, Reel and Line

Before we go out and hook into a big fish, we must know how to handle a spey-rod intelligently. Newcomers to the sport of speyfishing will experience some difficulty in handling the rod, reel and line when casting, controlling line and playing the fish for the first time. Even though you are using both hands, there are times when an extra hand would be useful. Unless you are related to an octopus, you must learn a number of new procedures. The techniques required can be divided into... *handling the rod, using the reel and handling the line*.

There are no rigid rules for rod, reel and line handling. Whatever suits your style of fishing will do, providing it produces the desired results without tying yourself in a knot. While guiding a very experienced angler, speyfishing for the first time, it was a total surprise to see him holding the handle of a fifteen foot rod in his mouth, as he tailed his fish with both hands.

HANDLING THE ROD - *see Photo* 15A. Long cork handles confuse the beginner. When casting, the hands should always be close to the reel with the right hand uppermost. This position is to allow maximum flexibility of a true speyrod and to allow full arm extension when 'push casting'. The extra length of the cork handle is for playing large fish.

 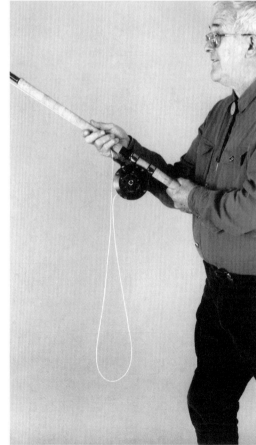

Photo 15:
ROD, HAND AND
LINE POSITIONS

A - Casting and mending   *B - Feeding line*

HOLDING THE ROD AFTER CASTING - During line control procedures, the rod should be held as for casting. Some styles of fishing require the fly to travel downstream and then swing in with virtually no mending. This can be tiring due to the size of the rod and the length of line being fished. Moving the left hand to the top of the cork grip and resting the weight of the rod on the body will reduce angler fatigue. This now frees the right hand for reeling, palming or hand lining.

SHOOTING, FEEDING AND MENDING LINE - *see* Photos 15B *and* 15C. Some styles of fishing require both shooting and feeding to be made in the same presentation. This will require a different method of holding the line. The shooting loop is held under and released by the right hand. The feeding loop is held under and released by the left hand. Don't worry about getting it wrong. You won't do yourself an injury and any mistakes will be immediately apparent.

HANDLING THE REEL - *see* Photo 15D. For most of the time the line is trapped under the right hand and the reel is not touched, as line is pulled off and fed downstream with the left hand. When the fly reaches the primary target area and the fish takes, the left hand should move to the top of the cork grip, trapping the line. The butt of the rod should be against the body with the right hand touching the reel, staying clear of the handle. With the left hand at the top of the cork handle and right hand close to the reel, it is possible to palm the reel. Reel in line and hand line with the right hand.

WHY WIND RIGHT-HANDED? - There are many valid reasons for fishing with the left hand at the top of the cork and the right hand close to the reel. The use of the weaker left hand reduces the tendency to 'rip the lips off' a fish that has taken the fly. If your hooks are kept needle sharp, there is no need to set the hook.

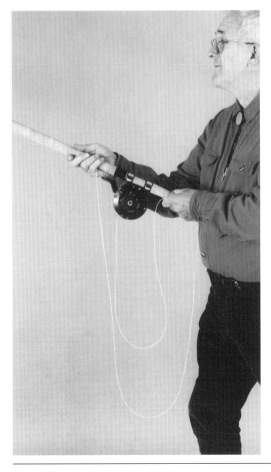

C - *Shooting line, feeding line*   D - *Controlling fish, palming reel*

Once the fish is on, it is possible to land it by applying very little force providing it is applied intelligently. The right hand is always available to 'spell' the left hand if required. After playing an active fish into the bank and back across the river a few times, palming, reeling, hand lining, etc., it will become obvious why the most sensitive and agile hand is used on the reel. Many a fish has been treated to an LDR (*long distance release*) because of tired left hands. When the fish is ready for tailing, the right hand is still free to accomplish this tricky procedure.

Why Do We Flyfish?

There must be some good reason why seemingly intelligent people should be wading around in a raging torrent of near freezing water with wind blowing from all directions at the same time, casting artificial flies to unco-operative and sometimes non-existent fish. There are times when they must begin to question their own sanity. What is it that prompts anglers to inflict this punishment on themselves? Apart from satisfying 'homo sapiens' natural genetically imprinted instincts to hunt, flyfishing is one of the most absorbing escapes available to contemporary man. It is the thinking man's sport, does not rely on machinery or electronic gadgets and requires an understanding and appreciation of nature. It does not matter who you are or how affluent you are. 'All are equal in the eyes of a fish'.

In all true sports, there are certain handicaps imposed so that it does not become too easy or boring and depreciate any sense of achievement. Flyfishers set their own handicaps to make it more difficult, not easier. It is acquiring the knowledge and skills to overcome these self-imposed handicaps that makes flyfishing so absorbing and rewarding. Flyfishing is one of the few sports in which you can never be proved to be entirely wrong and never prove that you are entirely right. This often leads to some highly suspect and entertaining fish talk after a day's sport.

A PERSONAL PHILOSOPHY OF FLYFISHING - Everybody has their own ideas of why they flyfish and how they go about it. Your ideas and methods may be far removed from mine, however, it is imperative that my methods are carefully explained so that you are better able to understand why my speyfishing takes the particular form that it does and why I fish that way. You are under no obligation to agree. Many of my current methods and ideals are the result of observing other, more talented anglers and discussing methods with other speyfishers.

WHAT IS FLYFISHING? - Flyfishing is the art and science of catching fish with an artificial fly intended to represent the size, color, shape and behaviour of the fish's natural food. The fly must be presented to the fish with a fly line, cast with a flyrod. Many anglers using flies that do not represent any known fish food without any knowledge of why the fish take them, feel superior to those using lures or bait while they are using 'so-called flies'. If you don't know what your fly represents or why the fish takes it, you are lure fishing with a flyrod, 'short changing yourself' and missing the very 'essence of flyfishing'.

If flyfishing is an escape from the stresses of the modern world, the last thing you should do is introduce the element of competition. The desire to compete is insidious. It can vary from setting personal goals as to size and number of fish to comparing your catch with your companions. An angler having had an enjoyable day with modest success can be 'put off' by the angler who has 'hit the jackpot'. There is much more to the enjoyment of flyfishing than catching fish. Don't let others spoil your fishing.

ARE YOU REALLY FLYFISHING? - Originally all fly lines sank. Flies were fished on the bottom or rising to the surface. When anglers began to grease their line (*to make them float*) or used the recently invented floating line, the 'old school cried foul'. It seemed that unless your fully sunk line was hooked around a rock or fouled up in the weeds, you were missing the fun of flyfishing. When some enterprising fellow invented the sink tip line, it was taken as a direct insult to the self-styled 'sunk line purist'. The final insult to the 'full sunk line, mind lock folk' was the introduction of the strike indicator. They bleated that strike indicators are the same as the floats used in bait fishing. The curious thing is that many who say the strike indicator is float fishing, are using a floating line themselves, which in reality is a very efficient long float. Providing the fly represents a fish's natural food in color, size, shape and behaviour, and is presented with a fly line and flyrod, it is flyfishing.

Prime Fall Male...

A beautiful summer steelhead of the Skeena River system being released in the early fall. Although this male has acquired its distinctive fresh water adaptation colours on its 200 mile journey up the Bulkley River, it will not spawn until early next year.

Part Four ~ Chapter Nineteen
About Fish Behaviour

So FAR WE HAVE BEEN CONCENTRATING on the techniques of speycasting, how to change the angle of cast and to make aerial and water mends to present the fly to the fish in the most tempting way. If we are to catch fish intelligently, we must understand more about their eyesight, how they process sound and how important their sense of smell is.

FISH CAN'T THINK - A fish's brain is about the size of a pea and is incapable of making decisions. The tiny organ is genetically programmed to react to certain external stimuli and nothing else. According to the late angling author *Charlie Brooks* of Montana, fish have only three things on their mind... *feeding, spawning and nothing*. This is a bit of an over simplification, however, it does help to illustrate the low level of intelligence of fish.

FISH DON'T ACT... THEY REACT - When a fish's brain receives a signal - sight, sound or smell - it reacts instantaneously. These reactions are based on the following circumstances...

- Is this food coming my way?
- Is this thing going to eat me?
- Can it be driven away?
- Is it time to get going?
- Is it time to spawn?

In plain words... *feed - fight - flight - reproduce*

How a Fish Sees the Fly and the Angler

All our previous work on casting and line control will be reinforced if we understand how a fish sees the approaching fly. It is natural to imagine that a fish below water can see objects as we do above it. A working knowledge of how a fish does see is essential in understanding its behaviour when intercepting food or avoiding the angler. How a fish sees above and below water is partly due to the properties of light entering a liquid and the amazing adaptation of the fish's eyesight to underwater life. A fish's ability to see and focus out of each eye independently with monocular vision on each side and binocular vision to the front gives us clues to the best fly presentations. Their ability to see out of the water (*through a window*), *see Sketch* 29A *page* 153, tells us when we can be seen above water. Fish see underwater objects reflected in the mirrored surface of the water. This tells us why they have difficulty in detecting food (*or our feet*) under certain water conditions. The fish's ability to see depends on the properties of light above and below the water and the amazing characteristics of the fish's eye. It is important not to confuse these subjects.

THE FISH'S EYESIGHT - Fish have relatively poor eyesight compared to us, however, they have a much wider field of view. As the eyes are positioned on each side of the head, they must protrude for the fish to see over a wide angle. In order to gather light from every point in the wide field, the lens of a fish's eye has developed into a sphere unlike the human lens which is a disk. In humans, focusing is obtained by changing the shape of a disk like lens. The significant thing about the human eye is that all objects within our field of view are also in our depth of focus.

To continue in camera terminology, a fish can focus by moving its spherical lens back **and** forth just like a camera. Unlike the human eye, the fish's depth of focus will change considerably at each length of focus just like a camera. For example, a fish focused at ten feet may be able to see clearly for a considerable distance. A fish focused at one foot may only see for a few inches either way. In other words, as the focal length gets shorter, the focal depth

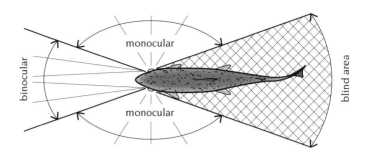

A - *Field of View*

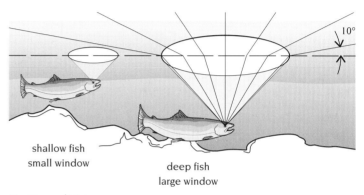

B - *Cone of Vision*

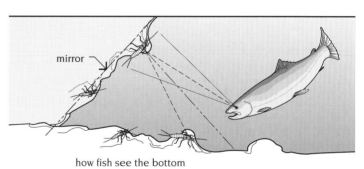

how fish see the bottom

C - *Mirror*

Sketch 28
Fish's Sight

gets smaller. This phenomenon partially explains why a fish will come from the depths and drift downstream with the fly on the end of its nose to check it out (*no, it's not smelling it*). Just because a fish is not focused on an object does not mean that it cannot detect movement of anything outside its depth of focus. Fish focused at their maximum range (*approximately thirty feet*) can also detect objects at a much greater distance.

There have been numerous experiments to determine whether or not fish can see colour or distinguish one colour from another. Without doubt, they can to a remarkable degree. Another set of experiments, far more practical, has demonstrated that the most significant question is... *can the fish see the*

Adult Stone

Acroneuria
Abnormus... the
natural adult
female stonefly
used as a model
for the 'Telkwa
Stone'.

colour against a similar background? The answer is yes, depending on how well the fly is camouflaged.

Having already discussed the function and effect of the spherical lens of the fish's eye, we must now understand how both eyes are used together. It can be seen from the sketch that fish have an almost complete field of view, leaving only a small blind area to the rear; *see Sketch 28A, facing page*. This is very different to us, our peripheral vision does not reach past our shoulders *(unless you possess the proverbial eyes in the back of the head)*. We, of course, have the ability to turn our head to increase our field of view. A fish's large peripheral view has developed to allow it to conserve **ene**rgy without the need to constantly move its head and body to see what could be threatening it from the side. It can also be seen in the sketch that each eye can work independently to each side - *monocular* - and combined in front - *binocular*. It must also be realized that the field of view is not a flat plane as shown. In reality, it is cone shaped rather like the beam projected by a wide angle flashlight *(fish, of course, do not project light)*.

A fish's brain must process a vast amount of information gathered from all around it at the same time. It must react instinctively *(not think)* to the fight, flight or food stimuli, or die. It is useful to imagine that the peripheral monocular vision is an early warning radar beam and the forward looking binocular vision 'locks on' and identifies the target. So far we have only discussed a fish's eyesight. It is now time to discuss the basic physics of light, which is independent of eyesight.

THE PROPERTIES OF LIGHT (REFRACTION) - Even our primitive 'hunter-gatherer' ancestors must have known that when they pushed their spears into the water, they bent and straightened out again when pulled out. This magical effect must have stimulated intellectual conversation around the camp fire in between chewing on mastodon burgers. Nothing seems to have been done about it until a Dutch mathematician, *Snell (died* 1626 AD) pointed out that if a beam of light travelling through air hits the water at an angle, it will break into two components: a beam reflected back above the water at roughly 90° to the beam of light and a beam refracted *(bent)* down into the water. Snell postulated a mathematical solution to calculate just how much each ray will bend depending on its angle to the surface and the density of the water. From these calculations, it was possible to determine that a vertical beam would not bend and that beams below approximately 10° would not enter the water at all, however, they would reflect upwards.

When it came to explain the significance of light waves and refraction to the angler, it was an open field. The great British angling writers of the last century *Halford* and *Ronalds*, and the no less great American writer *Marinaro* of this century, have contributed to our understanding of a fish's eyesight. The relatively recent publication of 'THE TROUT AND THE FLY' (*Goddard and Clark*) is without doubt the most practical explanation of how a trout sees and its significance when fishing. A glance at the sketch shows the light rays as they penetrate the water and hit the fish's eye. This is not a property of the fish's eye as precisely the same thing would happen with an underwater camera lens. It can be seen that all the rays above water must be compressed into a cone shape when they enter the water. It will also be seen that no light rays below 10° will enter the water.

THE CONE OF VISION AND THE MIRROR - *see Sketch* 28B *and* 28C, *page* 150. The effect of the cone shape field of the light rays produces a circular window above the fish's eye enabling it to see out of the water. Since light can still penetrate all of the water outside the window (*but not reach the fish's eye*). The bottom will be reflected on the underside of the surface as a mirror. Underwater photographs show that objects on the bottom, are quite clearly identified in the mirror providing the water is clear and smooth. They also show that the surface of the mirror is bent downwards to a foreshortened horizon. Since the cone of vision begins at the fish's eye, it will become smaller as the fish gets closer to the surface and larger again as the fish sinks deeper.

The fish's window allows it to locate and identify aerial or land predators (*including the angler*) and any potential food floating downstream on the surface. A glance at the sketch shows that a fish can gather information from a much larger area than its window and also see across the water due to the bent shape of the lower light rays. The fish's ability to see 'up and across' the water due to refracted light, is extremely important when fishing the dry fly.

Snell proposed that when a beam of light strikes the water, it splits into two components and that light beams will not enter the water below a certain angle. What happens to all this low angle light that beams into the edge of the window? Most of it is reflected upwards and concentrates around the edge of the window. Snell demonstrated that when a beam of light passes into another medium (*water*) at a low angle, an iridescent glow is produced. As light rays from the blocked lower angle rays are prevented from entering the water all around the edge of the window a ring of concentrated light is produced, enabling the fish to see colour. Fish must conserve energy or perish and not waste time rising to the many non food items floating down towards it... *leaves, twigs, etc.*

The process of identification is...

- Check feet or body shape in the mirror.
- Check wing and body above the mirror as the fly approaches the window (*the fish is still on the bottom*).
- Rise and check the colour as it enters the illuminated circle (*fish cannot see colour before it passes into the window or or after it passes out of the window*).

A fish's eyesight becomes keener the closer it is to an object. Therefore, a motivated fish will rise to get a better look and be in position to eat it if it is the right food. Anadromous fish will frequently drift down the river with the fly touching it's 'nose' and, in some cases, push it across the water. Could it be that it is keeping it in the illuminated circle to 'double check'?

THE FISH USES BENT LIGHT - *see Sketch* 29A *and* 29B, *facing page*. The sketch shows that the light rays entering the water are refracted downwards. This enables a fish to see you well before you are visible with a direct sight line. This is particularly important when walking along a river's edge with steep banks or close to underwater drop-offs. Look for fish well before you reach the edge of the water. The fish will probably see you first as its survival depends on rapidly identifying danger. You are a threat to it - it is not a threat to you.

FISH ARE NOT WHERE YOU SEE THEM - *see Sketch* 29C, *facing page*. The sketch shows the angler looking at a fish which appears to be well out into the stream. The true positions of the fish is much closer and deeper than the angler thinks. These phenomena can cause the inexperienced angler no end of trouble and are the main causes of spooking fish, approaching too close to the real position of the fish, thinking it is much farther away, or casting too far, allowing the leader to float over the fish.

How Fish See Sunk Flies - *see Sketch 28C, page* 150. All sunk flies will be reflected in the underside of the surface. This mirror effect is due to the weakening of the light rays as they bounce back off the bottom and are unable to pass through the surface again. As a sunk fly comes towards a fish, it will see it first as a reflection in the mirror (*an early warning system*). As the fly comes closer, it will see it by direct sight. Unfortunately, the mirror is often blurred by choppy current, rain, wind, etc., which distorts the warning system. This explains why the more visible flies are more effective under these conditions.

How the Fish Takes the Fly - In our study of a fish's eyesight, we know of their amazing ability to see out of the water, observe an approaching underwater object in the overhead mirror and focus to any object within their field of view. How does a fish utilize all this life preserving information? Fish seeing an interesting object coming straight downstream towards it, will leave its hold, drift down with the current and rise to inspect it. The fish will be tilted up and, in some cases, pointed somewhat downstream.

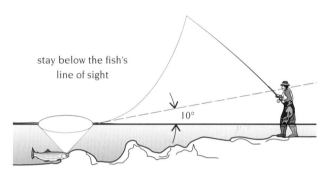

A - *Fish Can See You*

The object of the rise is to focus on the fly and eliminate all the additional information that its brain has to process when in 'wide angle focus'. A further reason for the close scrutiny is to hold the fly in the 'illuminated circle' to check out the colour of the fly. Fish seeing a fly swinging across their field of view may also leave their hold and rise to inspect the fly. Fish that have followed the fly for a longer distance will 'take' during the controlled downstream drift or controlled across stream swing. Most fish anxious to return to their 'safe hold' will suddenly twist and dive (*swirl*). This movement can be very subtle like a dimple or a huge bucket-sized hole in the water. This is where the speyfisher's steel nerves are required. *Don't set, don't strike!* Fish will often repeatedly come to the fly and swirl during the same presentation.

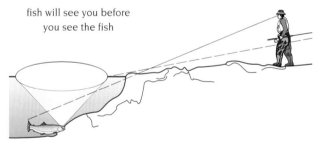

B - *Fish Hidden - Can See You*

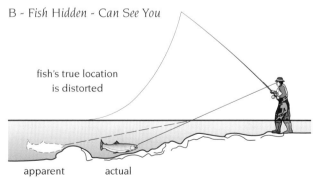

C - *Fish Not Where You See It*

When attempting to convince a student that there really was a large fish present, I had raised a fish on a dry fly (*with an intentionally bent up hook*). The

Sketch 29
Fish's Sight

fish would take the fly on the downstream drift and the bent hook would pull out of the fish's mouth. The fish would then return and have another go at this pesky fly during the across stream swing and again on the retrieve. During the last couple of attempts, it did not even dive, making huge wakes as it made high speed power turns back onto the target. This fish was either totally motivated or suicidal. The point of this story is... *once it had made its close range leisurely inspection and decided that this was the correct fly 'nothing was going to take it away'!*

A Fish's Other Senses

FISH CAN DETECT NOISE - Even though fish have no 'ears' they have the ability to detect both air-born and water-born noise travelling through the water as sound waves (*vibrations*). Sound waves are received and transmitted to the brain for processing by an electrochemical action. The signals are received by the skin and transmitted to the brain. Fish can detect noise much more efficiently than humans. Air-born sound is usually not a problem as sound waves do not translate to water very well. However, just because you think you are not making much noise as you wade, making waves, kicking rocks and banging around with your wading staff does not mean that you have not alerted or spooked the fish. Fishing in rough water such as riffles or rapids does not present much of a noise problem. The water crashing over the rocks is usually enough to mask any noise you may make.

When fishing in calm clear water, move very carefully. Remember... *you are nearly always hunting for fish, don't alert your quarry.*

A FISH'S REMARKABLE SENSE OF SMELL - A fish's ability to detect the various scents present in water is thousands of times more acute than that of human beings. Although it can process and react to the smell of its natural food and our artificial offerings, it is the fish's ability to detect the constantly changing chemical scent of its parent river as it migrates upstream to spawn that gives us our most reliable method of locating fish.

Part Four ~ Chapter Twenty
Know Your Fish and Your River

HAVING WADED THROUGH all the previous seemingly endless technical detail, it is time to talk about the fish and the river. To avoid further confusion, we will re-define the subject of speyfishing.

WHAT IS SPEYFISHING? - Speyfishing allows the angler to see a 'different river'. Reading the river and formulating a plan for each section to be fished can be based on the characteristics of the water and does not rely on the ability to make long overhead back casts (*fish do not only hold in front of wide gravel beaches*). The ability to control line encourages the extremely effective art of making the fly behave the way the fishes natural food would behave. The ability to control fish with a long, limber resilient speyrod (*used intelligently*) allows the speyfisher to concentrate on beaching the fish efficiently. This enhances its chances of survival on release without undue worry about 'breaking off' when using small flies and light tippets.

Newcomers to speyfishing eventually realize that they now have an entirely different concept of flyfishing and will start to re-examine their previous techniques. They will be asking themselves such things as... Is *my usual way of presenting the fly really the best way, or was it dictated by the use of my short single-handed rod and overhead style of casting?* It does not matter if you are going after Atlantic salmon in Norway, steelhead in British Columbia or exotic fish in the crocodile infested saltwater marshes of Australia, knowledge of the genetic background, seasonal life cycle, feeding habits and behaviour of your quarry is essential.

ALL YOU NEED TO KNOW TO CATCH FISH - There are only five things you need to know to catch fish. If you neglect either one of these important items you will be wasting your time speycasting. They are...

- What species of fish are we after.
- Where are they holding and why.
- Does your fly imitate their natural food.
- Can you present the fly to the fish and activate it to represent natural food.
- Can you land your fish after hooking it.

Anadromous Fish

Although speyrods (*salmon rods*) were developed to catch Atlantic salmon, they are now used for many other anadromous (*ascending rivers to spawn*) species such as the sea-run brown trout of Chile and Argentina, and the magnificent steelhead and Pacific salmon of North America. Since these widely differing species have remarkably similar life styles, we will lump them together in our study of their genetically controlled behaviour. Those who 'take offence' at this approach should remember that this book is about speycasting and speyfishing. Fishing for most species of fish available to the speyfisher is covered in many fine books by much better authors; *see page* 227.

GENETIC DEVELOPMENT - Assume that we are examining anadromous fish returning to their natal river system and spawning areas. Rivers will have tributaries close to saltwater or hundreds of miles inland. Some have gentle gradients with no natural obstacles to the fishes upward migration. Others rise several thousand feet, have steep gradients, cataracts or rapids that impede the migrating fish and make the return to the spawning beds a herculean effort. Over the millennia that fish have taken to adapt to the rigors of their parent rivers (*by natural selection*), their physical characteristics and behaviour will be different for each tributary. Fish with an easy return develop into large heavy 'footballs' that slug it out with you when hooked. Those with the obstacle course will develop into slim aerial torpedoes. A knowledge of a fishes genetic makeup is useful in determining its behaviour. Predicting the behaviour of (*heaven forbid*) a hatchery-produced fish is difficult if the brood stock are not taken from the same parent river or the fry are released at a location other than their natural spawning beds.

Steelhead
A prime female from the Skeena River system

Steelhead fry

LIFE CYCLE / SEASONAL TIMING - Migratory fish are spawned, then spend their juvenile years close to the area where their own parents began life. They will remain in the river until they are strong enough to withstand the rigors of the downward migration to the sea. The juvenile freshwater period may be as short as one year or as long as five years, depending on the fish's growth rate. Rivers with long ice-free periods and warm temperatures will produce abundant food for the juvenile fish and accelerate its growth. Rivers at higher elevations with short ice-free periods are much colder and do not produce as much food as the warmer rivers, which slows down the fishes growth rate, requiring it to remain in the river for an extended period in order to gain the strength to withstand the arduous return to the salt water.

Once in the salt water, anadromous fish will swim off or be carried by ocean currents to their feeding areas. Those who survive their natural predators and commercial netting will arrive back at the mouths of their parent rivers when sexually mature. There are hypotheses suggesting that the timing of the arrival is partly magnetic navigation, partly yearly rotation of the ocean currents and partly the fish's incredible ability to detect the scent of its parent stream. Once again the timing of the return and sexual maturity varies from one year to five, even though they were spawned in the same year. Could this be nature's way of protecting the species against a natural catastrophe in any one year? (*eg., Mount St. Helen's eruption*).

FISH NAVIGATE ON CHEMICAL SCENT - When migratory fish enter the freshwater and start their upstream journey to their spawning beds, they navigate on chemical scent. Fish have evolved genetically to respond to the numerous 'road signs' provided by the various scents encountered on the way home. They will remain downstream of the confluence of a tributary until they get the green light to move up the correct stream. They will usually stay put when high or muddy water dilutes or obscures the road sign. Some short rivers have long, low, water periods with the fish stacked up at the estuary mouth, being attacked by various predators (*including commercial fishermen*). When these rivers receive a flush of rain or snow melt, somewhat muddy, the fish will sometimes press on regardless. These fish have survived by being genetically imprinted to react to the stimulant of the extra flush of water even if visibility is not conducive to travelling.

Migrating fish seem to travel in the fastest water, probably because it carries the strongest scent or road signs. Fish have been seen bypassing man-made fish ladders and swimming or jumping over waterfalls. Travelling up the river highway in the fast lane requires the fish to find a rest area (*or motel*) at frequent intervals.

FEEDING HABITS - It is generally supposed that steelhead and Atlantic salmon do not feed once they enter freshwater. This information is confusing and misleading. How can fish spend so long in freshwater, swim two hundred miles upstream, spawn and return to the ocean again without some form of nourishment?

There are numerous cases of fish found with food in their stomachs. There are just as many with empty stomachs after actively feeding minutes before autopsy. Could it be that these empty fish were just sucking the juice out of the food? Fish have been observed squeezing roe bags (*used by bait anglers*) without being hooked.

A recent hypothesis suggests that anadromous fish undergo a form of anorexia (*ability but no desire to feed*) on entering freshwater and that this effect is not totally complete in all fish of the same species, migrating at the same time. Could it be that natural selection has made sure that some species can survive the demanding requirements of spawning, yet retain the strength to return to the ocean and repeat the performance a few years later? Perhaps the anorexic effect will be complete on the second visit. There is no doubt that a non-feeding migratory fish will come to a fly. There is strong evidence that this is an inherited instinctive reaction to take the fly into its mouth, even though it is not going to eat it. There is definite evidence that fish have a preference for one fly on one river, an entirely different one on the next. Juvenile fish will feed on insect larva, nymphs, crustaceans, minnows, etc. in freshwater. The adult fish feed on crustaceans, squid, and small fish of many shapes, size and colour in the salt water. It seems logical that if a fish spends more time in freshwater as a juvenile, than salt-water as an adult, it will have a preference for freshwater imitations and vice versa.

A fish that has a long fresh-water – short salt-water cycle seems to prefer flies resembling river organisms, while fish with a short fresh-water – long salt-water cycle prefer imitations of salt-water organisms. Perhaps this is why anadromous fish show a preference for a dry fly on one river and bait fish imitations on the next.

TEMPERATURE EFFECTS - Air and water temperatures affect the ability to catch anadromous fish. By far the greatest effect is on the angler, not the fish. Who can concentrate with numb fingers or frozen feet? Fish will become sluggish in the extreme low or high water temperatures that occur seasonally. They will also become inactive with a sudden change in water temperature (*until they get used to it again*). Fish of the same species are genetically adapted to the temperatures of their separate natal rivers. Seasonal temperature fluctuations and average temperature can vary widely from one geographical area to another. What would be considered warm water on one river would be cold for another. Don't make the mistake of using temperature effects observed on one specific river and apply it to one with totally different characteristics. To sum up, air temperature has little effect on the fish, great effect on the angler.

Solution... Providing you or the river are not frozen, take the air and water temperatures and go fishing regardless. If you fish in extreme cold, watch out for icy lines, frozen reels and loose rod joints.

HOOKING / LANDING FISH - Many fish 'go away' unhooked or are lost after a 'brief encounter'. This can happen if the angler forgets that the fish is not actively feeding. Anadromous fish do not always close their mouths after mouthing the fly. Attempting to strike or set the hook will usually end in failure. This is extremely difficult for skilled trout anglers who compulsively strike to set a hook in microseconds. A fish will leave its resting place, then move to inspect a well-presented fly. By instinct, hunger, curiosity, territorial defence or other reasons, it will sometimes take the fly into its mouth, return to its hold with mouth partly open and inadvertently hook itself. Fish have been known to repeatedly 'pluck' a dry fly as it drifts downstream. Other fish seem capable of taking the fly back to their hold and chewing on it without hooking themselves. These situations require the angler to be mesmerized or possess a 'will of iron' not to set or strike. Attempting to manually hook the fish usually results in an insecure lip hold instead of the unshakable corner of the jaw grip. Modern, well-designed, sharp-pointed hooks will bed into the corner of the jaw by the pull exerted on the line by water drag as the fish swims back to its hold.

A fish adequately hooked should be landed quickly and safely in order to enhance its survival rate on release. This process is a combination of common sense and a knowledge of a fish's behaviour after hooking. The use of the term 'fighting a fish' should be discouraged. How can a contest between a twenty pound fish in the water and a two hundred pound angler on shore be described as a 'fight'. Perhaps it would be a fair fight if the angler cut off the leader after hooking a fish, attached another fly, stuck it in his own jaw and jumped in the water with the fish to even up the odds.

Know Your River

Rivers are drainage systems for their catchment areas, used by anadromous fish as spawning grounds, incubators and nurseries. The volume of flow, seasonal variation, width, depth and current speed will vary widely for each geographical area. Having fished on a placid lowland stream will not prepare you for a brawling mountain river. Many anglers are intimidated at the first sight of a new river, simply because they were not mentally prepared for its peculiarities.

Rivers, dictated by their geological formation, can vary from wide, slow, low gradient to fast, narrow, steep gradient on the same river. These varying conditions can divide the water into flats, riffles, rapids, etc. and provide varying suitability of fish holds. Wading conditions should be checked before fishing any river. Seasonal changes can rearrange the river bottom and produce some nasty surprises. Use the correct wading gear with appropriate traction devices, wading staff and flotation device.

READING THE RIVER - To many anglers, the river is a closed book. To an accomplished angler, it is an encyclopedia containing the information that allows catching fish with skill and confidence, not 'blind luck'.

It is relatively easy to read the water if the angler follows a logical sequence of observations. Most established pools do not require much study, except in changing water conditions. When anyone does what everyone else is doing or have been doing for donkey's years without much knowledge of why, they are not reading the water, they are following a script. The speycaster will often be fishing difficult water where the script is not available or was written for overhead casters. Don't proceed until you have 'opened and read' your river. Many anglers concentrate on the river surface not realizing that anadromous fish are all on the bottom. This is similar to reading the front cover of the book and not caring what the book is about.

To read the bottom of a river and to understand how it was formed and its occasional seasonal change, it is useful to mentally remove the water. Nature has an unhappy knack of doing this for us during low water conditions. Low water may not be the best time to fish, however, it provides an excellent opportunity to examine the construction of the river bottom. Since fish can hold in places that are impossible to detect from the surface, low water can often solve these mysteries. If you are lucky enough (*or unlucky*) to find low water, photograph it or sketch it in your angling diary. Rivers vary considerably from placid to brawling, narrow to wide, shallow to deep. Make sure you are appropriately equipped and mentally prepared for your river before you get there. Many rivers are notorious for their seasonal, sometimes rapid variations in water flow. Find out what state your river is in beforehand. Don't get stranded on a gravel bar when fishing a river subject to rapid flow increases.

A Speyfisher's Dream...

A hazy sky, gold trees, cool clear water, the right fly and your favourite speyrod.

Photography © Maxwell

THE SHAPE OF THE RIVER BOTTOM - The shape of a river bottom is determined by the scouring action of the water and its geological make-up. Rivers flowing through hard rock canyons will take millions of years to change by water action. Those flowing through alluvial plains or in predominantly loose gravel areas will be subject to considerable seasonal change. This is not difficult to understand, once having observed the scouring action of flood water carrying sand and gravel or the ploughing action of an ice flow during spring breakup. It is impossible to describe all variations in the shape of the river bottom, however, a few hypothetical examples are illustrated below...

A - *Solid Bottom, Straight Course*
Usually has a level cross-section. Little change in depth from bank to bank, sometimes contains projecting ridge rock or loose boulders. Not much seasonal change.

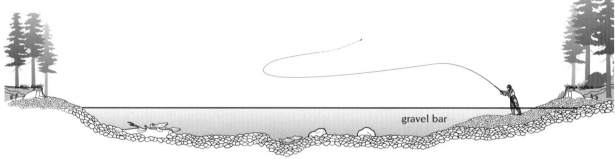

B - *Loose Bottom, Straight Course*
Has a level cross-section. Little change in depth from bank to bank, erratic gravel deposits along the bank, often contains loose boulders. Seasonal changes can produce underwater gravel bars.

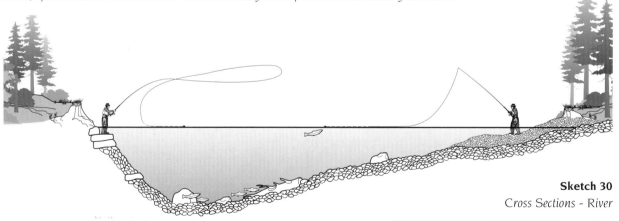

Sketch 30
Cross Sections - River

C - *Loose Bottom, Meander Course*
Has a wedge shaped cross-section. May have a gravel bar on one side, cut bank on the other. May contain large boulders that have fallen out of the bank. Seasonal flows can deepen or fill in the wedge. Unstable seasonally in alluvial areas.

LONGITUDINAL VARIATIONS - Rivers can vary from slow, flat, to fast, steep gradients, each producing its own form of longitudinal variation in shape. Low gradient rivers resemble flat highways while steep gradients can be described as stairways (*rapids or riffles*) with frequent landings (*pools or flats*) as illustrated below...

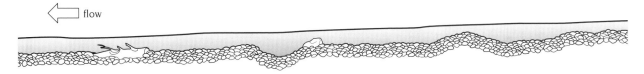

A - Slow, Flat Gradient
Solid bottom rivers with flat gradients do not produce much variation longitudinally unless there are projecting ridge rocks, boulders or occasional sand and gravel deposits. This type of bottom is very hard to read, usually neglected by the inexperienced angler. Can hold many fish. Slow flat gradients with soft gravel bottoms can form themselves into shallow or deep pools, flat runs or riffles, gravel pockets. Not easy to read in high water conditions.

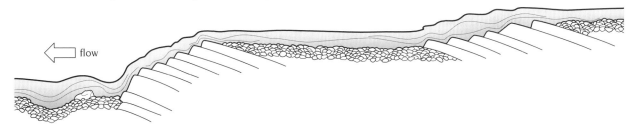

B - Fast, Steep Gradient
This type of river is formed into its staircase configuration by steps in the bedrock. Extensive gravel deposits can be swept around seasonally. This is the easiest type of water to read with the head, body and tail of the pool clearly defined.

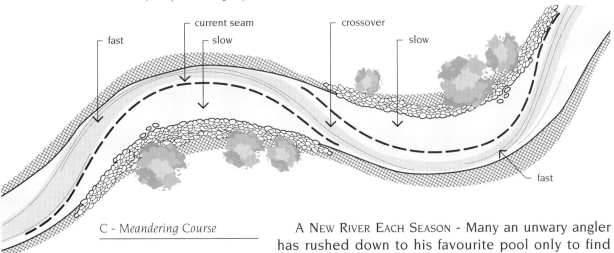

C - Meandering Course

Sketch 31
Longitudinal Variations

A NEW RIVER EACH SEASON - Many an unwary angler has rushed down to his favourite pool only to find that it has changed completely and no longer holds fish. Rivers that 'ice over' can place large rocks at strategic fish-holding locations and dig deep gouges. A large boulder shaped like the rear end of an elephant became a 'fish magnet' after mysteriously appearing on a British Columbia steelhead river. Its location was carefully marked by some anglers, to assist them when returning next season. For the next five years, this rock travelled in stages over half a mile downstream, finally disappearing altogether. Its location each year would produce its own crop of 'rock fans' who would also mark its position for next year. This produced a ludicrous sight... *groups of anglers distributed down the river, fishing over a rock that was not there*. River bottoms change constantly and produce a new river each season. Don't fish last year's river.

Locating Fish - Anadromous

Trout in a river require a holding station which provides relief from the current, protection from predators, oxygen to replenish expended energy and close to an adequate food supply. Anadromous fish have similar requirements to trout without the necessity to feed. Migrating fish are dominated by the urge to return to their natal spawning beds and reproduce. During the journey, as short as twenty miles or as long as two hundred miles, they must rest and recuperate at frequent intervals. The need to rest will depend on the distance travelled, the speed of the current and the natural obstacles encountered along the way. Fish that are native to slow estuarial rivers will not require rest as often or as long as a fish negotiating a mountain torrent. Migrating fish navigate on chemical traces occurring at various stages during their journey and react instinctively to the constantly changing conditions. Since the greatest flow carries the most 'scent', fish will travel in or just on the edge of the fastest water.

Fish will not proceed up rivers if exhausted or if water conditions are not adequate, such as: high water, low water or muddy water. Occasionally a bright sky and exceptionally clear water will delay fish. A heavy flow from a feeder stream will confuse fish until they finally read the signs correctly and proceed again. Radio monitoring has shown that fish will spend weeks in one area, drop back downstream and only continue when conditions are favourable. Fish that require places to hold or rest are usually located close to the travel lane for easy access to the fast water if threatened or to monitor the chemical scent. Don't look for them in deep pools unless it is downstream of a rapid or riffle, containing the required oxygen. Nature being what it is and fish being what they are, it is impossible to predict all the curious places that anadromous fish will rest. The following is a list of typical holding stations...

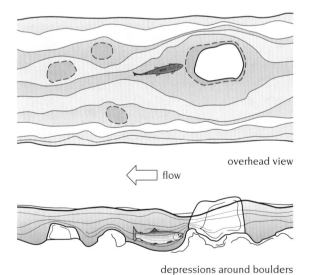

overhead view

flow

depressions around boulders

Sketch 32
Boulders

CURRENT SEAMS - *see Sketch 31C, page 161.* Any seam or foam line between fast and slow current indicating a changing river bottom or drop off.

BOULDERS - *see Sketch 32.* Large boulders or ridge rocks usually have satellite rocks downstream which may not be visible in the downstream slick. Current speed and refraction of light may give you a false impression of the location of a large rock which does not project above the surface, as it is usually closer and farther upstream than it appears to be. Water velocity is reduced to almost zero at the river bottom due to the drag effect of the rough bottom. Fish can be held behind rocks by vortex currents, without having to swim while they regain the strength to continue up river.

GRAVEL BARS - Can form just about anywhere. They can project from the bank, form an island, be above or below water. In any event, they create enough disturbance and vortex currents to be very productive fish holds. Seams and foam lines will indicate the prime spots. Gravel bars just downstream of a feeder stream, side channel or back water should be fished.

CROSSOVERS - *see Sketch* 31C, *page* 161. When fish travelling in the fast lane on the outside curve cross over to the fast lane on the other side of the river, they frequently hold where the seam comes close to the other bank. This is prime water, especially if it contains rocks or other obstructions.

FEEDER STREAMS - Feeder streams with heavy flows can confuse migrating fish by obscuring the road signs (*scent*). As these streams usually produce gravel bars at the mouth, the fish will hold there until they get the right signal to move.

GRAVEL DEPOSITS AT BANK SIDE - *see Sketch* 30B, *page* 160. Slow, shallow flat channel rivers with no visible fish holds will sometimes contain fish close to the bank, resting between gravel deposits precipitated by high water. These mounds and depressions can be very shallow, hardly noticeable, yet hold fish. As you move down the pool, maintaining your distance from the bank, you will notice that you are rising and falling as you proceed. Almost any change in depth indicates that there is a depression that will create a vortex and hold a fish.

JUVENILE HABITAT IMPRINT - Anadromous fish are hatched and spend their early juvenile life in and around large gravel (*from tennis to basketball in size*). The gravel must be located to provide oxygen, food, protection from the current and from aerial and water predators. It is fortunate, that large stonefly nymphs have exactly the same habitat as the fish. They feed on each other in a perfect symbiotic relationship. In some rivers food is not abundant, requiring the juvenile fish to remain close to their living quarters for a long period of time (*up to five years is not unusual for some species*). Returning fish can often be found holding close to gravel suitable for juvenile habitat with no apparent protection or reason for being there, even though their spawning areas are many miles upstream. Could it be that they are genetically imprinted to stop and check out anything that looks like home? Look around the beach for discarded exoskeletons of large stoneflies, clinging to the rocks on dry land. You are in the right place if you only find one.

EFFECT OF WATER CONDITIONS - Human nature proves that water conditions can never be just right. The best time to fish is when you can. Knowing how the water conditions affect the ability to catch fish is vitally important unless you prefer to stay home and wait for that elusive perfect day. Adverse water conditions can vary from water too high or low, too muddy or too clear, too warm or too cold.

- WATER HEIGHT - Any change in water height will require reading the river over again. In general, high water brings fish closer to the bank, low water will move them farther out to escape real or imagined predators.

- WATER CLARITY - The more coloured it becomes, the closer to the bank the fish hold. The clearer it becomes, the farther out they will hold.

TEMPERATURE - WATER AND AIR - The colder the water, the more sluggish the fish (*and the angler*). Providing your lines and reels are not frozen, keep fishing. Air temperature seems to have little effect on anadromous fish and a considerable influence on the angler. Fish will take the right fly presented correctly on the bottom of the river at any water or air temperature. Under certain circumstances, they will also take a surface or true dry fly at near freezing water and air temperatures. An angler fishing close to shore in 'murky' water, air and water temperature, 36°F. was astonished to see a large fish mouth his dry fly and hook itself. What was intended to be the last cast of the day developed into about two more hours of uncomfortable 'last casting' before returning to the camp fire.

THE TAIL - A clearly defined pool can usually be divided into sections. Tired fish enter the pool by climbing the fast water of a riffle, or rapid, and rest in the first available hold (*large fish can be observed displacing smaller ones*). Tails of pools usually contain boulders trapped by the obstruction that formed the pool. Do not neglect the 'tail out'.

THE BODY - Fish not quite so tired will move up the pool and rest in any convenient spot... *boulders, depressions, large gravel bars and small intermittent gravel deposits along the edge.* Many of these holds are not visible, do not cause any surface disturbance and are difficult to locate. Just because you can't see the hold does not mean that they are not there. Fish all the water.

THE HEAD - This water contains fish in various stages of the journey... just arrived and resting, gathering strength to rush up the next obstruction, dropped back after failing to make the climb. Large fish can often be found in head water (*perhaps their bulk is a handicap in climbing steep slopes*). Pay particular attention to the head of the pool just before dark. Fish preparing for upstream travel at night can congregate there.

Part Four ~ Chapter Twenty-One
Think Before You Fish

MANY ANGLERS ARE SO EXCITED at the first sight of the river that they just can't wait to 'fish it all' or have a go at those tempting rocks or fishy looking slicks. Keep in mind that the pool is only fishable by speyfishing and has not been named or mapped by others. Without another thought, they wade out to cover the entire river and probably disturb the fish holding along the edges. To make matters worse, they will flail away at any likely looking area and wade down the river like a grizzly bear. The final waste of water is getting the line out there any way possible without any attempt to determine the correct presentation or to control the line and the fly. This is just 'chuck it and chance it' angling and an insult to the river.

It does not usually take long for our 'trusting to luck' speyfisher to realize that the fish are not playing fair and are not where we would like them to be. Don't forget that speyfishing is the thinking man's (*or woman's*) sport and that more fish have been caught by planning and persistence than by haphazard methods. Always remember that although we have studied the geological make-up of the river and can 'read the water', we are looking at the surface and do not know or can't see every potential fish hold under the water. It follows that we must make an intelligent plan to cover all fishable water logically and thoroughly.

Photography © Enrique Izquierdo

Make a Game Plan

Now here is a golden rule of spey-fishing... *examining and analyzing the river before fishing will be the major factor of the success of your fishing. A second rule is... setting up and following your game plan is a further key to your success.*

Tea Time Again...
Mike introduced Frank Neunemann to the invaluable custom of taking 'time out' during a long day's fishing to rest the water (and the angler)... make it part of your Game Plan.

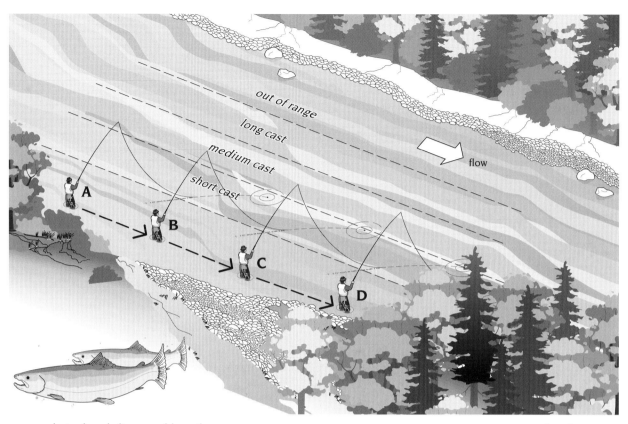

- obstacles define pool length
- A, B, C and D are casting stations
- divide river into strips

Sketch 33
The Game Plan

SETTING THE BOUNDARIES - Having decided to fish an area of the river, determine the boundaries of the 'pool' you can fish in the time you have allowed yourself; *see Sketch 33…*

- Your start point could be a rock or riffle or a tree on the other bank.
- The end of your pool could be at rapids or any other distinguishing marker.
- The reachable width of the river is usually determined by the length of your optimum controllable cast.

DIVIDING THE POOL INTO LENGTHS - Short pools can often be fished from one casting station, however, long pools must be divided into reasonable lengths. Choose markers across the river to locate each casting station. Give each casting station equal time.

DIVIDE THE CASTING AREAS INTO STRIPS - Each casting area is divided into short, medium and long casts. Each area must receive equal attention. If you make three presentations at your short cast, make the same number on the medium and long casts. Give each length of cast equal time.

MOVING DOWN THE POOL - The time taken to cover each casting station will depend on your method of presentation. Dry fly techniques may take longer than wet fly, etc.

DON'T STEP CAST - Unless you have the pool all to yourself, it is good form to move down the pool to allow other anglers to fish. Some anglers seem to be in such a hurry to get down the river that they take a step downstream on each cast.

These speed demons often restrict themselves to only one cast length and can't be bothered to change. A speyfisher can move downstream to the next casting station, say one or two rod lengths, and be moving just as fast as the step caster. It is a good idea to inform the following anglers what you are doing to prevent any unpleasantness, especially if you are more successful than they are (*or smaller*).

FOLLOWING OTHER ANGLERS - Excessive wading is the trademark of an untrained angler. It is almost as if a powerful electromagnet on the other side of the river is acting on the heavy metal festooning their fully equipped fishing vests. Don't worry about following the deep wader, just take your time, carry out your game plan and perhaps catch fish behind him. The number of times this has happened is too numerous to mention.

DON'T JUST FISH THE 'HOT SPOTS' - Having formulated your game plan and divided your river into casting stations and strips, you should carry out your plan, giving equal time to each area. There are going to be 'those fishy looking potential holds' at each station such as rock or slicks that will draw your attention and in many cases waste your time. **Remember...** *fish will hold where they want to, not where we would like them to be.*

PRESENTATION METHODS - Success in flyfishing depends on presenting the right fly in the right place, at the right depth and activated to represent the natural. It is obvious that the method used to transport the fly correctly will vary according to the type of fly, wet or dry, and the depth and speed of the current. Each of these circumstances will dictate a different style of fishing.

IT'S NOT JUST FISHING DOWN AND ACROSS - Before we discuss all the effective presentations possible when speycasting, there are some misconceptions about speyfishing that must be laid to rest. Many styles of fishing, wet fly or dry, are based on making a downstream and across cast. This style of cast has developed over the years to allow the caster to get out line when backcast distance is restricted. It seems to have been handed down through the years and is now the most popular method. Among the numerous drawbacks to the down and across approach is that the fly is nearly always swinging across current in front of a fish instead of coming straight downstream as the majority of food does.

USE SKILL... NOT WEIGHT - Unfortunately there are still many double-handed casters who are using 'magnum' rods, heavy sinking lines and heavyweight 'flies' to get their offering down to the fish with a downstream cast and across stream swing. This style of fishing is restricted in its ability to present the fly naturally and tiring to perform. A skilled speyfisher would be fishing to the same fish with a less powerful rod, a much lighter line, a much smaller fly and less fatigue. With an across or upstream cast, followed by skilled line control, the fly can be sunk to the correct depth and presented to the fish naturally 'by skill, not weight'.

QUESTION... *Why do so many double-handers persist in the downstream only cast when using dry fly, surface fly or sunk flies?*

- Is it the only presentation they know?
- Are their rods too stiff for effectively making an upstream double spey?
- Are their rods flexible enough for effortless line control?

Speyfishing Styles

Speyfishing allows choosing the correct fly, fished with the appropriate style, relying on skill not weight or the use of attractor flies. Any style of fishing can be accomplished by the skilled speycaster with ease, grace and efficiency.

Speyfishing styles can be categorized as...

- DRYFLY - Imitating emerging and ovipositing aquatic insects or terrestrial blow-ins and fished with a floating line.

- SURFACE WET FLY - Imitating small bait fish feeding on emerging insects, also fished with a floating line and a lightly dressed wet fly.

- MID-WATER WET FLY - Imitating bait fish swimming around, looking for food or escaping from predators. Fished with a wet fly and a dry line in shallow water and if necessary, a sink tip in deeper water.

- BOTTOM WET FLY - Imitates any food organism crawling along the bottom - being swept along by strong current or migrating to shore to emerge. Fished with a heavy hook or lightly weighted fly. Can be fished with a floating line in shallow water and if necessary, or sink tips of different lengths and densities to suit the depth and speed of the current.

THE TROUT STREAM ANGLER ADVANTAGE - Experienced trout stream anglers coming into speyfishing have very few problems adapting to the methods used as most of them have already been making the necessary presentation and line controls with their single-handed rods on their trout streams. It does not take long for the more accomplished short rod trout angler to realize that he has finally found the ultimate instrument for any presentation and line control required, that is of course, a long limber true speyrod.

LET THE FISH SEE THE FLY - To induce any fish to take a fly, it is necessary to mobilize its instinctive genetically imprinted reactions to 'check it out' or eat it. To fully motivate the fish, the fly must be presented to imitate its natural food in size, shape, colour and behaviour. It is even more important (*and often neglected*) that the fish gets the best possible view of the fly for the longest possible time. We will now discuss the many different techniques of presenting the fly to the fish to 'make it take it'.

Presentation Methods

The style of presentation adopted by the speyfisher is mostly a matter of personal choice. Many of us finally end up fishing the method that gives us the most pleasure and success for the least effort.

WHY SO MANY DIFFERENT PRESENTATIONS? - A fish's desire to feed can vary from gluttony to finicky to anorexia. Each degree of reluctance to take our fly will require a more careful presentation if we are to tease a lethargic fish into taking it. Another equally important factor in deciding the appropriate presentation is the speed, depth and variations of the current. What works in one situation may be totally wrong for another. Searching for the correct presentations for each change in the river is one more reason why speyfishing is so absorbing; *see Sketch 34, pages* 169 *and* 170.

BEWARE OF THE SPECIALIST - A specialist can be defined as one who knows 'more and more' about 'less and less'. When selecting your method of presentation, use your own judgement. Don't be intimidated by the 'self-styled' experts who are just about ready to dunk you in the river if you don't use the particular method that they habitually use for every presentation regardless of water conditions or degree of difficulty in hooking fish.

Method 1

- THE DOWNSTREAM PRESENTATION

  In this style of fishing, the line is mended to make the fly swing across the fish's field of view. The problem with this (*all too prevalent*) presentation is that the fish only has a momentary look at the rear end of the fly as it swings across its limited field of view. This method is a perfect example of line control and a bad example of fly presentation. It is predicated on the misleading idea that the line must be kept tight at all times with no thought of how the fish sees the fly.

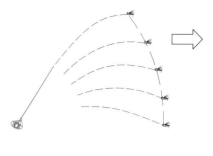

A - *Method* 1

Method 2

- ACROSS & UPSTREAM MEND DIAGONAL PRESENTATION

  After casting directly across stream, the line is continuously mended upstream. This procedure allows the fly to drift downstream and in towards the fish diagonally giving the fish a much longer time and a somewhat side view of the fly. This method is an example of good line control and an attempt at giving the fish a better view of the fly.

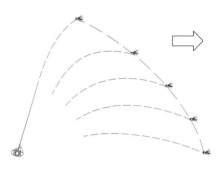

B - *Method* 2

Method 3

- UPSTREAM - COMBINATION MEND PRESENTATION

  Stage 1
  After an upstream cast, additional line is fed out and continuously mended to send the fly straight downstream. The object of this stage is to show the fly to as many fish as possible coming straight downstream towards them in direct sight for the longest possible time. The length of cast is increased periodically to cover more water farther out. The length of downstream drift depends on the anglers ability to control line. A motivated fish will leave its hold and drift downstream to inspect the offering.

  Stage 2
  When all feeding line is out, the line is continuously mended upstream to send the fly diagonally downstream and towards the bank. This will allow a fish, enticed downstream, to make a further inspection and to cover additional fish holding closer to the bank.

  Stage 3
  When the line has finally drifted downstream, it is allowed to hang there for about ten seconds. The additional feeding line is then slowly retrieved. A fish that has followed the fly and is not yet fully

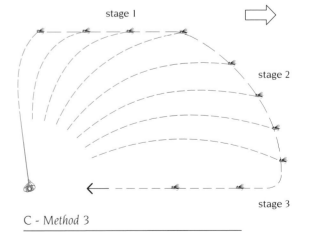

C - *Method* 3

Sketch 34
Presentations

motivated will often strike as its potential food appears to be escaping upstream. This method fishes the fly three different ways with one cast, covers an enormous length of travel and more potential fish holds than other methods.

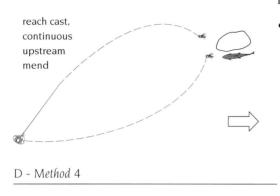

reach cast,
continuous
upstream
mend

D - *Method 4*

Sketch 34
Presentations, cont'd

Method 4

- HANGING THE FLY

Fish will sometimes hold in locations where it will only see the fly momentarily as it flashes past its restricted field of view. Unless the fish can see and recognize the fly for a sufficient length of time, its instinctive reactions will not be mobilized. By skilful mending, the fly can be made to swim around in front of the fish for as long as you keep mending (*without making another cast*).

This technique can form part of any presentation (*wet or dry fly*) or to concentrate on that 'special rock' that you have been saving. Hanging the fly with a long limber speyrod is child's play. Watch out for the fish that just grabs it without warning.

ONE MORE WORD ABOUT SPEYRODS - It must be obvious by now that success in speyfishing is dependent on your ability or willingness to control the line and the fly. It will become painfully obvious that line control will be difficult with stiffer rods and easier with more flexible rods. Don't let the stiffness of your rod prevent you from using the presentation and line control technique that you have selected.

THE SPEYCASTER'S ADVANTAGE - Using a true speyrod, keeping the fly in productive water and controlling its behaviour is the name of the game. An accomplished speycaster is able to feed the fly to the fish with any presentation required and enjoy the advantage of intelligent line and fly control.

THE VALUE OF LINE CONTROLS - The importance of aerial and water line controls cannot be overemphasized. It will become obvious that all presentation methods consist of speycasting in any required direction and then controlling the behaviour of the fly by aerial and water mending. These subjects were covered in Chapter Seventeen.

Remember... *the rules for success in motivating and hooking fish...*

- Cast in the required direction.
- Make an upstream aerial reach cast.
- Control the line by water mending.
- Repeat this process on every presentation.

Part Four ~ Chapter Twenty-Two
Angling Techniques

WHAT FLY LINES ARE REQUIRED? - Before we investigate the various techniques of speyfishing, it is necessary to examine the specialized lines required. Fishing with the wrong type or design of line is the road to frustration.

THE EVOLUTION OF THE FLY LINE - The braided silk line, the original line used for speycasting was either a slow sinker or a poor floater even if dressed with a floatant. The dressing was marketed under various trade names, the basic ingredient being lanolin, a by-product of the sheep wool industry, hence the term 'greasing your line or your fly'. The slow sinking rate of the silk line required the use of mammoth hooks (*up to* 9/0) to get the fly down. Double or treble hooks were also used so that the weight was still there even if the hook size was decreased.

With the relatively modern introduction of the true floating line, the subsequent development of sinking lines in various densities and finally the use of sink tip lines with various lengths of sink tip, the angler was faced with a bewildering array of fly lines and a considerable drain on his finances. Anglers are very innovative and it did not take long to boil down the mess of available lines to the bare essentials. It is now possible for a speyfisher to 'get by' with a floating line and a few detachable sink tips of various lengths and densities to cover all necessary presentations. Line types for flyfishing...

❖ SINKING LINES - The traditional method of fishing wet flies was with a slow sinking line and heavy fly. This style of fishing is highly skilled and extremely difficult for all but the experienced wet fly man. To be able to swim the fly at the exact 'taking' depth and speed without hooking the bottom, requires unlimited patience and a sixth sense. Those who do not have the necessary time and resources to perfect this technique will just have to find a better way. There is a better way.

❖ FLOATING LINES - Double taper lines are the logical choice for speycasting. They allow the smooth generation and concentration of line energy during casting and the ability to control the line after casting. Unfortunately the authority who chose the length of taper for the larger double taper lines did not do a very good job, causing the end of the line to 'wimp out' unless considerable force was used or splash down (*similar to a level line*) when cast with excessive power.

- IMPROVED TAPER - *See page* 208. The development of the improved compound taper[2] solves this problem allowing the acceleration of the line due to energy concentration to proceed smoothly and efficiently without the use of excessive power. The ability to straighten out the line and the leader at the final delivery of a long cast is extremely important and very difficult for the novice speycaster using a standard double taper line.

- FIXED SINK TIPS - There will be times when the fly will not get down with the normal leader and sunk fly technique. This problem is partially solved by the use of floating lines with tips that sink. Lines are available with the tips permanently fixed to the line in varying lengths of sink tip and different sink rates. The problem with this system is that a different line and spool is required for each depth and rate of sink. Imagine the cost, expense and time wasted in changing lines for each situation. Most anglers eventually tire of constantly changing spools and carry on using the same sink tip. They are using the wrong tool for the job.

- DETACHABLE SINK TIPS - *See page* 211. Changing spools with a short single-handed rod is time consuming. Changing spools on a long spey rod seems to take forever and makes considerable inroads into the effective fishing time. This problem has been solved by the use of easily detachable sink tips of various lengths and densities. As the sink tips can be used singly or in combination[3], it is possible to cover every situation with one reel and line and a few lengths of sink tip without the hassle of rethreading rods or carrying spare spools.

THE FLOAT FISHING CONCEPT - There is a method of fishing that although not fly-fishing can serve as a near perfect example for our floating line speyfishing. This traditional and contemporary method of fishing with monofilament line, float and leader with some sort of lure or bait, is not flyfishing, however, it is one of the most efficient methods of hooking fish. Its success is not due to the type of lure used. The secret of the method is the complete coverage of the water and total control of the lure at all times.

Float fishers instinctively divide their water into slots extending down river. They fish each slot in turn, starting close to the bank, the last slot at their maximum controllable cast. When the float and lure have been cast to the slot being fished, the mono line is fed out so that the float proceeds directly downstream for a considerable distance. The length of the leader can be adjusted for each cast, so that the lure is fished at the exact taking depth. At the end of the downstream float, it is allowed to swing in shore, retrieved and cast out again. The key to this method is that the lure is presented to the fish floating directly downstream towards it, not swinging across its vision in an unnatural way.

A further highly significant similarity between float fishing and speyfishing is the ability to make any angular change in casting direction without the need for an overhead backcast or false cast. Since some of the lures used are remarkably like flies and that float fishing is so efficient, it seems reasonable to learn from this and derive a similar system of flyfishing. The logical conclusion was to use a floating line for the float, a leader or sink tip to get the fly down and present the whole thing floating downstream, just like float fishing with a fly line.

---

[2] *Mike Maxwell* 1984
[3] *Mike Maxwell* 1985

The advantages of using the float fishing concept when speyfishing with fly line and fly are...

- Using the line as our float and the fly as our bait.
- Sending the fly straight down the current flow by skilled mending.
- Adjusting the length of leader or sink tip to get the fly to the 'taking depth'.
- Allowing the fly to drift directly downstream towards the fish, not swinging past it.

It is probable at this time that you are saying to yourself that this sounds a bit far fetched. Let me assure you, it is a fascinating and efficient method of speyfishing. When guiding and teaching speyfishing at our Bulkley River lodge, we allow the students to familiarize themselves with the river by letting them make any presentation they choose. If there are plenty of fish around, they usually 'luck out' and hook fish. This is probably due to the more active and competitive behaviour of fish when other fish are close by and not entirely due to their speyfishing skills.

When our students are finally at home on the river and their casting is adequate, we introduce them to the float fishing concept of speyfishing. This timely information produces mixed reactions varying from... *"Now I know how to fish those difficult fish on my home river"*, to... *"That looks too much trouble, so I will carry on in my usual way"*, which is more often than not a simple, down-and-across and swing in presentation.

To illustrate the mixed reception of the float fishing with a fly line concept, let me relate the following 'fishing story'...

When guiding a very experienced angler and his less skilled partner, I had the gall to suggest to the expert that he would do better if he used the float fishing concept. The silence following this advice was deafening and the air temperature dropped about ten degrees. He, of course, continued to use the presentation he always used, regardless of what river he was fishing or the speed or depth of the water. His partner, not knowing any better, immediately started off with the float fishing method. Three days later, after watching his inexperienced, 'former friend' outfishing him three to one, he was heard to say, "Hey, Mike... what was that about float fishing with a fly rod?"

As we shall see later, the float fishing concept can be used to present a dry fly, surface wet fly and sunk fly with equal precision and success. Of course, when fishing dry fly or surface wet fly, the sink tips are removed. Now let's see how far we have progressed in our speyfishing studies.

What Skills Do We Now Have?

After wading through all of the previous chapters of the book, it is time to make a list of our accomplishments so far. They are...

- To select the appropriate tackle.
- To make all necessary speycasts.
- To read the river as a speyfisher.
- To make all necessary presentations.

This is a formidable array of skills and knowledge, however, there are a few more important things that we will need to know if we are to put our accomplishments into practice and hook fish intelligently.

Presenting the Fly the Correct Way - So far we have learned that anadromous fish on their way upstream will hold just about anywhere. We are also aware that they may take a true dry fly on the surface, wet fly below the surface, sunk fly down on the bottom with the preference for a particular group of flies pre-determined by their genetic background. Each specific fly must be presented to closely resemble the natural food being imitated, at the correct depth (*except dry fly*) and with the correct behaviour. Each type of fly will require a different technique to keep it up or get it down and make it move right. All anglers have their favourite angling techniques. Some become 'mind locked', never having known or forgotten why they are fishing that way. Others have blindly followed others and so on, hoping that it is the correct thing to do because everybody else is doing it. In many cases the angling technique used has been dictated by a restricted backcast. Speycasters have virtually no limitation on casting, controlling line or using any style of angling necessary to hook fish.

All references to flies will be generic. As it is beyond the scope of the book to suggest specific flies for each technique.

When selecting your fly, keep in mind that you are attempting to imitate the natural in size, colour, shape and behaviour. Make sure you understand why the natural is, or was, where it is and what it is doing. Having selected your fly, the next problem is deciding what presentation is the most effective in imitating the behaviour of the natural. Always start with the fly, then decide the presentation required. 'Give the customers what they want, serve it to them correctly'.

What Techniques Are Possible? - Anadromous fish have been genetically imprinted to take flies on and below the surface. Our artificial flies must be served to the fish to represent the natural movements of a living organism and at the correct depth of water. This can be...

- Right down on the bottom.
- At mid-water between the bottom and the surface.
- At or just below the surface.
- Floating on or in the surface.

We will examine each technique in detail.

Fishing the Bottom

Includes organisms crawling among the rocks, drifting downstream or migrating to shore. Includes nymphs, crustaceans and leeches.

The Line - As the fly must be drifted along the bottom at various depths, use floating line and variable sink tips. The correct length of tip must be decided by allowing the fly to 'tinkle' along the bottom without hooking too many rocks. Use a short leader to prevent the fly being swept back upwards by vortex currents occurring along the bottom. In very shallow or slow water, the sink tip can be dispensed with.

Modified Nymphing Technique - Starting at your 'short cast', cast slightly upstream and reach cast upstream. Hold the rod high to keep most of the line off the water to allow efficient mending (*This is easy with long speyrods*). Allow enough line on the water to act as the 'float'. Assuming that your fly is at the correct depth, let it drift downstream, mending upstream without pulling the fly off its drift line. This can be achieved by raising and lowering the rod slightly as the fly comes past you, gently making short mends. As the line and fly proceed downstream, mend and feed line, so that the fly drifts down the taking strip as long as is practically possible. Remember... *this is float fishing with a fly rod.*

At the end of the downstream drift, the line will start to swing inshore and drag the fly unnaturally. Mending outwards will delay the inward movement of the fly to give the fish a better view.

If the fly is not 'getting down' or is hooking on the bottom, cast farther upstream or downstream, until the required depth is reached. If this procedure does not work, change the length of the sink tip. The modified nymphing technique relies on the utmost control of the line and fly. It is not suitable for long distance presentations. About three times the rod length is the longest cast that should be attempted. Start your presentation about half a rod length in front of where you are standing. You may be pleasantly surprised.

Telkwa Nymph

A versatile searcher when fishing deep.

HOW FAR APART SHOULD THE DRIFT LINES BE? - A fishes field of view is dictated by the depth of water that it is holding in. Fish in deep water will have a wide field of view, drift lines may be spaced well apart. Fish holding in shallow water will have a narrow field of view, drift line must be closer. As a general rule... *drift lines should be spaced about twice the estimated water depth at the drift line.*

WHAT WILL THE FISH DO? - If the fish is motivated to inspect the fly, it will leave its hold and drift down behind it to make an inspection. It could follow the fly down the drift line during the controlled swing to shore and on the slow retrieve. If not sufficiently interested, it will swim back to its hold.

Once the fish becomes agitated, it may take the fly at any stage of the proceedings with a slight preference for the beginning of the controlled swing. If you cannot find any takers, continue fishing the next strip. Do not cast any farther than your ability to control line.

Fishing the Mid-Water

Includes anything swimming or drifting around between the river bottom and the top water, either migrating or feeding (F*ish food must also feed*).

THE LINE - Once again this is decided by the depth and speed of the water. As the fly must be kept well down below the surface, a variable sink tip is preferred in heavy water with only a leader in slower or shallower conditions. Leaders may be longer to enhance the swimming action of the fly.

THE SWIMMING MINNOW TECHNIQUE - Whichever strip you are fishing (*short, medium, long*), start by casting slightly upstream. Allow the fly to sink well below the surface, however, not catching on the bottom (*you may have to change sink tips to accomplish this*). Mend the line so that it proceeds straight downstream for a short distance with the rod held high. As the fly approaches the target area, twitch the rod tip to animate the fly without pulling it across stream or pulling it to the surface. When the line starts to swing in, mend it to delay its progress or to produce the diagonal presentation or the combination presentation. Throughout the process, keep twitching the rod tip to imitate a swimming minnow and draw attention to your fly. The historical and contemporary popularity of many colourful Atlantic salmon patterns imitate some form of food encountered during the fishes years at sea. On the other hand many rivers contain minnows that are of more sombre hues. The fishes preference will also be influenced by its fresh - saltwater cycle.

WHAT WILL THE FISH DO? - The motivated fish will drift down and across stream to inspect the fly. If not interested it will swim back to its hold. The interested fish, probably attracted by the twitching fly will take the fly at any stage of the process with a definite preference for the beginning of the controlled swing. Fish all casts right through. Fish usually slash at an animated minnow (*to prevent its escape*) which enhances the self-hooking process.

'Fish your minnow to make it live', if no takers continue fishing the next strip. Do not cast any farther than your ability to control line.

Fishing the Top-Water - Wet Fly

Includes minnows feeding on insect hatches, drowned stoneflies or sinking terrestrials just below the surface.

THE LINE (FLOATING ONLY) - Double taper line with modified tapers are all that is needed for this type of fishing. Longer leaders, perhaps a rod length long are useful in clear calm water.

THE FEEDING MINNOW TECHNIQUE - This method appears to be simple to the novice speycaster. The skill to keep the fly just inches below the surface as it swings across stream is only acquired by constant practice. Once again, the speyrod allows perfect line control for short, medium and long casts. Cast the line across stream, making an aerial mend upstream. Keeping the rod tip high and pointing slightly upstream. As the line proceeds down river, it will start to swing in towards the bank. By gentle upstream mending (*imparting a little twitch to the fly*) and leading the fly around with the long rod, the fly can be made to 'swim' just below the surface in a diagonal direction giving the fish a good view of the fly for a long time.

WHAT WILL THE FISH DO? - An interested and correctly motivated fish will drift down and across to inspect the fly. It may do this time after time, sometimes sucking at it, pushing it with its nose or boiling under it. Keep a constant watch for this behaviour and don't strike. Fish will take just about anywhere with a strong preference for that magic moment at the end of the swing. At this point, leave the fly alone, count to five and slowly strip in one yard of line with the rod held high. This seems to trigger off a hesitant fish, perhaps imitating the minnow escaping upstream. If no takers, continue fishing the next strip. Don't cast farther than your ability to control line.

**Thunder &
Lightning**
*Mike's favourite
mid-water and
top-water fly.*

Fishing the Surface - Dry Fly

Includes all insects floating on the surface, ovipositing stonefly and caddis adults or terrestrial blow-ins (*hoppers, bees or wasps*).

THE STONEFLY ADULT - Anadromous fish seem to have a natural tendency to rise to a carefully presented adult female stonefly as she drops down onto the water to lay her eggs. The ability to imitate the many stages of the stoneflies return to the river, with a long limber speyrod is a winning combination.

THE LINE AND LEADER - Make sure your floating line is in good repair and dressed to float high. A modified end taper is required to fully utilize the rapidly reducing energy as the end of the line rolls out and to prevent the splash down effect of large double taper lines. The combination of dry fly and speycasting requires special attention to the leader. They must be easy to install, strong enough to hold large fish, long enough to avoid spooking a fussy fish, heavy enough to accept the jolt of energy from the line and tapered to drive a large air resistant bushy dry fly.

THE PRESENTATION (NATURAL WAY) - The object is to imitate the female stonefly when on the water, ovipositing. The presentation is made to represent the three stages of the process.

- Splashing and fluttering downstream.
- Blown, washed or fluttering to shore
- Struggling to fly upstream again.

Although each stage is fished consecutively, it is sometimes difficult to determine when one stage finishes and the other begins. When compared to other presentation techniques, it will be seen that the 'natural way' allows you to fish the same fly, three different ways with one cast. How's that for conservation of energy?

THE CONTROLLED DRIFT - Whichever 'strip' you are fishing, pull out enough line to reach it then an additional twenty feet of line (*let all the line float downstream*). Now strip in the extra twenty feet and trap it under the right hand. Cast out directly across stream, making an aerial mend (*with the rod held high*) so that the fly is ahead of the leader, the leader ahead of the line. The moment the fly starts to be dragged sideways, mend it back on course again, feeding a little of the extra line at the same time. Continue this process until all the feeding line has gone. If the rod is held high, it is relatively easy to mend and feed line (*exceptionally easy with a true speyrod*). Don't worry about dunking the fly when mending, this imitates the clumsy natural. A well-designed dry fly will pop up again.

Telkwa Stone
A dry fly for Atlantic salmon and steelhead.

THE CONTROLLED SWING - By the time that all the feeding line is out, the fly having travelled a considerable distance downstream will start to swing back to shore. As the rod is still held high, it is possible to control the speed of the swing by mending. Once again, don't worry about dunking the fly or if it is not visible when fishing a long line. The tension of the line will pull the fly into (*not under*) the water surface, making it difficult for the angler to see, but very attractive to the fish. There is no need to resort to planing discs or riffle hitches during this stage. The rod must still be held high.

THE CONTROLLED RETRIEVE - When the line and the fly are downstream close to the shore (*providing there is enough water*), pause for a few seconds then slowly strip in the feeding line, pausing after each strip with the rod held high. If no takers, turn towards the river again and repeat the casting and line control procedure.

WHAT WILL THE FISH DO? - If the fly is behaving correctly (*animated to represent the egg laying stonefly*), a sufficiently motivated fish will leave its hold and drift down behind it to make a closer inspection as it floats downstream during the controlled drift stage. It may also continue its inspection during the swing and the retrieve. During the inspection, the fish may come close to the fly then suddenly swim away leaving a tell tale swirl, then repeat the process right through the presentation, finally swimming away unhooked. This 'cat and mouse game' can continue until you or the fish gives up. If you give your fly 'sufficient water time', an over-active player is going to make a mistake, take your fly and swim back to its hold without closing its mouth and hook itself as we shall see later.

COVERING THE WATER WITH THE 'NATURAL' METHOD - Assume that you have read your river and decided on the casting stations. Remember... *you are going to fish along the bank first*. The number of stations will depend on the length of the pool. The water in front of each station is then divided geometrically into short, medium and long casts. A typical set of casts would be thirty feet then forty-five feet followed by a sixty foot cast. Make at least three identical presentations at each cast length.

The complete set of casts covers an enormous area. After thoroughly covering the first station, move down to the next station and repeat the process; *see Sketch 33, page* 166. Don't forget that the head and tail of the pool are just as important as the body. Don't concentrate (*or neglect*) those fishy-looking hot spots.

THE SPEYCASTER'S ADVANTAGE - Fishing the natural way allows the speycaster to utilize all the skills and advantages of using the true speyrod. Being able to cover all water from right at your feet to way out without wasting time false casting, etc. just about doubles your effective fishing time (*compared to the overhead caster*). The ability to control line, making your artificial do what the natural would have been doing is the epitome of flyfishing. The final advantage of the long limber speyrod is the ability to control and land the fish after it has hooked itself.

Part Four ~ Chapter Twenty-Three
Hooking, Controlling and Landing Fish

HERE WE ARE, FINALLY OUT ON THE RIVER, SPEYFISHING. We have selected the right tackle and fly, have just made the correct presentation for the river conditions and a fish has shown itself and taken our fly. By now, the adrenaline is flowing and our inherited cave man instincts take over. The natural reaction of a novice angler is to strike so hard that they 'rip the fish's lips off'. If lucky enough to actually hook a fish, you could lose it again by 'horsing it in' to shore, or worse still, take so long to land it that it 'dies of old age' before it can be released. The final blow is losing your fish by clumsy fish handling methods. What is the point of learning speycasting, line control, etc., if we can't *hook, control* and *land fish*?

Hooking Fish

When angling for anadromous fish, it should always be remembered that they are not really feeding. Fish will take a fly for numerous reasons, either territorial defense, juvenile competitive feeding response or to feed, etc. Unless the fly is presented 'right on the nose', a fish must leave its hold to take the fly. A tired fish that has just arrived upriver or is in very cold water is often reluctant to move.

Once the fish has been sufficiently motivated, it will gently suck the fly in or grab it with a powerful thrust. In most cases the fish is not feeding (*just checking out the fly*) and does not swallow or close its mouth completely. Once the fish has taken the fly, its survival instincts take over again, causing it to swim back to the safety and comfort of its hold. The return may be a gentle slow swim or a sudden rush depending on water conditions or length of swim required. As the fish returns to its hold with a partly closed mouth, many different things can happen. It may foul hook itself outside the mouth, bed the fly into the mouth by line drag or take it back home and chew on it.

As a general rule, the longer the return swim, the greater the drag on the line, the better the chance of the fish hooking itself. Hooks should be super sharp hard wire and strong. If blunted on rocks, change your fly. Don't attempt to sharpen hooks when fishing.

How Do You Know? - When surface or top water fishing, there is usually an obvious visible swirl or boil when the fish goes for the fly. Unless the fish refuses or rejects it, there will be a slight tug or a strong pull on the line as the fish swims back to its lie. As the pull is generally caused by water drag on the line, it will be influenced by the length of line and strength of current. A sensitive, limber spey-rod will enhance the delicate pull that some fish can produce.

When fishing sunk flies near or on the bottom, it is extremely difficult to detect a take. The paradox is that you don't want to get your line and fly hooked in the rocks on the bottom, yet that is where it must be because that is where the fish are. This is almost impossible with full sunk lines. The problem is largely solved with the use of floating lines and variable sink tips together with the float fishing concept. The take can usually be detected by any hesitation or tightening of the floating line. This effect can often be felt, however, the key to this style of angling is observation.

Don't cast farther than your ability to see the end of the floating line. Fish holding directly on the bottom are often reluctant to move to a fly. This style of angling is highly skilled and difficult, however, it is often 'the only game in town'.

Once again use super sharp hooks. As your fly must be down in the rocks, it will be blunted quickly, discard it. Don't let the cost of a fly lose that next fish.

What Do You Do? - To many anglers that magic moment when you 'just know' that the fish has taken the fly is the pinnacle of flyfishing. To these happy people, everything else is downhill. All previous activities have been aimed towards this moment, all primitive hunting instincts are activated. This is the nemesis of the novice angler who is in such a hurry to hook the fish that the most important fact is overlooked. Anadromous fish seldom close their mouths after taking the fly. Any attempt to strike or set the hook will result in an insecure hook up or pull the fly out of the fish's mouth. Novice anglers (*for anadromous fish*) will often lose three out of four fish hooked. Some of this will be due to poor fish control, most of it will be the result of insecure hookups due to impatience and striking the fish. This is very discouraging and usually unnecessary. The next question is... *if it is wrong to strike or set the hook, what do you do when the fish takes the fly?* The answer is 'nothing'... *hold your breath and look the other way.* The fish will hook itself on its return to its hold, or when it first feels the point. The self-hooking technique results in fewer fish hooked and more fish landed (*experienced anglers will lose about one fish in four*). It does not seem reasonable to hook more fish only to lose them after disturbing other fish and fellow anglers.

Remember... *'sharp hooks, dull reactions'*.

The Player - Having motivated a fish to come to the fly, it is capable of some very strange behaviour. It has an uncanny knack of sucking, pulling, slapping or otherwise moving the fly without taking it into its mouth and hooking itself on its return to its hold.

A fish was once observed (*from a cliff*), moving thirty feet down river and twenty feet across to follow a floating fly, then swim directly under it and zoom home unhooked. This continued for about a dozen presentations before the ultimate mistake, it took the fly. On another occasion, a novice angler was convinced that a smolt (*they sometimes take the fly*), was playing with his fly. Each presentation produced a number of what felt like gentle taps on the fly. From a high vantage point, his guide could see that it was a good sized fish. The angler, anxious to move on to better looking water, had to be almost physically restrained to 'stay put' and work on 'his smolt'. After almost an hour of impatient casting, almost ready to terminate the guide, a 'smolt' of over twenty pounds was beached. It that was a smolt, the adult would be something to see.

A fish that can play with a fly is also playing with the angler and vice versa. Some anglers seem to establish a telepathic communication with the fish. There are even a few blase folk who take perverse pleasure in seeing how many times they can raise the fish before it finally makes a mistake or gets fed up and goes away. These anglers have reached the highest plateau of angling, not interested in how many or how big! Deciding to say 'good-bye' to a real player and move on to where there may be another fish is a tough decision. Surely it is better to work on a 'known fish' than go to where there might be one. It is good etiquette to let the angler who is following know that you are working on a 'live player'. He may decide to go ahead of you and take your place at the head of the line with the advantage of undisturbed water or wait and see if you are unsuccessful and have a go at your player when you move on.

Anglers will often raise an interested fish so that it comes to the fly, swirls and returns to its hold unhooked. Inexperienced anglers (*for anadromous fish*) will often assume that the fish was holding where it showed, particularly if it is adjacent to a rock. Too much time is wasted casting to a fish that is 'long gone'. If you raise a fish, carry out the original presentation until you hook your player.

Don't Strike or Set - The success of skilled trout anglers in hooking anadromous fish is dependent on their ability to restrain their acquired hook setting reactions. This reaction is by now involuntary, some deny having 'struck' when in fact, they have pulled the fly out of the fish's mouth. The following illustrates the importance of letting the fish hook itself...

Some time ago, a well-known and respected trout guide from below the border had raised a player on our beautiful Bulkley River. He was fishing for summer steelhead with a dry fly. It just so happened that he had phenomenal eyesight and the rare ability of seeing through water and spotting the fish. Despite his intense concentration, he just could not restrain that final strike when the fish took the fly. After half a dozen abortive attempts, the angler's confidence had sunk and the guide was less than complimentary. Knowing of the angler's interest in wildlife, the guide called his attention to a spectacular bald eagle flying overhead, just as the fly was proceeding down river on the next presentation. Picture the scene, the angler is staring up into the sky unaware that a large fish was mouthing his fly and subsequently hooking itself securely. For the rest of the trip, the guide shouted 'bald eagle' whenever a fish approached the fly. The angler, knowing very well that there was no bald eagle, could not resist looking and hooked the fish every time. If you cannot resist striking or setting, look for the bald eagle!

Controlling Fish With Speyrods

Once a fish is well hooked, it should not be allowed to go cavorting all over the river, disturbing other fish, breaking the leader, dying of old age before landing, beating itself to death on the beach or totally exhausting the angler. These unfortunate (*but often observed*) situations can easily be avoided providing you are using a long limber resilient (*shock absorbing*) speyrod and a modicum of common sense.

The moment the fish hooks itself, it has paid you the complement of taking your fly. It is now up to you to reciprocate, by landing it quickly and safely, to ensure its survival on release.

Anglers have been known to take 'forever' to land relatively small fish. Could this be the 'fear of failure' or is it 'this is probably my only fish of the trip so I am going to make it last'? Both of these mentalities make poor angling and bad sportsmanship. The prime concern when controlling a fish, is to get it to the beach when it is ready (*ripe*) for landing, not too soon (*green*), or too late (*near death*). In order to do this, the fish (*and the angler*) must expend energy. This means that, if the fish is not working by trying to pull away from you, you must be working to pull the fish towards you.

ELIMINATE USELESS FORCES - It seems logical that if the object is to get the fish to the beach, the best way of doing it is to pull it sideways, by the most effective method. This is so self evident, that it is difficult to imagine why it is not universally understood. Most anadromous fish are caught in relatively weed free water, unlike trout which will dive for weed cover when hooked. Anglers (*skilled in trout fishing*) will try and lift the fish's head up with a vertical lift (*out of the weeds*). This spells disaster when hooked into a large angry migrating fish. Don't do it, unless you are practising your LDR technique... *long distance release*.

As the pull on the fish is usually inclined in three directions, it is useful to examine the simple statics of these forces. Any inclined force can be replaced (*equilibrated*), by other forces acting in a vertical, lateral and horizontal direction. The magnitude of these forces can be obtained by vector diagram, as indicated in sketch below...

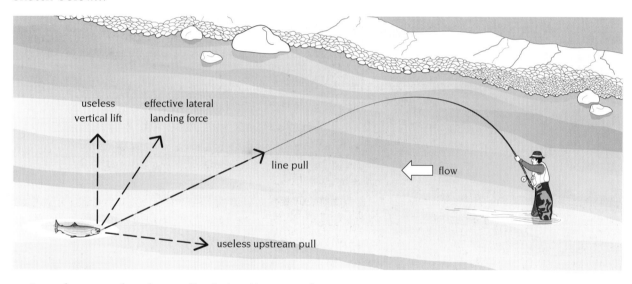

In other words, the pull of the line can be replaced by one force trying to lift the fish, another force trying to pull it upstream and still another force pulling the fish towards shore. This means

Sketch 35
Vectors - Effective & Useless Landing Forces

that for every pound of pull applied in the correct direction, there could be pounds of useless force, applied in other directions. For example, a fish being pulled at an angle of 45° to the current and 45° to the surface, with a ten pound pull, could produce less than five pounds effective lateral force. This is a great deal of strain on the leader, for very little effective effort.

By the way, a five pound weight will produce an enormous bend in a well designed speyrod. Try it with your own rod, you won't be able to lift it. It follows that landing large fish with only a light pull on the line, is going to require skill, not raw power. Inexperienced anglers seem to have an uncontrollable urge to pull the fish upstream to help it swim or lift it out of the water. Get it to the beach as soon as possible with a lateral pull.

THE EFFECT OF THE LATERAL PULL - Apart from providing the most effective way of getting the fish to shore, the method has the additional advantage of preventing the fish from dashing up and down the river. A fish that has spent so much time and effort swimming up river and selecting a resting area, is more inclined to stick around its temporary home, than be forced to do otherwise. In simple terms:

- Don't pull it upstream, it won't pull you downstream.
- Don't pull it downstream, it won't pull you upstream.
- Pull it directly sideways, it will stay put, or jump about.

A hooked fish will generally keep pace with the current, however, it will drift downstream when tired. This is not a problem if the fish can be pulled into slacker water or you can walk down to keep directly opposite the fish. The most important advantage of the lateral pull, is the effect it has on the fish's ability to replenish its oxygen supply during the struggle to escape the hook. A strong lateral pull bends the fish's body sideways, closing one gill, restricting the oxygen supply at the very time the fish 'most needs it'. In order to overcome this and to maintain station, it will move inshore to straighten its body. This has a dramatic effect on large fish, providing steady reeling pressure is maintained.

Applying Pressure...

Gary Woodward putting lateral pressure on a securely hooked steelhead.

Important...

do not pump the rod, it will allow the fish to straighten its body and take another breath.

The Maximum Effective Lateral Force Method
See Sketch 36, page 185...

Although tradition is an essential part of our speyfishing heritage, it must be adapted to suit our contemporary situations. In those circumstances where killing fish is permitted or mandatory, it seems natural to 'play' a fish to death before beaching it. An old school 'sport', taking forever to land a fish, remarked that after paying so much for his fishing, he was going to have fun 'playing' it. Needless to say, he did not fish with me again.

On the other end of the scale, those anglers using the lateral force technique should be able to land fish in about half a minute for each pound of fish. The time taken will vary somewhat due to obstacles as we shall see later.

The effectiveness of the lateral force technique was demonstrated when one of our guests had hooked a large steelhead which immediately took refuge behind a submerged rock directly downstream. Being of the old school and not wanting to waste his time walking to shore, he carried on a 'tug of war' with the fish for twenty minutes to no avail. When finally convinced that the line must be hooked around the rock, he reluctantly consented as a last resort to give the lateral force method a try. His sixteen pound fish was brought to shore, revived and released in a further ten minutes. We will now examine the effective lateral force method in detail.

Helping Hand
Anne Voss Bark, angler, of the Arundell Arms Hotel, Lifton Devon, England, being assisted by guide, Denise Maxwell, on the Bulkley River.

The Pay Off
A glance at Anne's very large fish, being released by Mike Maxwell, Jr., explains why she required a little extra muscle.

It is vital that the rod is held sideways at all times, with a constant pull on the fish. Do *not*, I repeat, *do not* pump and reel the rod. Any slackening of the rod pull, even momentarily will allow the fish to relax and regain oxygen and strength. When the fish comes in for the first time, it will be too 'green', take one look at the shore and zoom out again. This is exactly what you want it to do, in order to let off a little more steam.

This process may have to be repeated, until the fish can be made to hold a few feet from shore. Whatever you do, don't play with a fish until it is exhausted and near death. The advice to 'wait until the fish can be brought in floating on its side', belongs to those uninformed and primitive 'sports' who kill fish. Should the fish swim upstream, it may be necessary to switch the rod downstream again, and vice versa.

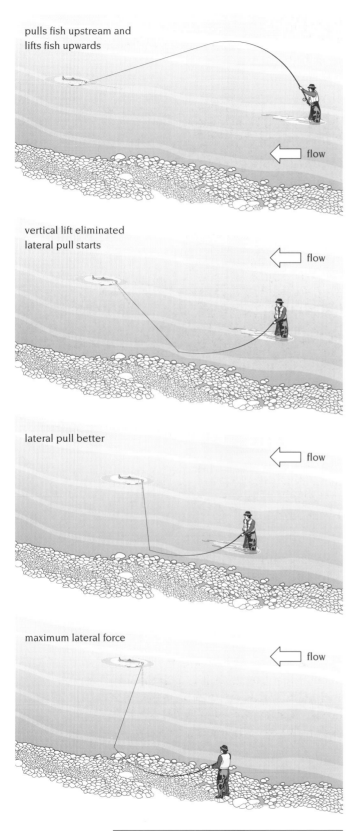

pulls fish upstream and
lifts fish upwards

flow

vertical lift eliminated
lateral pull starts

flow

lateral pull better

flow

maximum lateral force

flow

Sketch 36
Effective Lateral Pull

STAGE 1

A fish that has taken the fly is capable of doing some very strange things… going back to its hold and chewing or worrying the fly, like a dog with a rabbit, ripping off line like an express train, a slow steady pull away (*an indication of a tired or large fish*), an acrobatic display worthy of an Olympic diving event. Controlling the initial run, is an important part of the proceedings.

STAGE 2

The moment a fish is hooked, start walking to shore with the rod bent sideways towards shore, the left hand at the top of the cork grip, the right hand palming the reel. Make the fish work for every foot of line, without breaking off. Whatever you do, don't just stand there, and see how far the fish will run, unrestrained. The water drag on large double taper lines and an excessive length of heavy backing, can easily unseat a not too well bedded hook. It is also bad sportsmanship, to allow your fish to swim into another anglers' water. Fred Harrison of California, a highly skilled and courteous angling guest of ours, will frequently break off his fish rather than let it go down into the next man's water.

STAGE 3

It must be remembered that speycasters are usually working on difficult water, with obstacles along the bank of the river. This can make the sideways pull of a long speyrod difficult. There are also deep water areas and accumulated debris, logs, etc. along the banks of every river, that make landing fish difficult. It is sometimes necessary to locate possible landing sites, during your analysis of the pool, before fishing. As you are walking to shore, head for your landing area, while still reeling with the rod bent sideways.

STAGE 4

Having hooked your fish, controlled its initial run, selected a landing site, walked to shore, directly opposite the fish, applied maximum effective lateral force by bending the rod sideways, the fish will come to shore quickly.

OBSTACLES - *see Sketch* 37A. Although the lateral pull must be maintained whenever possible, be careful of visible, or hidden obstacles. Fish will sometimes seek the safety of a large rock and snag the line. Lift the rod momentarily and return to the lateral pull when the fish is clear of the obstacle. 'Take heart', everyone loses fish on rocks and sunken logs, etc.

JUMPING FISH - *see Sketch* 37B. One of the joys of angling is the jumping fish. What fish accomplish above the water testifies to their strength and endurance. Controlling a jumping fish is largely a matter of common sense, however, a long limber resilient speyrod gives the speycaster an enormous advantage. It is common practice (*with stiff rods*) to lower the rod tip (*bow to the fish*), when a fish jumps. The idea behind this procedure, is to prevent the fish falling onto a tight line and 'throwing' (*their words, not ours*) the hook. In many cases, when 'bowing', the fish falls on a slack line, is temporarily out of control and unseats an insecure hook.

When using a true speyrod, raise the rod to a near vertical position and keep the line tight when the fish jumps. When the fish falls back to the water, it does not matter if it lands on the line, as all shock will be absorbed by the limber speyrod. Just raise the rod, hang on to it, watch the show. Remember... *a long speyrod has no more power than a short rod for the same line weight. It does have many times the shock absorbing qualities.*

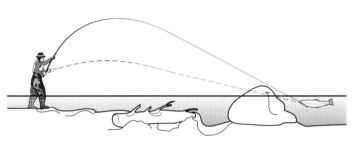

A - *Lift the line over obstacles*

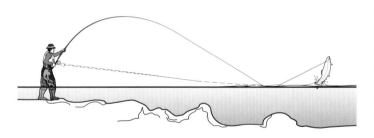

B - *Don't bow to the fish or drop the rod tip*

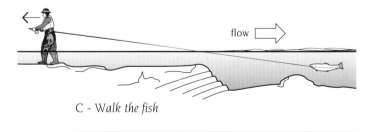

flow ⇨

C - *Walk the fish*

Sketch 37
Lift/Don't Bow/Walk

WALKING FISH - *see Sketch* 37C. Always check (*part of the game plan*) that you will be able to land a fish from any angling location. To watch your catch disappear over a waterfall, or down a vertical sided canyon, will have you questioning your own common sense. Occasionally a large fish may take you around a bend in the river, head for the rapids or run past an unwadable section of river. If you try to follow the fish, you may drown or end up in the salt water, miles downstream. There is a much better (*not always successful*) solution. As the fish proceeds downstream to where you cannot follow, well into your backing, point the rod directly at the fish and palm the reel until the fish stops moving downstream. Do not reel in the line, do not bend the rod. This procedure has a dramatic, unexplainable effect on fish. One hypothesis suggests that as the fish's original intention was to migrate upstream, it will swim, back up again, if given any incentive. Since the straight line pull does not represent any interference from a live 'enemy' and helps the fish to beat the downstream current, it will follow the pull on the line. If the angler turns around (*to prevent tripping*), walks slowly upstream, does not reel in or allow line out, does not jiggle the rod, the fish will follow. When you have finally towed the fish far enough upstream, land it and release it.

Remember... *don't waste time on impossible landing locations.*

HAND LINING - *see* Photo 15D, *page* 145. How the rod is held and the line controlled, is extremely important when landing fish. As the most agile and sensitive hand must be reserved to control the reel and the line, the left hand is placed at the top of the cork grip. The butt of the rod should be against the body. The right hand is free to reel in, when retrieving line and palming to allow line out under tension. Occasionally a fish will swim towards you faster than you can reel, resulting in a slack line. This can cause an insecure hook to drop out, or snap the leader if the fish makes a sudden dash for freedom. If the line is still trapped under the left hand, the slack line can be quickly retrieved, by stripping in line with the right hand . The moment the fish runs again, the line is allowed to slip under the left hand, taking care not to let it shock the rod as the slack finally runs out. The right hand should be used to feed out the slack and be ready to palm or reel immediately.

TAILING FISH - *see Sketch* 38. Landing fish with long speyrods requires the angler to use slightly different procedures and a great deal of common sense. The use of landing nets is not encouraged for the following reasons...

- It is a carry over from the 'kill 'em all' period.
- It can seriously injure a fish.
- It is an insult to the skilled angler who reserves the right to tail and release his own fish.

Adequately sized landing nets are cumbersome and usually require another person to handle them. Assume we have brought our fish close to shore, to be hand tailed. The rod should be in the left hand, trapping the line. The rod should also be bent sideways upstream and kept low. The fish should be upstream and allowed to float down to the angler, extending the rod to the shore. As the fish comes within reach, grasp it firmly by the tail. It is vital that the human hand is insulated from the fish's nervous system, by the use of a cloth, or better still, an old wool glove (*keep it on your wader belt*). If the fish is gripped firmly, just in front of the tail with thumb and forefinger, (*practise gripping a tennis ball with thumb and forefinger*), it immobilizes a fish. If you release the pressure momentarily, the fish will struggle again. Don't try and land fish in fast current, there is usually slack water close by. Keep the fish in the water, lay your rod down on the shore, allowing you to place your left hand under the fish's belly. Do not relax your tail grip.

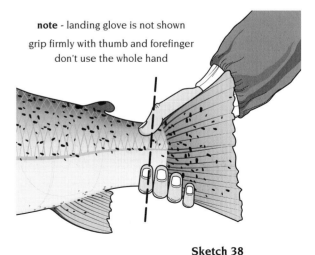

note - landing glove is not shown
grip firmly with thumb and forefinger
don't use the whole hand

Sketch 38
Tailing Fish

Matepedia Atlantic
Dr. Carlos Montero of Argentina (r) and his
guide, Guy Ramon, with a 25 pound Atlantic
salmon taken on the Matepedia River, June 1994,
using a 15 foot rod and #10 line; two other fish of
over 30 pounds were also landed and released.

For the Future
Proper care
when handling
and releasing
fish will ensure
there will be fish
for the next
generation.

RELEASING FISH - Those who still continue to kill anadromous fish, believing that it helps to defray the cost of their fishing, should seek the services of a good accountant. Those who kill fish to massage their deflated egos, should consult a psychiatrist. Don't take your frustration out on innocent fish. Assuming that you have risen above the 'gut 'em and eat 'em' stage and are going to release your fish, keep the fish in the water to help it to regain oxygen. Remove the hook, or cut the leader if too deeply imbedded (*barbless hooks recommended*). Measure the fork length with a dressmaker's cloth tape.

Photograph the fish in the water with a polarized lens. If you must lift it up, do so by supporting the fish's weight under the belly with the left hand (*do not relax the tail grip*). There is no need to lift the fish for more than a few seconds and for a few inches above water. At no time should any fish be lifted by the tail, hanging down like a rubber chicken. This unnecessary procedure (*a great macho pose*) is damaging to a fish's internal organs.

Release the fish under its own steam. Do not grab hold of a limp fish and shove it out into the current, like launching a toy boat. Check the progress of your released fish. The ability to land and release fish efficiently and safely, is the hallmark of a true sportsman. Knocking a fish on the head is not.

LOSING FISH - A true sportsman is never totally disappointed at losing a fish, except with himself for 'goofing up'. The essence of flyfishing is, inducing a fish to come to your artificial fly and hook itself. This is the supreme moment. The shock

produces the maximum bend in
the weakest part of the rod

Sketch 39
Break Rod

will temporarily awaken your submerged primeval hunting instincts and get all those intoxicating natural juices flowing (*not bottled or packaged*). It is some consolation, that no angler (*except around the dinner table*) lands every fish hooked. It should also be noted, that you can make your 'lost fish' any size you would like it to be. It should always be twice the size of the day's largest fish. While secretly observing an old gentleman skilfully controlling a jumping fish from the opposite bank, it was disappointing to see the fish break loose and swim away. However, it was heartwarming to see this true sportsman turn to the river, raise his hat and bow to the fish.

ROD SAFETY AND STRENGTH - Well-designed and constructed speyrods are strong, but not indestructible. Intelligent handling will guarantee that you will not break you rod during the crucial landing process.

The prevalent cause of broken speyrods, is the inexperienced angler's urge to lift the fish up out of the water when it is almost lying at his feet; *see Sketch* 39. This is partly due to the mistaken belief that a double handed rod has unlimited power and strength, regardless of what line weight it was designed to cast. Unless you have unlimited financial resources, use skill, not muscle. When tailing and releasing fish, place your rod on the shore, out of harm's way, ready to grab it again if the fish wants to 'go another round'.

There are many fine rod companies, who for no fault of their own, have been plagued by broken rods. These rods are usually trashed by clumsy, insensitive anglers. The abuse includes trying to cast a forty-yard, fast sinking double taper line, right off the bottom of a deep pool or assuming that they are fighting a five hundred pound marlin. When faced with attempting to design an 'idiot proof' graphite rod, rod makers have a number of value judgements to make. Should they spoil a perfectly good rod by wrapping on extra fibreglass, etc., use a little fibreglass and compromise, or leave a good design alone and hope that it will be used by an intelligent, not necessarily skilled angler.

ON ANGLER FATIGUE - Apart from the ease of casting and controlling line with a true speyrod, there is one characteristic of a well designed speyrod that is important and seldom understood. It can be seen from Sketch 40 on the following page that there is a considerable difference of bend between a stiff rod and a limber (*not soft*) rod. The shape of bend (*action*), will affect the amount of power required to hold the rod (*with equal fish pull*). It is obvious that the push and pull exerted by the angler, is a function of the effective length of the bent rod. Since the limber rod, will bend to a shorter effective length, than the stiff rod, the push–pull power required by the angler will be smaller, even for the same fish pull. Simply put, the limber rod bends out of the way when loaded, greatly reducing angler fatigue.

Most beginners are surprised (*and alarmed*) at just how much a well designed speyrod will bend. Try lifting a one pound lead weight on dry land. Those who question the flexible speyrod's ability to land fish should understand that the dead weight of a fish is considerably less in water due to the flotation caused by the water displacement of the fish's volume (*Archimedes*).

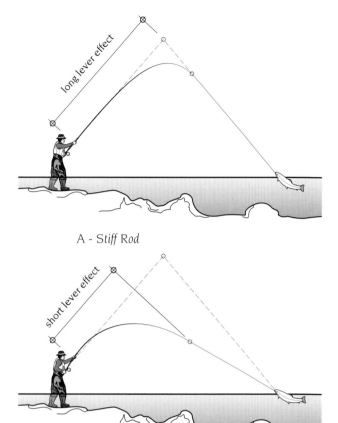

A - *Stiff Rod*

B - *Limber Rod*

- same rod length
- same line weight
- same size fish

Sketch 40
Angler Fatigue

Evaluate Your Performance

Take the time to reflect on your day's fishing. Was your speycasting as good as you expected it to be, were your speyfishing techniques adequate?

After landing a fish, it will prove valuable to evaluate your performance, from the time the fish took the fly, to the moment it swam away upstream on release. Did you control the fish, or let it dash about spoiling everyone else's fishing? Did you take advantage of the shock absorbing characteristics of your speyrod and land your fish with skilfully applied lateral power. How was your fish tailing technique? Did you release the fish prematurely, or only when it could swim away upstream with powerful strokes. Did your reel have sufficient capacity to prevent the line jamming under one side of the frame, when reeling in, without manually level winding? Could you control your fish with just a rim control? If your reel had a mechanical drag, was it too tight or too loose? Did you rely on it too much? Was it too expensive or delicate to lay down on the shore when releasing the fish?

A fish can place a considerable strain on your equipment. The euphoria of landing a large fish, can temporarily cause a normally cautious angler, to lose touch with reality, continue fishing and lose an even bigger fish due to the failure of tackle damaged on the last fish. Don't forget that rod joints can work loose. Check the leader for cuts, abrasions and tangles. Check your fly, did you bend it when taking it out of the fish? An ounce of prevention is better than all that (*post* LDR) picturesque language.

PART FIVE ~ EQUIPMENT

CHAPTER

Twenty-Four   *Design and Construction of Speyrods*

Twenty-Five   *Selecting a Speyrod for Speyfishing*

Twenty-Six   *Reels for Speyfishing*

Twenty-Seven   *Lines and Leaders*

Twenty-Eight   *Hooks for Speyfishing*

Twenty-Nine   *On Flies and Local Rivers*

A PAIR OF CONTEMPORARIES...

Speyfishing for steelhead, salmon and trout is becoming a popular method of angling. Using graphite as the rod blank demanded evolving the design approach to produce a true speyrod that emulated the very best fishing qualities of graphite's predecessors without the compromise of weight.

Above:

3 piece, 10-weight, 15'−0" and 5 piece, 6-weight, 11'−6" speyrods.

Part Five ~ Chapter Twenty-Four
Design and Construction of Speyrods

THE OPTIMUM ROD for learning and practising speycasting was covered in Part One, however, there are many other very important subjects that must be considered and understood if you are to make an intelligent and practical choice when selecting your double-handed rods for fishing.

SPECIAL PURPOSE RODS - There are as many different types of double-handed rods as there are different styles of fishing. Some manufacturers successfully cover all styles of fishing with rods specifically designed for each special purpose, however, their catalog terminology can be confusing and misleading to an uninformed beginner. The unfortunate practice of calling any double-handed rod a speyrod has led to the disappointment of many would-be speyfishers. Calling a double-handed rod a speyrod does not make it into one.

The primary consideration in choosing a double-handed rod is 'fitness for purpose'. In other words, what style of casting and fishing was the rod designed for and is this how you intend to use it? You could play golf with a hockey stick, however, it would not make a very pleasant game. Make sure you are selecting the correct rod for the style of casting and fishing that you intend to adopt. The following is a simplified description of the many types of double-handed rods currently available.

TYPE ONE - Overhead Casting

This rod seems to be the choice of anglers who still believe that the fish are all on the other side of the river or that it is necessary to use overweighted flies. The main attraction seems to be that the stiffer overhead double-hander has a similar action to their single-handers. Unfortunately it is also the natural selection of those anglers who are not aware of the advantages of spey fishing or are unwilling or unable to learn. Attempting to speycast with an overstiff, overhead rod has the following disadvantages...

CASTING

- Double speys would be next to impossible.
- Single speys are possible but tiring.

FISHING

- Line control would be very tiring.
- Many fish lost due to overstiff rods.

Attempting to speycast with an overhead style of rod would be as awkward as flycasting with a spinning rod.

TYPE TWO - In-Betweener

Some manufacturers are attempting to cover the market with an all purpose, double-handed rod. There is nothing really wrong with this approach and although it is a step in the right direction towards a true speyrod, the following important facts must be understood...

- The closer the action is to an overhead rod, the more difficult it is to spey-cast.
- The closer the action is to a true speyrod, the easier it is to speycast.

The following disadvantages must be considered...

- Speycasting will be tiring.
- Line and fish control will be tiring.

TYPE THREE - True Speyrod

This limber yet powerful type of rod is specifically designed for speycasting and speyfishing, and has the following advantages...

WHEN SPEYCASTING

- Allows relaxed and graceful speycasting.
- All double and single speys on both banks.
- Short line casting for 'close in' fish.
- The restricted backcast procedure.

WHEN FISHING

- Effortless aerial line controls.
- Superb water mending.
- Total control of the fly presentation.

WHEN CONTROLLING FISH

- Limber yet powerful.
- Very effective shock absorber.
- Will tire the fish - not the angler.
- More fish landed - after hooking.
- Fish landed quickly and humanely.

WHY SO FEW TRUE SPEYRODS AVAILABLE - It must be obvious that if you are going to take advantage of the desirable characteristics of a true speyrod when casting and fishing, you must use a rod specifically designed for that purpose. If you do your homework when selecting your rod, you will begin to wonder why there are so few true speyrods available on today's market. Could it be that so few anglers are able to cast and fish with a true speyrod or is it due to the scarcity of qualified and accomplished speycasting instructors? Perhaps it is the difficulty of selling a limber flexible rod to a customer who is looking for a double-hander that 'feels like' a stiff overgrown single-hander. Unfortunately there are too many anglers looking for the 'quick fix', are not prepared to learn speyfishing and are fair game for rod salesmen.

On Rod Jointing Systems
See Security of Speyrod Joints, page 200...

Due to the enormous bending and twisting effects of long limber speyrods, careful consideration must be given to the security of the joints. No other style of rod requires such careful attention to joint design. There are two popular jointing systems. They are...

THE TOP OVER BOTTOM JOINT - *see Sketch* 41A. The practice of connecting rod sections by pushing a lower section of a rod up into an upper section produces an overstiff length of rod at each joint. This system of jointing is generally used by rod companies who produce the stiffer action rods intended for overhead casting, therefore the interruption to the bending curve due to the overstiff joints is minimal. The disadvantage of the swelled out, overstiff top over bottom joint is its lack of resistance to the twisting effect of double speycasting. Some 'authorities' recommend the use of electrical tape to prevent joint loosening or 'twisting off' part of the rod.

If your present rod is connected with top over bottom joints, there is no reason why you can't cast or fish with it (*when correctly assembled*) providing you take into account and adjust for the peculiarities of this jointing method.

THE INTERNAL SPIGOT FERRULE - *see Sketch* 41B. Graphite speyrods specifically designed for speycasting, line control and controlling large fish can be jointed by the internal spigot system. This method, time-consuming, expensive and highly skilled, consists of cementing a short section of a thick walled smaller diameter tube in to the bottom section of the rod and inserting it into the top section to join the two sections. As the spigot is designed to bend to the same curve as the adjacent rod sections, there is no interruption in the rods curvature or sensitivity and minimal stress concentration under dynamic loading. The principal advantage of the internal spigot joint is that it does not slip (*when correctly assembled*) and does not require taping.

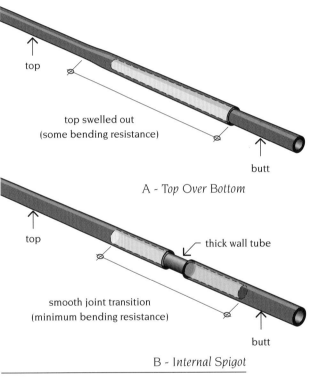

top

top swelled out
(some bending resistance)

butt

A - Top Over Bottom

top

thick wall tube

smooth joint transition
(minimum bending resistance)

butt

B - Internal Spigot

Sketch 41
Rod Jointing Systems

PART OF THE 'PLAN'…

Aaron Reimer, outfitter and guide in Ketchikan, Alaska, fishing a typical southwest Alaskan river. These short brushy streams hold just about every species of local and anadromous fish. An intelligent game plan and a long limber speyrod are essential where delicate, accurate presentations are necessary.

Part Five ~ Chapter Twenty-Five
Selecting a Speyrod for Speyfishing

BEFORE PROCEEDING, IT MUST BE UNDERSTOOD that just as in single-handed flyfishing, there is no such thing as an all purpose rod. It is also obvious that you must match your equipment to the size of fish you are after, your own physical characteristics and last, but not least, that most all important and illusive subject of... *your own personal preference*. It should also be realized that the size of the river is not significant as there are as many narrow rivers with big fish as there are wide rivers with small fish.

A glance at the table on page 198, shows the selection of rods made to my design which should cover just about any speyfishing situation. The number of speyrods you will eventually own will depend on how many different types of rivers you are working on and the species and size of fish you are after.

Former speyfishing student, *Aaron Reimer*... instructor, outfitter and guide of Ketchikan, Alaska, lives and fishes in what must be an angler's paradise. Apart from four different families of Pacific salmon, he has steelhead and cutthroat trout available virtually all year around. Over the years, he has built up his 'arsenal' of speyrods, to enable him to match his equipment for any speyfishing situation and now owns and fishes with every rod shown in the previously noted table. Wouldn't we all like to have the opportunity, resources and dedication of Aaron?

Things to Consider When Selecting a Speyrod

RELATING POWER WITH LENGTH - Assuming that we are considering true speyrods, there must be a relationship between the length of the rod and the line weight it was designed for. To go to the extremes, a twelve foot rod for a twelve weight line would be ugly to cast, impossible to control line with and a guaranteed fish loser. On the other hand, a sixteen foot rod for a four weight line would be next to impossible to cast and control line with and a very efficient fish killer, even if the angler is wearing running shoes.

RELATING YOUR PHYSICAL CHARACTERISTICS - Never make the mistake of assuming that short rods are easier to cast and fish with than long rods or that age or strength is the deciding factor in choosing your speyrod. You will find that the longer your rod, the easier it will be to cast in 'those impossible places', to control line and land fish.

MATCHING THE ROD TO THE FISH - The only sensible way of choosing speyrods is to match the power of the rod with the size of the fish you are fishing for. Attempting to control very large fish with light line rods is as unrewarding as landing very small fish on a very powerful rod.

THE EFFECTIVE RANGE OF A SPEYROD - *The effective range of a speyrod is the distance from the shortest to the longest cast, over which the line and fly can be effectively controlled.* Do not make the mistake of confusing the controllable length of your cast with the maximum length you can cast (*rod salesmen, take note*).

It is natural for a novice to concentrate on speycasting and neglect the vital procedures of line and fly control. Some will rate their performance on how far they can cast without regard for how many fish they hook. On the other hand, it appears that the more experienced a speyfisher becomes, the shorter the cast becomes and the more line control is used. American angler, *Harry Lemire*, is probably North America's most knowledgeable and successful steelheader, and an accomplished speycaster. Although Harry is capable of making very long casts, his short line speycasting, careful line control and superb fly control are a delight to see.

THE LENGTH OF A CAST - All casting distances are measured from 'your feet to the end of the line'. The fly will travel farther according to the length of leader being used (*dry fly or wet fly*).

EFFECTIVE RANGES OF EACH ROD - The practical ranges for each length and power given in the rod selection guide table are based on the capabilities of an accomplished speycaster. Don't expect to cover a lot of water until your speycasting skills develop. If you can't reach your target area without exceeding your maximum controllable cast length, you are in the wrong place. A glance at the table will show that the maximum effective range of a true speyrod is five times the length of the rod.

MAKING A DECISION - Assuming that you are dealing with a rod company that produces true speyrods, with the length of the rod correctly related to the power of the rod, the following table should be useful in selecting your rod.

Selecting a True Speyrod

Fish Weight	Line Weight	Rod Length	Effective Range *
5 lb.	#6	11 foot	15 to 55 feet
10 lb.	#7	12 foot	15 to 60 feet
15 lb.	#8	13 foot	20 to 65 feet
20 lb.	#9	14 foot	20 to 70 feet
25 lb.	#10	15 foot	20 to 75 feet
30 lb.	#11	16 foot	20 to 80 feet

*   *Length of leader must be added.*

THE FLEXIBILITY OF YOUR ROD - Make sure that your rod is limber enough to make the very short casts shown in the table. Many of the stiffer rods on today's market, make short line casting difficult or impossible.

Remember the golden rule...

A short line cast to where the fish are, is better than a long cast to empty water.

SPEYCASTING WITH SINGLE-HANDED RODS - Double-handed speyrods for very light lines are impractical, however, there are many long light line, medium action single-handed rods available that allow speycasting. Many of my speycasting students are now speycasting for trout on smaller streams with shorter rods and lighter lines and fishing those impossible places that we all know on our favourite streams. On the other hand, many accomplished single-handed casters are surprised to discover that they have been using a form of speycasting without realizing it. Many of the line pick-up and cast directions changes required on brushy streams are, in fact, single or double speycasts. There is no reason why you can't speycast with a single-handed rod, however, you must remember that the shortness of your rod depends on how much you are prepared to handicap yourself when speyfishing. You must also understand that stiff single-handed rods chosen for their distance casting characteristics will make speycasting difficult, line control tiring and fish control disappointing.

An accomplished speycaster, using a well-designed single-handed rod is capable of making very long speycasts well beyond the limit of adequate line and fly control. The following fish story should illustrate this...

Denise Maxwell, my dear wife for the past twenty years and considerably younger than my advanced years, is a former World champion distance and accuracy caster with a single-handed rod, and the first woman to hold a steelhead guide's licence in British Columbia. When developing our speyfishing line control techniques, Denise would cast with a ten foot, single-handed rod to a known fish hold and do her best to control the line to activate the fish.

Robust Brown
A moment to be admired, then released.

After resting the water, I would follow with my fifteen foot rod, the same length cast, the same fly pattern and presentation technique, and hook fish. This test produced the same results more often than not and indicates that all other things being equal, long rods are better line controllers than short ones.

It should be emphasized that speyfishing is not just for steelhead, Pacific salmon or Atlantic salmon. Any freshwater gamefish can be caught on a speyrod. *Paul Brown* of Montana, a respected angler and instructor, fishes his local brushy mountain streams for rainbow and brown trout, with a long six-weight double-handed speyrod. As Paul points out, the Blue Ribbon Montana and Wyoming streams are crowded at the height of the trout season. Speyfishing allows him to get away from the crowd and fish undisturbed water.

What Brand of Rod is Best?

My original intention was to field test and comment on as many different rod manufacturers products as time would allow and make recommendations on which rods are suitable for true speycasting. This has proved to be an invidious task. As of today there are at least a dozen reputable rod companies around the world producing double-handed fly rods, suitable for true speycasting to an equal or lesser degree. Added to this there are rod companies who are constantly changing their rod actions to keep up with the demands of the growing number of true speycasters.

NOT A CATALOG - In view of the previous discussion, it would not make sense to recommend any specific rod maker or any particular rod when it is more than likely that it would not be available later on. However, a short list of recommended rod makers is given on page 229.

Don't forget that each speyrod maker will have somewhat different action, however, you should be able to use and enjoy the true speyrod of your choice if you patronize any of these fine companies.

When being advised by other anglers, make sure that the older graphite rods that they are showing you have not been discontinued and replaced by a more advanced design.

HAS YOUR DEALER READ THIS BOOK? - When dealing with your local tackle store, make sure that they are able to select a true speyrod from their many other double-handed rods. Perhaps you should ask them if they are familiar with the recommendations of this book?

YOU MUST BE THE JUDGE - Once again, the more you try to describe a reasonably simple subject the more complicated it seems to be. If you have done your homework, you should now be able to select your true speyrod based on the following criteria...

- It should have a full flex action.
- It must also have a powerful butt action.
- The length must be related to the fish size.
- The line weight must be related to the fish size.

A few words of advice! *Be careful when being advised by unqualified rod salesmen or inexperienced self-appointed experts as they seem to be behind every rock. Above all, look out for the excessive distance casting only speycaster.*

Security of Speyrod Joints

Many novice speyfishers are in such a hurry to 'get going' that they do not pay enough attention to setting up their tackle or assembling their speyrods correctly. Casting off part of your rod and seeing it knock off your fly and disappear forever, is a very expensive lesson. Joints will also slip due to rough casting and temperature changes, as we shall see later.

PUTTING YOUR ROD TOGETHER - Before starting, lubricate the spigot with ordinary white candle wax (*not bees wax or canning wax*). Push the spigot in, misaligned about a quarter of a turn (*good speyrods will have lining marks*). Grasp the sections firmly, stay clear of the guides. Start to twist the sections and push the joint even tighter. Aim to complete the twist at the same time as you complete the push with lining marks opposite each other. The security of this system relies on simple physics. The friction of the 'twist and push' creates enough heat to soften the low melting point candle wax, creating a lubricant. The cooling wax sets and grips the rod firmly. Obviously the joint must be twisted again before undoing it.

ROUGH CASTING - Rough casting and the use of excessive power can produce ear splitting noises and vibrations that could shake the fillings out of your teeth and loosen the rod joints. Well-designed spigot ferrules should not loosen if correctly installed, lubricated and checked occasionally for temperature effect.

TEMPERATURE EFFECTS - Variations in temperature can cause problems with speyrod jointing systems and has been the main cause of loose or stuck ferrules. Graphite joints will tighten when heated and loosen when cooled. This is no problem if you remember the following...

- RISING TEMPERATURE - If you assemble your rod on a cool early morning day, you will have problems getting the joints apart if the day becomes warmer.

  Solution... cool the rod off in the river.

- FALLING TEMPERATURE - If you assemble your rod on a warm afternoon, your joints will loosen as the temperature falls. Also, you will need to check your joint security after taking your rod out of a warm car on a cold day.

  Solution... sight down the rod occasionally to check the guide line up and tighten the joints if necessary.

Construction Details

Speyrods are long and cumbersome when compared to single-handed fly rods and must be able to take a certain amount of abuse and rough treatment when fishing or just getting down to the river. Banging your rod against a rock, hooking into a tree or slapping it down onto a gravel beach when tailing a fish could be disastrous for a poorly built speyrod.

CORK HANDLES - Speyrod handles have developed into the practical shape used today. Custom rod builders should restrain themselves when trying to improve something of such a basic nature which has taken hundreds of years to evolve. The cardinal sins are: placing the reel seat at the top of the cork grip or shortening the length of the cork grip so that it more closely resembles a single hand rod. A speyrod should look like one, not like a bait or spinning rod.

REELSEATS - Nothing is more frustrating than reelseats that do not hold the reel securely, jam when removing the reel and with locknuts that can't be turned with cold hands. The ingenuity of rod manufacturers know no bounds when it comes to reelseats. The designs vary from beautiful and accurately machined all metal reelseats, to functional, easy-to-use and maintain, stainless steel and graphite seats. Custom rod builders should not use reelseats taken from old heavy cane rods so that the new lightweight graphite rod will hold that old heavyweight brass and ivory reel inherited from their grandfather.

GUIDES - True speyrods require special attention to guides. The action of a speyrod is somewhat dependent upon the self-weight momentum of the rod. A skilled designer can adjust this effect by varying the weight and number of guides used. Long limber speyrods are continuously bending in each direction to a much greater degree of curve than any other type of fly rod. The effect of alternately compressing and stretching the guides must be taken into account.

Care of Speyrods

Graphite rods are strong when casting, controlling line and landing fish. As they are constructed with relatively thin walled tubes, they do not take kindly to big feet, car doors, exuberant children, big ugly dogs or being whacked by an over-sized weighted fly when casting in the wind. Accidents will happen to the best of us. A very experienced angler, friend and author was very proud of his newly acquired rod (*after waiting months for delivery*). When tailing a large fish, perhaps a little too green, he placed the rod on a gravel bank close to the water out of harms way. His attention was diverted while gently laying down the rod and his tail grip relaxed. Now, any normal fish would take this opportunity to escape, this one decided to get a little of its own back, jumped up in the air, deflected off the astonished angler and landed on his rod. This was not very healthy for the fish and disaster for the rod.

ASSEMBLY / PUTTING AWAY - It is natural that the safety of the rod is not uppermost in the mind, when gearing up before fishing and farthest away when taking off all that heavy clothing etc. at the end of the day. The potential danger to the rod is increased in proportion to the potency of the liquid used to toast the river. It makes sense to leave the rod in its case until you are fully clothed, wadered and geared before assembling your rod. Clumping around, looking for a misplaced item after making up your rod prematurely spells trouble. Don't assemble your rod until you are ready to fish. Conversely, put your rod back in its case before doing anything else (*even if it's already poured out*). Stumbling around in the half dark with your rod lying around is a disaster waiting to happen. An angler whose rod 'just broke for no reason' could be unaware that it had been previously damaged, unintentionally by someone else. Guard your rod, don't let it out of your sight once it is assembled.

USE A CARRYING CASE - One of the easiest ways of damaging a fly rod is to put it away in its bag and then have someone lean on it and press the guides into the adjacent section of the blank. Speyrods with relatively large guides are particularly susceptible to this form of damage. Obviously a rod case would prevent this.

The selection of rod tubes requires discussion. Many aluminum tubes, suitable for short single-hand rods are not adequate for long speyrods due to their relatively soft metal and thin walls. Anyone seeing a five foot aluminum tube neatly folded in two will understand (*airports have specialists trained in this procedure*). Thin-walled plastic tubes are also suspect. Rod cases of modern impact resistant materials are now available in any length and diameter which are virtually indestructible

An Angler's Artisan
Don Horsfield (r) with Mike Maxwell and one of Don's leather rod cases.

Photography © Kelly Fisher

and inexpensive. The cases can be made to hold any number of rods (*speyfishers are also tackle junkies*). Those who feel that a plastic case does not fit their image should consider the handsome leather-covered cases available.

Anglers who find it difficult to resist the seductive effect of fine leather work should stay away from the work of *Don Horsfield* - speyfisher, saddlemaker, master craftsman and artist in leather work. Working in his little shop close to the Skeena River in the coastal mountains of British Columbia, he produces a limited number of custom rod cases, reel boxes, tackle bags and fly wallets that would make your mouth water. Don ships to his many customers around the world.

Protect your rod bag from dirt and rain by stuffing it back in the tube before assembling your rod. Should it get wet, dry it out the moment you are indoors again. A wet bag inside a warm case is rather like a pressure cooker.

Above all... protect your rod, there is nothing like the sickening feeling of realizing that your favourite (*sometimes only*) rod has been mortally wounded.

CHECK BEFORE YOU GO - It makes sense to thoroughly check your rod before that upcoming fishing trip. It is also very easy to forget. Pay particular attention to the following...

- Tip top and guides - security and wear.
- Rod shaft - abrasions, cuts, nicks.
- Ferrules - security, lubrication.
- Cork handle - separation, cleanliness.
- Reelseat - security, lubrication.

Any legitimate rod maker will stand behind a warranty if the damage can be firmly attributed to an inferior product or workmanship. 'There's the rub'. How does the maker determine what is a manufacturing defect and what is abuse of the rod? No rod maker 'worth his salt' will try and make money out of your misfortune should you break your favourite rod. Report the matter accurately and ask for his help. Don't forget rod makers have heard every possible reason for rod damage and will turn a deaf ear to the 'my rod just broke for no reason' excuse. A valued customer was treated gently when rabbits ate the cork handle off his rod.

OLD TIME REELS...

Part of Mike's fly reel collection - a solid brass Malloch (centre) circa 1895, 4 1/2" diameter, made in Perth, Scotland; a Hardy Perfect (left) circa 1910 bearing the original Hardy trademark, 4 1/2" diameter, with brass side plate and ivory handle; and a Hardy Perfect (right) circa 1930 bearing the new Hardy trademark, 3 1/2" diameter, with the original Hardy finish.

Current day reels are considerably lighter as a result of materials used in contemporary construction. Combined with the lighter rod weights, this spells comfort for speyfishers spending a full day on the river.

Part Five ~ Chapter Twenty-Six
Reels for Speyfishing

CHOOSING A FLY REEL is like choosing a car. There are those who are happy with good reliable transportation, others who enjoy and appreciate fine workmanship and those who require a status symbol. Fly reels come in just about every shape, size, design features, standard of workmanship and with 'all the bells and whistles' and price ranges imaginable. Take your time with reel selection, however, buy the best you can afford.

It is beyond the scope of the book to discuss or recommend any specific brand or type of fly reel for speyfishing. There are so many excellent reels available today, from very low cost and quite serviceable to extremely expensive works of art, take your pick and pay your money.

THE REQUIREMENTS OF THE REEL - Although the reel is used to store the line and dispense it as required, the primary object is to assist in controlling the fish after hooking. Reels must have adequate capacity for both backing and line, a reliable method of breaking the speed of a running fish and a simple winding system for retrieving line. The reel should have at least half an inch clearance between the fully wound in line and the frame. This is to guard against the line jamming during the final stages of landing a large fish (*you have no way of level winding a reel with a speyrod during this crucial stage*). The reel should be rugged and able to withstand being tossed onto the shore while releasing fish without the owner worrying more about the reel than the survival of the fish.

CONTROLLING FISH - Outdoor writers are apt to exaggerate and dramatize the experience of hooking fish regardless of how big it may be. They write of bone jarring strikes, screaming reels, fish that exhaust every ounce of the angler's skill and strength as it rips off every inch of their five hundred yards of fifty pound backing before conceding defeat (*the fish, not the angler*). This is 'piffle' and belongs in the funnies, not on the river. Make your fish work for every inch of line. If it is well-hooked and your knots were correctly tied, you will not lose your fish. Your reel is one of the key elements in fish control.

RIM CONTROL - The absolute minimum requirement for controlling the run of a fish is an adequate rim control system. Holding the line or fingering the inside of a rapidly revolving reel can be painful. Palming or thumbing the rim is an efficient and delicate method allowing you to feel each surge or slackening of the power of the fish.

MECHANICAL DRAG - Drag systems can be very effective providing they are mechanically sound and handled intelligently. Slow starting or sticky drags have lost many fish. Over or under-tensioned drags have lost even more. The best all-around practical control system for speyfishing is a combined mechanical drag and rim control reel. This has the advantage of slowing the initial run, before the right hand can be used for palming. Having been fishless for a while, an unexpected 'take' by an active fish can sometimes stun you momentarily, letting the fish take you 'well into your backing' before you can palm your reel.

The combined system will prevent this, use the reel as follows...

- Strip off the length of line you will be casting, adjust the drag for about a one pound pull (*this takes practice*). Do not touch the drag again.
- The initial run will be slowed by the mechanical drag alone and then stopped by drag plus palming. Don't touch the drag.
- If the fish makes additional runs during the landing stage, it will still be working against the light drag initially, then stopped by palming. Don't touch the drag.

ANTI-REVERSE REELS - This type of reel may have its place on saltwater, with single-handed rods. It most definitely does not belong on a river with a speyrod. Picture the following scenario... the drag has been set, the fish is much larger than you think, takes off down river into fast current, well into your backing. The fish stops, you start reeling like crazy, the reel goes around, the fish keeps on going. Only thing to do, tighten up the drag. In comes the fish, sees you, makes one more run against an over tightened drag, good-bye fish!

Reel Protection... *Perhaps the ultimate in reel cases... one of Don Horsfield's leather cases.*

MAINTAIN YOUR REELS - Check that your reel has not been damaged in your tackle bag or inadvertently dropped on the ground. Many high priced reels have delicate cast aluminum spools and frames. Others have a multiplicity of small screws or rivets that can work loose eventually. Make sure that your spool is securely latched into the body of your reel. Some quick-change spare spools do not always seat adequately. Check before you buy.

Some reel makers deliver their reels stuffed with a rust inhibiting grease. This compound, good for preserving the reel on the dealer's shelf has a magnetic effect on sand and grit and solidifies in cold weather. Check your reel for dirt, impacted grease or stale oil. Clean with a good solvent (*remove and check your line beforehand*). Modern chemistry has given us lubricants with almost magical powers. These compounds are able to remove dirt and rust, penetrate metal and plate it with lubricant. Keep your reel in 'tip top shape'.

Photography © Calen Darnel

Part Five ~ Chapter Twenty-Seven
Lines and Leaders

THE ROLE OF THE FLY LINE - Before we get down to line design, we should define the requirements of a fly line. Speycasting depends on the smooth generation of line energy during the casting stroke, then directing the energized line towards the target allowing the energy to concentrate and carry the line out above the water. A further and equally important requirement is that the line can be mended and controlled after casting.

WEIGHT FORWARD LINES - Weight forward lines are inadequate as the main weight is concentrated forward and it is impossible for energy to be uniformly distributed along the line during casting. It is also impossible to control the thick head section of a shooting head line with the thin running line. Simply put, the thin running line cannot drive the thick head section when speycasting. It should be obvious that if we are to make smooth controlled speycasts, improved double taper lines must be used.

INADEQUATE TAPERS ON LARGE LINES - The object of the end taper is to ensure that the line will continue to straighten out, as the energy reduces (*the line gets thinner as the energy reduces*).

All your efforts will be wasted if the end of the line just splashes down without straightening. Large double-taper lines are not generally used for delicate casting with single hand rods. When speycasting with standard lines, it is obvious that something must be wrong with the design of the front taper. Unless the angler has perfect conditions and is highly skilled, the end of the line will die before straightening or splash down like a lead weight.

About ten years ago, I set out to investigate the possibility of designing an improved taper which would allow a relatively unskilled speycaster to straighten the line and leader at the end of a long speycast with a double taper line. The final design proved to have more advantages than originally intended. My design was based on the following data...

It has been demonstrated that energy is uniformly generated along the length of a double taper line during the forward stroke. It has also been shown that as the loop proceeds, it slows down due to the air drag on the long moving portion and accelerates again as the moving line shortens. As the cast proceeds, some of the energy is absorbed by air drag and the work required to continuously bend and straighten the line as it rolls out. The equation for kinetic energy ($E = \frac{1}{2}Mv^2$) can be transposed to show that velocity $v = \sqrt{E/\frac{1}{2}M}$. What this means is, with E remaining as near constant, the reduction in the length of the live line, will cause it to accelerate (*a slight pull on the rod tip will be observed*).

The amount of energy stored in a fly line is a function of its mass, which is related to its cross-sectional area... $A = \pi D^2/4$. The air drag on a line is a function of its surface area, which is related to its circumference... $C = \pi D$.

It can be seen that although the area of a circle increases by the power of two, the circumference only increases by the power of one. This means that lines with larger diameters are capable of containing more energy with relatively less air drag, re-accelerating sooner and retaining energy for a longer period. Since a relatively large amount of energy is still present towards the end of an efficient cast, it is possible to lengthen the end of the taper to take advantage of this phenomenon, hence the improved taper.

Design of the Improved Taper

The design of the improved taper[4] is an extremely complex subject. The problem is to adjust the diameter of line so that the mass to surface area ratio is related to the diminishing energy. Simply stated, the line must get thinner as the energy fades out, still leaving enough kick to straighten the leader. The problem is further complicated by the fact that the energy diminishes with an inverse exponential relationship and not at a constant rate. Even if the correct taper could be calculated, it would be a line manufacturer's nightmare to produce.

As necessity is the mother of invention, it was discovered that adding a section of a lighter line produced a definite improvement to the final stage of the cast. After countless hours of casting and fishing, the final details of taper length and weight of line it was cut from was decided. A table of main and improved taper line weights, and taper lengths is provided for those who wish to build their own.

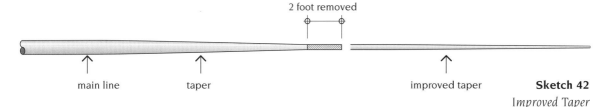

2 foot removed

main line   taper   improved taper   **Sketch 42**
Improved Taper

It is obvious that the hybrid tapers produced do not conform to the theoretical taper, however, they have given good service over the years and are a considerable improvement over the tapers on standard lines. The end

Main Line	Taper Line	Length of Taper
#11	#9	16' – 0"
#10	#8	15' – 0"
#9	#7	12' – 0"

Lines below #9 do not require modifying.

tapers can be cut from the ends of a double-taper line, one of your old lines or perhaps a lower grade line. There are further advantages of the improved taper...

- The taper can be used as an indicator of the correct anchor length when casting, better still if cut from a different colour line.
- There is considerably less splash down as the business end of the line is two line weights smaller than the main line.
- Beginners (*and experienced casters*) can strip off the coating at the end of the line in the wind. Replacing the improved taper saves money.

[4] *Mike Maxwell* 1984

Recent Developments in Speyline Design

Notwithstanding the discussion on weight forward, double taper and improved taper lines, it would be unfair not to mention recent developments of the major line companies. There are a number of special purpose lines intended for double-handed flyrods. Some are designed for maximum distance and minimum line control, while others permit long accurate effortless casts and superb line control. It must be kept in mind, however, that we are discussing speycasting lines designed for smooth casting and line control – *not distance casting*.

Selecting the correct weight and taper for your particular rod will depend on what you believe is most important to your presentation and line control techniques. You need to ask yourself... *which casting and fishing method do you endorse and select your lines accordingly.*

At the time of writing this book, the AFTMA method of calibrating lines by weighing the front thirty feet is not applicable as some speylines have tapers longer than thirty feet. Also, as each line company uses a different method of designating the weight of a speyline (*one company's 10-weight could be another's 8-weight*), check your taper design and try the line on 'your rod' before you buy.

The Triangular Taper - Never having been unduly influenced by the multiplicity of 'wonder products' on the flyfishing scene, it took Joan Wulff's gentle persuasion for me to try out the triangle taper speylines. Having calibrated the correct line weight for my particular speyrod, it was a complete surprise to discover that my speycasting had suddenly improved and required much less effort. It did not take long to analyze what was happening and to isolate the advantages of speycasting with the triangle taper line...

- The principal advantage is the ease of placing and pulling the anchor portion of the line during the upstream side cast and the forward delivery of the speycast – the front end of the triangle taper is considerably lighter than the end of the equivalent double taper.

- As the triangle taper line close to the rod tip is much heavier than the equivalent double taper, more line energy is generated on the forward stroke, driving out the tapered line at about an equivalent speed in proportion to the decreasing energy.

What Line Makers Should You Consider - As speyline designs and line weight designations are in such a 'state of flux' at this time, it would be inappropriate to recommend any specific line maker. However, if you stay with any of the fine, well-established line companies and do your homework, you should not go far wrong.

Loop Jointing System - *see Sketch* 43. The improved loop jointing system produces virtually no drag in the guides and absolutely no interruption in the energy flow or cast. Those who can remember the wonderfully smooth casting possible with an almost worn out silk line (*a continuous string of hinges*) will understand why the hinge effect of the improved loop is not significant.

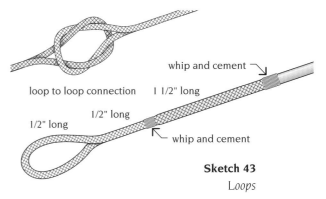

whip and cement

loop to loop connection   1 1/2" long

1/2" long

1/2" long

whip and cement

Sketch 43
Loops

Building the Improved Loop...

- Push the braided mono onto the line.
- Thread the other end of the braided mono back inside itself to form a loop.
- Whip finish where shown in Sketch 43.
- Cement the whip only.

Note... *use a tapestry needle (blunt-ended point with a large eye) to open the braided mono when forming the loop.*

Marking Lines - *see Sketch* 44. The many variables affecting the efficiency of speycasting make it imperative to know just how much line is to be aerialized. Every extra foot of wading depth will reduce your efficiency and every increase in current speed will make speycasting easier. It is very difficult to know just how much line you are working with when speycasting with a long rod. The sketch shows the line divided into ten foot lengths, marked concentrically from the centre line (*commercial lines vary in length*). It is easy to see how much line you are handling by checking the line code nearest to the reel. When calculating the length, don't forget to include the length of the added improved taper. Sooner or later the front taper of your main line will start to show signs of wear no matter how good a caster you are. Simply change ends, the marking still applies (*you will have to attach another improved loop*).

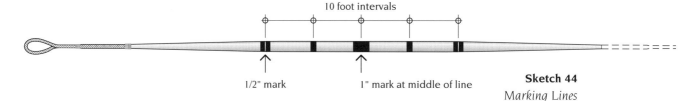

10 foot intervals

1/2" mark   1" mark at middle of line   **Sketch 44**
Marking Lines

Care of Fly Lines - Premium fly lines are expensive and not always obtainable in the larger double-taper weights required in speycasting. A few moments taken to inspect and dress your lines will definitely pay dividends as follows...

- The line will last longer.
- Pick-up 'off' the water is easier, as it does not sink.
- Shoot better by reducing friction.
- Avoid premature guide wear.
- Pack onto the reel better.

Some line makers claim that their lines don't need dressing, this may be so for lighter lines in crystal clear chalk streams. Experience has shown that this is not so with larger lines used under unfavourable conditions. Any line dressing is better than no dressing (*a mild soap will do in an emergency*). A good dressing should have the following requirements (*not all do*)...

- Easy to apply.
- Not add weight to the line.
- Not wash off.
- Not be sticky.
- Repel water.

Any fly line will retain some memory from the time spent wound around the spool in your tackle bag. This coil spring effect must be removed to allow the 'miraculous gravity defying' process of speycasting to be fully mobilized. If you have the time, the space and a helper, run all the line out and stretch it. If you cannot stretch the full line, tighten down the reel (*or drag*) by palming and stretch the line as you pull it off the reel. Allow it to float downstream through the guides. Don't forget to readjust your drag again (*if you have one*) before fishing... *many fish are lost on overtightened drags.*

FULLY SUNK LINES - There are those traditionalists who prefer to fish with heavy sinking lines to get their flies down to the river bottom. They invariably make a very narrow angular change of direction and rely on the weight of the line to get the fly down to the fishes level. Having fished this way quite successfully for some time, it occurred to me that there were many disadvantages as follows...

- The line could easily tangle around rocks or sunken logs.
- The fly was easily blunted as it dragged along the river bottom.
- Fish were often difficult to motivate as the fly remained in their narrow frontal field of view for such a short time as it swung to shore.
- Unless the current flow was very fast, it was tiring to bring the sunk line upstream again at the beginning of the next cast.
- Heavy sunk line fishing required a much stiffer and more powerful rod that wore me out after a few hours of 'power speycasting'.

FIXED SINK TIP LINES - It did not require a genius to produce lines where the majority floated and the front end sank. Although this system was a vast improvement over the 'rock catching' full sunk line, it had one major annoying and expensive disadvantage. In order to cover varying water depths and current speeds, it was necessary to carry at least three different lengths or densities of sink tip lines which of course required carrying extra spools. You were in no danger of floating away. A further disadvantage was the time-consuming process of reeling in the line and re-threading the required sink tip line. Moving down the pool often required changing the line again to suit the new water conditions. After one or two line changes, the angler could tire of re-threading lines and carry on with the wrong length of sink tip.

HYBRID SINK TIP LINES - Many experienced anglers, tired of hauling around spare spools and different sink tip lines, made up their own hybrid lines with detachable sink tips of varying lengths. The connections were made quickly and efficiently by a loop to loop method. This allowed using the same reel and floating line, without having to carry extra spools or re-threading lines. Unfortunately this system of detachable lines encouraged the use of 'heavyweight' sink tips including bottom dredging lead core sink tips. There are those who do not seem to be happy unless they are playing 'Russian roulette' with a length of lead core buzzing around them. It is virtually impossible to speycast comfortably and accurately with an overweight sink tip due to the inability of the lighter floating line to drive the heavy sink tip on the forward delivery... *to say nothing of difficulty of pulling up the anchor.* Once again, this type of line is usually fished with a down and across presentation, making an upstream double spey would be certain suicide.

Designing a Better Sink Tip System

It occurred to me that it should be possible to design a better sink tip system[5] that covered just about every depth of sink required, make any presentation necessary and allow me to enjoy my speycasting and speyfishing, without having to carry additional reel spools or the nuisance of constantly changing lines.

[5] *Mike Maxwell 1985*

Instead of just experimenting and seeing what happens, I set up the following guidelines. The system should...

- Allow sinking a fly by skill, not just weight.
- Allow any speycast required.
- Have sink tip lengths from 5 feet to 30 feet.
- Be readily available and easy to attach.
- Be enjoyable to cast and control.

After many trial designs, hours of testing, miles of discarded line, sore muscles, the final solution evolved.

THE VARIABLE SINK TIP SYSTEM - *see Sketch* 45. Three short lengths can be cut from a standard 30 foot shooting head. Loops are attached to each end, the main floating line and leader are also looped together. The following illustrates the main advantages of the system...

IMAGINE... *you are fishing a river with variable depth and current speed, are using a full floating line and wet fly, and find that you are not getting your fly down to the fish, even though the water is shallow. Without reeling in, you retrieve the line, remove your fly, leader and improved floating taper. You then loop on your five foot sink tip, add your leader, retie your fly and continue casting. As you move down the pool, you find it necessary to switch to your ten foot or fifteen foot sink tip to fish the really deep runs. In a particularly deep pool, your fifteen foot sink tip is still not getting the fly down, so you add the five foot or ten foot section.*

The important thing to remember... *you are now able to fish with a floating line and modify it quickly into a sink tip line of six different lengths with only three pieces of sinking line. Sink heads of different densities can also be used.*

5 feet   10 feet   15 feet

From a 30 foot shooting head...
- use a head one size lighter than the main line.
- use an appropriate sink rate.

improved loop   improved loop

How DO THEY CAST? - It soon became obvious that heavy sink tips were difficult to cast due to the excessive anchoring effect during the initial stages of any speycast and uneven energy concentration on the forward delivery.

Sketch 45
Sink Tips

These problems are somewhat alleviated by making the tips from a line one size smaller than the main floating line. With a little practice, you will be able to choose the correct length and density of sink tip, make any speycast you require and put your line out to any angle of cast and control your fly perfectly.

WILL THE LOOPS AFFECT YOUR FISHING? - If the loops are correctly made and your rod guides are of normal size, you will not notice any difference when reeling in a fish or putting away your rod. It seems that everyone is worried about the 'hinge effect' of the loop-to-loop connection. Having read questionable magazine articles on leaders, they are convinced that a hinged leader connection will upset the cast and assume that it would be even worse in a fly line. Fortunately this misleading information is not born out in scientific fact as the following example should explain...

When fishing with the old silk lines, they had to be carefully dried and dressed to prevent deterioration of the organic fibres. As the lines started to wear, they became very limp to the extent that they finally resembled a continuous chain of hinges. The curious thing was that as they wore, they were easier to cast. This is difficult to understand unless you go back to the physics of a flycast. As the energized line rolls out, it is slowed down by air drag and the energy absorbed by bending and straightening the loop. If the line was a chain, it would not require energy to bend it and would not impede the cast. It is obvious that hinges make no difference to the leader or sink tip connections and it can be argued that they are an asset, not a hindrance.

THE FLOAT FISHING CONCEPT... AGAIN - We have already discussed the value of this method of presentation. Assuming the line is a float and covering the water with long downstream drifts is probably the most effective method of speyfishing. Although it is an excellent dry or surface fly method, it is without doubt the most sensible and practical method of fishing a sunk fly. The use of adjustable length sink tips allows getting the fly down to the fish in just about all fishable water. The speed and ease of changing the sink tips allows the angler to use the 'right tool for the job, every time'.

SINKING THE FLY IN DIFFICULT WATER - There are going to be times when your fly does not get down to the fish due to the speed or depth of the current when using a thirty foot head. This problem could be solved by casting farther upstream, giving the sink tip time to get down. Another solution is to carry a 'sink tip set' with a faster sink rate. Don't forget it must still be made from a shooting head, one line size lighter than your main floating line. It is a good idea to colour code the heavier set by changing the colour of the thread wrapping at the loops.

Leaders for Speycasting

Leaders are probably the most important, misunderstood and neglected item in the sport of speyfishing. All your wonderful and carefully selected equipment will not mean a thing if the fly does not get to the fish correctly. What is the point of making a beautiful speycast if your leader does not roll out ahead of the line and deliver the fly right on target. Don't expect to hook a difficult fish if your tippet is too stiff to allow your dry fly to float freely or your wet fly to swim naturally. Having hooked a large fish, you will be lucky to land it if your knots are sub-standard.

LEADER DESIGN - A well-designed leader should have the following characteristics...

- Butt should be heavy enough to accept the jolt of energy from the fly line.
- Mid sections should taper down in proportion to the reduction in speed due to air drag and internal bending losses.
- Tippet should be as thin as possible to prevent 'spooking' fish and strong enough to prevent break-offs.
- Dry or surface fly leaders must be long enough to separate the fly from the splash down of the line.
- Sunk fly leaders must be short enough to prevent the fly from being lifted again by swirling currents. Line splash down is not a problem with sunk fly leaders as the cast is made well upstream of the fish.

LEADER CONSTRUCTION - It would be impractical to produce leaders to the exact theoretical tapers (*and a manufacturer's nightmare*). However, after many cut and try experiments, it was possible to produce a compound step tapered leader[6] closely matching the theoretical requirements. By the way, if you are doubtful about your present leader, try a long cast with a heavy floating line and a bushy #4 dry fly. Make your longest and best cast and check that your leader has straightened and your fly is ahead. If not... *it's time for 'super leader'.*

LEADER STRENGTH - As leader sections are chosen for their ability to accept and transfer energy, they are much stronger than any load they are subjected to. You will not break your leader if your knots hold. It can be seen from the table on page 216, the mass required to drive a large bushy dry fly needs an eight pound tippet. You will break any normal double-handed rod trying to lift an eight pound weight.

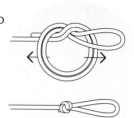

finished knot

Surgeon's Loop

LEADER MATERIALS - After field testing many 'new and improved' leader materials, most of them claiming unbelievable but unnecessary, breaking strengths, there was one that provided the most reliable and consistent results. This is a German monofilament material called Maxima (*No - this is not a paid endorsement!*). Here are the advantages of this product...

- It is consistent in diameter and strength.
- It has excellent wet knot strength.
- It is available in large and small diameters.
- It can be found anywhere in the world.
- It is economical in price.

LEADER KNOTS - It is safe to say that more fish are lost due to inadequate knots than any other circumstance. Unfortunately many of the knots in use today are a carry over from the old silkworm gut leaders used at the beginning of the century. To make matters worse, there are those who take a perverse pleasure in tying the most complicated and time-consuming knots without regard for the type of material used. Modern monofilaments can be produced from many different chemical formulae and with varying degrees of stretch when soaked in water. The variation in elastic properties have a major significance when considering knot strength.

finished knot

*Double
Surgeon's Knot*

WHY KNOTS FAIL - There are many reasons for knot failure, however, the practice of connecting two different brands of leader material is the most prevalent. A knot tied in air will stretch and tighten when loaded underwater. As the knot tightens, a certain amount of slippage occurs as it compacts. If non-compatible materials are used or the sections have large diameter differences, the most elastic section will slip causing a stress concentration and premature failure.

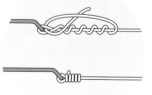

finished knot

Improved Clinch

RECOMMENDED KNOTS - Before recommending knots, it must be realized that how well you tie the knot is more important than what knot you tie. It is also assumed you are familiar with and proficient in contemporary knot procedures...

- Leader to line - surgeon's loop.
- Leader joints - double surgeon's knot.
- Tippet to fly - improved clinch.
- Don't forget to lubricate your knot with saliva (*spit*).

Sketch 46
*Recommended
Knots*

[6] *Mike Maxwell 1980*

The double surgeon's knot has a higher wet strength than any other monofilament knot used in freshwater fishing. It is also the most practical, easiest to tie and most compact of all leader knots. The following 'fish tale' will illustrate this point...

At our Bulkley River lodge, we provide all guests and students with the appropriate step-tapered leader. The knots, of course, are double surgeon's. A guest who decided to replace his tippet, insisted on using a double blood knot. Later on a large steelhead took his fly, put on a aerobatic display and broke off. Taking advantage of the angler's weakened state of mind, the guide replaced the tippet with a double surgeon's knot and tied on another fly. After regaining his composure, the guest resumed fishing. Imagine his surprise when another fish took his fly at exactly the same place as his previous fish. He was even more surprised to find that it had two identical dry flies imbedded in the corner of its jaw. The final shock was finding a tippet firmly attached to one of the flies, complete with the tell tale twisted end of a failed blood knot.

CHECK YOUR LEADERS - Once again, your leader is the least expensive and most fragile link in your angling chain. A well designed and correctly tied leader will give you a sense of confidence when speyfishing, however, it must be checked and serviced regularly, as follow...

- Leaders must be freed of memory when taken off the reel.
- Simple stretching should do the trick, be careful that you do not cut your softened wet hands on the knots.
- Do not use a rubber leader straightener, they can generate enough friction to 'burn' and damage the mono.
- Always check your leader before fishing and most definitely after landing a fish. Replace any sections showing roughness caused by snagging rocks, etc.
- Carry spare leader spools for the last three sections of your leader, keep them in your pocket out of the sunlight.
- Do not mix monofilament brands.

MAKE YOUR OWN LEADERS - Sketch 46 depicts the controlled energy leaders you will need for dry-fly, surface-fly and sunk-fly speyfishing; the tables on page 216 give construction details for both.

A - *Dry Fly/Surface Leader*

B - *Wet Fly/Sunk Leader*

Sketch 47
Speyfishing Leaders

When making your own leaders...

- The lengths of each section can be adjusted 'pro-rata' to produce longer or shorter leaders, to suit any special water conditions.
- Tippet lengths and strengths can also be adjusted to suit special conditions.
- Low, clear water - lengthen and downsize the tippet diameter.
- Heavy or bushy flies - increase your tippet diameter.
- The tables are based on using Maxima monofilament.
- If using other brands, remember... *diameters are critical, strength is secondary.*

Floating Line Leaders - Length 10 feet, Butt 40 lb., Tippet 8 – 10 lb.

Section	Length	Diameter	Strength
Butt	48"	0.024"	40 lb.
Transition	24"	0.022"	30 lb.
Taper	8"	0.020"	25 lb.
Taper	8"	0.017"	20 lb.
Taper	8"	0.015"	15 lb.
Tippet	24"	0.012"	8 – 10 lb.

Sketch 48
Floating Line Leader

Sunk Line Leaders - Length 5 feet, Butt 30 lb., Tippet 10 – 15 lb.

Section	Length	Diameter	Strength
Butt	24"	0.022"	30 lb.
Transition	12"	0.020"	25 lb.
Taper	6"	0.017"	20 lb.
Tippet	18"	0.015"	10 – 15 lb.

Sketch 49
Sunk Line Leader

Part Five ~ Chapter Twenty-Eight
Hooks for Speyfishing

HOOKING FISH has already been covered in Chapter Twenty-Three, however, a few more words on this important subject seems appropriate at this time. My experience in freshwater fishing has convinced me that you will land more fish by allowing the fish to hook itself. You could perhaps hook more fish with an 'eye crossing strike', however, you could also pull the fly out of the fish's mouth or lose it later on due to an insecure hook-up. Many of the hooking techniques, 'beloved' by outdoor writers and other 'learned authorities' are a carry over from the soft wire, blunt pointed hook days and are entirely unnecessary with today's hardwire super sharp hooks. The question usually asked at this time is... *"What do I do if when a fish pulls on my line?"* The answer is, nothing. By the time the fish pulls on the line and the signal goes to your brain and down to your arm again, the fish is either 'on or gone'. Look for the 'bald eagle', page 181.

A BRIEF HISTORY OF HOOKS - There are many super sharp, hard wire, well-designed hooks on today's market. There are also just as many relatively soft and blunt hooks in use today. There is no reason why you should not fish with the old traditional type of hook providing you realize and make allowances for its short-comings.

On Hook Making

SOFT WIRE HOOKS - Since medieval times, hooks were made of soft iron wire so that they could be bent and shaped by hand, then hardened by crude heat treatment methods. Later on, hook making machines, able to manufacture soft wire hooks were introduced and are still in use today. Hooks were made with thick wire to compensate for the low strength metal used. When examined under a powerful microscope, it can be seen that soft wire hooks have dull points to prevent premature blunting, during manufacture and packaging. There are also accumulations of coating on the microscopic burrs produced when grinding the point. The combination of the thick wire and the dull point makes it difficult to bed the hook into a fish's jaw without considerable force. It is easy to pull the fly out of a fish's mouth or foul hook it unless considerable skill is used in striking or setting the hook when using blunt, soft wire hooks.

HARD WIRE HOOKS - As the science of metallurgy developed, very hard wire for sewing needles was introduced to the hook makers. Hooks could now be made with thinner wire. As early wire bending machines could not handle the harder metal, it required the tedious and highly skilled process of making hooks by hand. Although these hooks were sharper than soft wire hooks, dulling due to the accumulation of coating on the grinding burrs was still a problem. Added to this was the problem of maintaining a consistent degree of hardness and strength due to archaic heat treatment methods.

IMPROVED HOOK DESIGN - As labour costs increased, it was no longer feasible to have rows of little old ladies hand bending and sharpening hard wire hooks, or let the old gentleman who knew how to do the tempering, retire. Modern technology has suppressed many traditional industries, however, it has been a godsend to the hook maker and the angler. We now have unbelievably hard wire hooks with points that can slice your fingers like a surgical scalpel. The use of sophisticated machinery has kept the cost of this new breed of hook to an acceptable level. The use of chemicals to remove the grinding burrs and give the finishing touches to the point must be a milestone in angling history.

Single or Multiple Hooks

There are many parts of the world where double and treble hooks are legal. It is not for me to criticize anglers who fish with these time-honoured hooks, however, it is hoped that the following 'discussions' will enable you to make up your own mind as to whether or not they are necessary.

If you research the origin of the multiple hook fly, you will find that its main purpose was to make sure that the fish had no chance of escape after being securely hooked. It must also be remembered that the multiple hook was invented for food fishermen and 'sportsmen' who traditionally killed all their fish. A further claim for using the multiple hook fly was that the additional weight allowed sinking a small fly when using a slow sinking silk line without much skill required. Why the fly was not weighted by other methods has never been logically explained. With the advent of full sinking and sink tip lines, it is no longer necessary to rely on the weight of the hook to get the fly down to the 'taking depth'. The only logical reasons for the continued use of multiple hooks seems to be...

- The angler does not know how to sink a fly.
- The angler does not know how to hook fish.
- The hooks are not sharp enough.
- The 'fear of failure' when controlling fish.
- The fish is going to be eaten.

Single Hook Flies

In countries where outside influences have depleted the stocks of freshwater gamefish, killing fish is no longer ethical or viable. Where these unfortunate conditions occur fish must be released humanely and with the least trauma if they are to survive and the fishery is to be sustained. It is obvious that the single pointed hook is the least damaging to a fish, however, withdrawing it from a fish's jaw can be time consuming and traumatic for the unfortunate fish. The obvious solution is to pinch down the barb of the hook.

FISHING WITH BARBLESS HOOKS - Barbed hooks are intended to prevent the hook from being withdrawn from the fish's jaw, however, it can also be argued that the barb makes hook penetration more difficult. Many anglers who have been required to de-barb their hooks are pleasantly surprised to find that they have no problems in landing fish. This could be due to the better penetration of the hook or more careful control of the fish, knowing that the hook is barbless. The satisfaction of knowing that you are releasing your fish virtually unharmed is well worth the trouble of pinching down your barbs.

COMPARING HOOKS - When developing and testing my angling and presentation techniques in the early days of our guiding on the Bulkley River, all guests would be given the same fly pattern and taught to perform the self hooking technique. Although our hooking to landing ratio of approximately 50 percent was above average for the river, we were still losing too many fish and came to the conclusion that the thick soft wire hook was the culprit.

When changing our hooks to hand made, thin hard wire hooks, our hooking to landing ratio increased to just over 65 percent, however, fish were often lost on broken or straightened out hooks (*heat treatment problems*).

After finally changing to a more advanced design of hard wire, chemically sharpened hooks, our hooking to landing ratio increased to over 75 percent with no bent or fractured hooks.

In conclusion, the type of hook used is far more important than the size of hook and just as important as the fly pattern used. Don't forget to de-barb your hook - these super sharp hooks will go right through any projecting part of your anatomy.

USE THE CORRECT HOOK - Assuming that you are using 'modern' hooks, it is important to use the correct weight, length and gape of hook for each intended use of the fly. Dry fly hooks should be very hard, thin wire to help the fly to float. Surface wet fly hooks should be slightly thicker than dry flies so that the fly will penetrate the surface quickly. Fully sunk and nymph hooks should be heavy to sink the fly and made from very hard wire to offset the blunting effect of river bottoms. Take the time to research and locate the correct hook for the 'job in hand'. The wrong hook is often the cause of losing a fish after a 'brief encounter'.

SPEYFISHING FLIES...

A selection of patterns from Mike's fly box that will serve you well, regardless of which depth in the river you fish... bottom, mid- to top-water or the surface.

BOTTOM FLIES - *Stonefly Nymph, Leech*
MID-WATER & TOP-WATER FLIES - *Rusty Rat, Silver Doctor, Blue Charm, Thunder & Lightning*
DRY FLIES - *October Caddis, Bomber, Tom Thumb, Mitch's Sedge*

Photography © Maxwell

Indian Summer...
The leaves have turned, the mountains are dusted with snow, the 'fish are in'.

Part Five ~ Chapter Twenty-Nine
On Flies and Local Rivers

THERE ARE AS MANY DIFFERENT SPECIES of freshwater gamefish as there are methods of angling for them. To further complicate matters, each geographical area and country has traditional or recently designed patterns designed for the characteristics of each separate river. It is obvious that a fly used successfully on a brawling mountain steelhead river would not work well on a 'gin clear', slow moving Atlantic salmon stream. Adding to the confusion is the fact that fish have developed, by natural selection, to survive in their natal rivers and could have totally different habits to another stream just a few miles away.

To advise you on books that would cover every fly pattern and local methods of fishing is unrealistic, therefore I have chosen a few books that should start you out in the right direction; *see Recommended Reading, page* 227. Books on European salmon rivers have not been included as my experience is now somewhat outdated, however, it should not take you long to locate suitable data on this subject.

Old Flies...

Early spey flies in an antique Hardy fly box.

Varzuga Silver...

Ehor Boyanowsky of Vancouver releasing a 20 pound plus Atlantic salmon on the Varzuga River in Russia.
Ehor, a past president of the Steelhead Society of British Columbia, is a tireless worker for the preservation of the magnificent wild steelhead and a skilled speyfisher.

Just one word of warning! The art and science of speyfishing seems to be in a state of transition at this moment. 'Thank God!' Always remember that the words of the angling masters are not written in stone. Many authors would dearly love to be able to turn back the clock and change some outdated advice. When confronted with conflicting information, take the time to analyze and compare, then decide which advice is the most logical.

NO NEED FOR ATTRACTOR FLIES - Flyfishing depends on catching fish with an artificial fly that represents its natural food at some time in its life cycle. The artificial fly must represent the natural in size, shape and colour. Last, but certainly not least, it must be presented to imitate the behaviour of the natural that it represents, this is where the true speyrod is so effective.

Anglers using so-called flies that do not resemble any known natural organism are only one step away from lure fishing and are missing the very essence and satisfaction of flyfishing. Those unenlightened anglers who rate their success on the number and size of their fish when using a big ugly attractor fly, with no idea of why the fish takes it, should be pitied and avoided. Don't make the mistake of believing that a gaudy attractor fly will somehow make up for a lack of flyfishing skills.

At a recent club meeting, a local guide was advising members on the best fly to use for coho salmon and how to determine the size and colour. There was a 'deafening silence' as he explained that the best way was to check what colour and size of the metal lure that the successful spin casters were using, then tie a fly to imitate the lure. Perhaps there are salmon out in the great Pacific Ocean that feed on schools of metal baitfish with hooks sticking out of them.

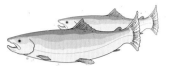

STEELHEAD RIVERS

SKEENA WATERSHED
1   Babine River
2   Bulkley River
3   Kispiox River
4   Morice River
5   Skeena River
6   Sustut River
7   Zymoetz (Copper) River

DEAN WATERSHED
8   Dean River

FRASER WATERSHED
9   Fraser River
10 Thompson River

VANCOUVER ISLAND
11 Cowichan River
12 Gold River
13 Stamp River

QUEEN CHARLOTTE ISLANDS
14 Copper River
15 Tlell River
16 Yakoun River

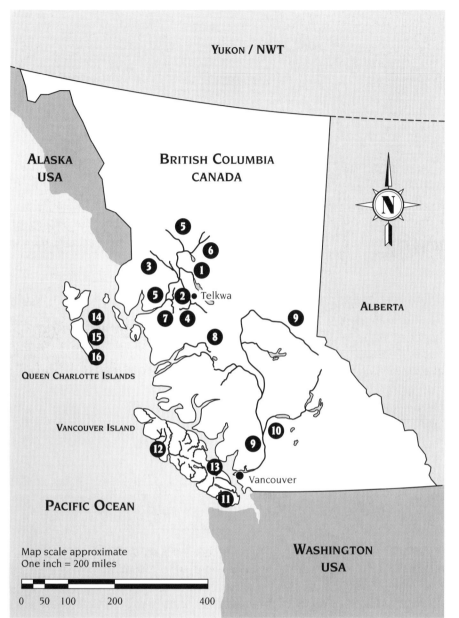

Sketch 50
Steelhead Rivers in British Columbia

WATERSHEDS IN BRITISH COLUMBIA - The western-most province of Canada contains some of the most diverse and dynamic watersheds in the world. These systems support an abundance of wild Pacific salmon – *sockeye, chinook, coho, chum, pink and steelhead* – as well as many species of trout and char – *rainbow, cutthroat, brook, brown and dolly varden.*

The principal salmon-bearing watersheds include the *Fraser, Dean* and *Skeena* rivers on the continental mainland, with smaller yet productive river systems on Vancouver Island and Queen Charlotte Islands. Each system has numerous tributaries that feed into the river from which the watershed derives its name and it is beyond the scope of this book to delve into the specifics of each.

Trey Comb's book, STEELHEAD FLY FISHING, is a virtual treatise on the truly great rivers in the Pacific Northwest... *Klamath, Rogue, North Umpqua, Deshutes, Clearwater, North Fork Stillaguamish, Skykomish* and *Skagit* in United States, and *Stamp, Thompson, Dean, Bulkley, Kispiox, Babine* and *Sustut* in British Columbia.

Photography © Myron Kozak

TIME FOR CONTEMPLATION...

The fresh water fishery in British Columbia is world class... something to be respected, cherished and nurtured. Wild steelhead, salmon and trout use the rivers for spawning and juvenile rearing. Clean water and silt-free gravel in the spawning beds are a must to ensure the survival of all species that inhabit the many and diverse watersheds throughout the province.

Numerous angler groups - non-profit societies, federations or clubs - serve as river guardians, keeping an ever-watchful eye on the resource.

Above:

Anglers on the Bulkley River enjoying a quiet moment.

CONCLUSION

WELL... Here we are at the end of the book. At this time, I would like to congratulate all who have had the 'intestinal fortitude' to wade through the rapids of the seemingly unending data and convoluted instructional procedures. You have both my sympathy and respect.

Don't be disappointed if you are not able to understand or believe the somewhat complicated physics or are unable to produce the casts shown in the sketches and photographs. Keep up your pond and river practice, and you will finally find that elusive perfect cast that you have been looking for. Above all, remember that no caster makes a perfect speycast every time.

As your speycasting and fishing skills develop, you will find that you are reading the river as a speyfisher, making a game plan, searching the river systematically, presenting the fly accurately, motivating the fish to eat it and finally, controlling, landing and releasing your fish quickly and humanely.

When you have finally reached 'the plateau' of accomplished speyfishing, you will find that you are not longer constrained by the shortcomings of your single handed overhead casting method of flyfishing. Eventually your speyfishing skills will become 'second nature' and you will find that you are catching fish safely, intelligently and successfully with the 'traditions of the past' and the 'technology of the present' and will enjoy every minute of it.

Writing these last few words, after so many years of research and writing, leaves me with mixed emotions. The anguish and disappointment of a failed hypothesis, the expense and time wasted on an unacceptable rod design or teaching procedure is somewhat alleviated by the thrill and sense of achievement of knowing that I have produced a range of true speyrods, and a simple, logical method of casting and fishing with them.

On completing this work, it is offered as a contribution, in general, to the sport of fishing with all double-handed fly rods and in particular, to the 'art and science' of speyfishing with a 'true speyrod'.

Last, but not least, to all my speyfishing friends and students who have been instrumental in developing many of the techniques and procedures given here, and insisting that I keep my 'nose to the grindstone' and finish the book.

Mike Maxwell
Vancouver 1995

RECOMMENDED READING

Several books and periodicals that will make interesting reading to round out The ART & SCIENCE of SPEYFISHING...

Books

- ATLANTIC SALMON, FACT & FANTASY. Gary Anderson 1990
  Salar Publishing

- ATLANTIC SALMON, A FLY FISHING PRIMER. Paul C. Marriner 1992
  Winchester Press

- STEELHEAD FLY FISHING. Trey Combs 1991
  Lyons & Burford

- FLY PATTERNS OF RODERICK HAIG-BROWN. Arthur James Lingren 1994
  Frank Amato Publications

- RIVER JOURNAL THOMPSON. Arthur James Lingren 1994
  Frank Amato Publications

- IN THE RING OF THE RISE. Vincent Marinaro 1976
  Nick Lyons Books

- ADVANCED FLY FISHING FOR STEELHEAD. Deke Meyer 1992
  Frank Amato Publications

- THE TROUT AND THE FLY. Goddard & Clarke 1980
  Ernest Benn Ltd.

Periodicals

- Tom Pero. WILD STEELHEAD & ATLANTIC SALMON

- Frank Amato. STEELHEAD FLY FISHING JOURNAL

- Atlantic Salmon Federation. ATLANTIC SALMON JOURNAL

LIST OF ROD MAKERS

The following is a list of recommended rod makers to be considered when selecting your 'true speyrod'…

- The names are arranged in alphabetical order.
- Do not interpret this as an order of preference.

Rod Maker	Mailing Address *
Bruce & Walker Ltd.	Huntingdon Road Upwood, Cambs. ENGLAND PE17 1QQ
Gold-N-West Flyfishers Ltd.	5169 Joyce Street Vancouver, B.C. CANADA V5R 4H1
G. Loomis, Inc.	1359 Down River Drive Woodland, WA USA 98674
Orvis	Route 7A Manchester, VT USA 05254
House of Hardy	
Hardy (USA) Inc.	10 Godwin Plaza Midland Park, NJ USA 07432
In Canada…	
H.C. Kennedy & Sons Ltd.	636 West 6th Avenue Vancouver, B.C. CANADA V5Z 1A3
Sage Mfg.	8500 NE Day Road Bainbridge Island, WA USA 98110

ROD MAKERS, *cont'd on page 230*

* *Addresses subject to change; current at time of publishing.*

LIST OF ROD MAKERS

Rod Maker	Mailing Address *
Scott Fly Rods	200 San Miguel Drive P.O. Box 889 Telluride, CO USA 81435
Thomas & Thomas Rodmakers Inc.	2 Avenue A Turner Falls, MA USA 01376
R.L. Winston Rod Co.	Twin Bridges, MT USA 59754

List of Speyline Makers

The following is a list of recommended line companies or lines to be considered when selecting your speylines for casting and fishing. The names are arranged in alphabetical order...

- Cortland
- Rio
- Scientific Anglers
- Wulff Triangle Taper

God's Gift to Speyfishers...

Good Weather,
Crystal Clear Water,
Lots of River to Search for Fish!